ANGIE B. WILLIAMS

JOY IN ADVERSITY

21ST CENTURY PRESS

Published by 21st Century Press

Springfield, MO 65807

ISBN 0-9728899-6-5

Cover: Keith Locke
Book Design: Jeremy Montz and Terry White

Visit our web-site at: 21stcenturypress.com
and 21centurybooks.com

For childrens books visit: sonshippress.com
and sonshipbooks.com

DEDICATION

I dedicate this book to Rivers, my dear husband of forty years, who has walked with me through adversities like a pillar of strength, dignity, and faith.

To our beloved sons, Barth and Bert, who were subjected to many hardships along with us. To our grandsons, Garrett Emerson and Parker Lee Williams, whose innocence and joyful spirit have comforted me; and our daughter-in-law, Angie, who has faced adversity with courage and faith. It is because of God's grace and my special family, that I am the woman I am today.

I dedicate this book, in the Name of Jesus, to all persons who hurt, and pray that you will be strengthened by the power of the Holy Spirit when you are called upon to face the trials of life. May you also have Joy in Adversity.

Angie Bass Williams

ACKNOWLEDGEMENT

I thank God for His enduring love and mercy in helping me to persevere when many things hindered my writing.

I acknowledge with thanks the contributions of all those who have believed in me, encouraged me, and prayed consistently about this project. For those who offered helpful suggestions, including Dr. Robert and Martha Reichard, Pastor Dave Eshleman, Pastor Ed and Eileen Heatwole, Evangelist Steve and Barbara Wingfield, Eunice Gilchrist, Donna Suter, and Barbara Borntrager, thank you.

Special thanks to Rivers who proofread the manuscript and took over household duties to free me to write, and my friend, Betty Hottinger, who assisted with typing and proofreading.

I acknowledge gratefully Daniel E. Atwell, Doctor of Chiropractic, without whose expertise it would have been very difficult to complete this book. I applaud his Christian character and compassionate spirit, as well as his assistant, Meredith. Doctor Atwell's treatment of my carpal tunnel syndrome has enhanced my ability to type, and other therapies have improved my general physical condition. Thank you.

May God bless each of you!

Angie Bass Williams

Rivers and Angie's 20th Anniversary

Rivers and Angie's wedding
June 22, 1963

Rivers and Angie's 28th Anniversary

TABLE OF CONTENTS

FOREWORD

During my thirty-eight years of ministry I have known few people who have experienced the degree of adversity and tragedy that Angie and Rivers Williams have endured. And most importantly, at the end of the day, they have emerged still standing. Many would say that is a miracle in itself, and rightly so. Hallelujah!

As you read through *Joy in Adversity*, you will likely experience the full range of human emotions. For instance, you will be moved to tears as Angie relates the premature loss of three babies. Anger may well begin to stir in your soul with the account of pompous, erroneous accusations of sexual immorality brought against a young Christian lady coupled with its ensuing humiliation imposed upon her. Within your heart, empathy for a sister in Christ will rise up as you read page after page, chapter after chapter, of the reality of deep prolonged, personal adversity as it is unashamedly revealed to the glory of God.

Age-old questions are resurrected as one reads this book. Why do the righteous suffer? How can a righteous God allow adversity and tragedy to plague His servants? These would be used as seeds of discouragement and defeat by our adversary, Satan, if he could. However, the answer to these and similar questions is so beautifully woven into the fabric of the entire work that the reader is never left alone with doubt, fear, or unbelief. Angie has remarkably allowed the Holy Spirit to fashion with every adversity a subsequent word of encouragement, exhortation, and glorious praise and thanksgiving to the King of Kings and Lord of Lords. Never is the reader left to his or her own devices of comprehension and determination, but rather is continually pointed to the One who is the Way, the Truth, and the Life (John 14:6). The Almighty God and Father who has never forsaken His own (Joshua 1:5,9; Matthew 28:20), nor allowed His children to go begging for bread (Psalm 37:25), confirms His promise in this book not to allow adversity to come upon us except that He necessarily provides a way to bear it (I Corinthians 10:13). The author has skillfully addressed this issue in the chapter entitled, "From Victim to Victor."

Having both faced the possibility of a terminal illness at an early age, both Rivers and Angie have exemplified by their perseverance through adversity what the Psalmist said in Psalm 118:16,17, "The right hand of the Lord is exalted: the right hand of the Lord doeth valiantly. I shall not die, but live, and declare the works of the Lord."

Throughout the book, frequently Christian brothers and sisters immediately came to the aid of the Williams family, and often that action was at the cost of personal sacrifice and inconvenience. For that we praise the Lord. Yet, often Angie and the family experienced the barbs, criticisms, insults, and wounds of well-meaning Christians. The message and lesson for the church is clear. We must recognize the magnitude and severity of the adversity of our brothers and sisters and then, with Holy Spirit sensitivity and wisdom, apply the "Balm of Gilead" to the hurts and wounds of our friends (Jeremiah 8:22).

The author, plainly and unhesitatingly, expresses the thought that pain is pain wherever and whenever it exists. Some Christians would take issue with that statement, declaring that one must never confess an adversity though it is very real in one's experience. This issue presents a simple, yet profound truth. It goes something like this, and the difference is very subtle. On the one hand, we call those things which are not as though they were, while on the other we call those things which are as though they were not. The former is clearly a powerful, definitive statement of active faith, and the latter is simply a lie.

After having read *Joy in Adversity*, I believe everyone should read it. In my estimation, it surely is a "must read" for every Christian, regardless of his or her involvement in the Kingdom. As you read the book, you will be astounded by the severity of the adversity suffered by Rivers and Angie Williams. You will be astonished by the glorious presence of God surrounding the author and her family in and through that adversity, and you will be amazed by the power of the Holy Spirit to remove obstacles, minister healing, and to empower God's children to rise above the fray. Angie Williams has, indeed, captured the essence of knowing "the power of Christ's resurrection and the fellowship of His suffering" (Philippians 3:10). As you read *Joy in Adversity*, may the Holy Spirit communicate His divine message to your heart so that you will never be the same.

—Robert H. Reichard, Ph.D.
President, Evangel Theological Seminary
Harrisonburg, Virginia

It has been a pleasure to read Angie's manuscript—the message is Biblically based and right on target. While none of us would choose suffering and adversity, it is the very ingredient God uses to cause us to grow spiritually. As milk for a baby and fertilizer to a plant, so is adversity to the soul—it brings growth. This is validated through the growth of the underground church in Africa, India, and Central Asia.

The power of this book is in knowing the author. I have known Angie for most of my life. However, I never knew the breadth of adversity and suffering the Williams family has faced. To the public eye, they reflected a very positive and joyful attitude. Their faith was vivacious and engaging, but through their story I am reminded once again that we are called to bear the cross joyfully.

As Oswald Chambers has said, "The true test of our spirituality is not how we do on the mountain tops of life, but how we live in the valley. The test of our spiritual life is the power to descend; if we have the power to rise only, something is wrong."

David said in Psalm 84:5-7, "Blessed are those whose strength is in You, who have set their hearts on pilgrimage. As they pass through the valley of Baca (weeping), they make it a place of springs; the autumn rains also cover it with pools. They go from strength to strength, till each appears before God in Zion."

I highly recommend this book to anyone who is being tested by adversity. Be encouraged—you can overcome! You can live in a place of streams amidst adversity. Angie's personal life is a testimony to this.

—Pastor Ed Heatwole
New Beginnings Church
Bridgewater, Virginia

Mrs. Williams presented to our office with difficulty writing her book because the intensity of pain in her wrists and back from previous injuries had gotten progressively worse. Through the power of chiropractic and her God-given ablity to heal, she has improved considerably. Angie has a beautiful spirit, and is a pleasure to work with, as she truly demonstrates *Joy in Adversity*.

—Daniel E. Atwell, D.C.

INTRODUCTION

I have often exclaimed, "We are what we are in adversity!" But *Joy in Adversity* sounds like a contradiction, an oxymoron, or an utter impossibility. Does the Lord expect me to be joyful when facing the myriad of pressures and disappointments that come my way? Am I to wear a smile when a migraine headache is pulsating and throbbing and my eyes are sensitive to sunlight? If I cannot conceive a child or lose my babies through miscarriage, does God really expect me to rejoice? Can't I even ask the rhetorical "why" question?

Jesus said, "These things I have spoken to you, that in Me you may have peace. In the world you will have tribulation; but be of good cheer, I have overcome the world" (John 16:33, NKJV). While adversity, tribulation, trials, and suffering come in many forms, they are universal—a part of the human experience. They don't discriminate based on one's social status or ethnic background. The Lord taught me that pain is pain, no matter what its origin.

The Apostle Paul said, "That you may walk worthy of the Lord, fully pleasing Him, being fruitful in every good work and increasing in the knowledge of God; strengthened with all might, according to His glorious power, for all patience and long-suffering with joy" (Colossians 1:10, 11, NKJV).

These and other scriptures warn us that trials will come; therefore, the Christian must be prepared. God did not leave us without means for coping with and overcoming adversity. While I don't claim to have all the answers to life's many problems, I have turned to the Answer. My faith has been tested, tried and retried, so I believe my words have a ring of authenticity.

The Lord convicted me about sharing more of my spiritual pilgrimage when I spoke to groups. Since I was joyful, without this exposure it was not obvious that I had walked through adversity or endured chronic pain.

While I tended toward perfectionism, I was by no means perfect. The Lord loved me enough to chasten me for trying to be the Holy Spirit to Rivers, and it hurt! He "slapped my little hands" when He found them in the cookie jar.

With a good Christian marriage, two healthy sons and good jobs, at one time I thought things could not get much better— life was simply wonderful, and we were riding high. Hold on! Little did I know what was about to happen to us. Even though it isn't easy, in these pages I share some of the adversities that we have endured and how God has led us through them. After a number of unexpected trials had tested us, in my youthful naivety I thought we had paid our dues and nothing else adverse could happen. How wrong I was! Through sharing these personal stories my objective is to encourage you to keep your eyes on Jesus, no matter what the test.

My story continues to unfold day by day as God gives me victory over life's trials. Some portions evoke strong emotions, and occasionally tears dim my eyes. But then, the Lord reminds me of why He has called me to pen these words. I believe II Corinthians 1:3,4 (KJV) offers comfort to the fifth power. "Blessed be God, even the Father of our Lord Jesus Christ, the Father of mercies, and the God of all comfort; Who comforteth us in all our tribulation, that we may be able to comfort them which are in any trouble, by the comfort wherewith we ourselves are comforted of God." As God has offered me comfort, I pray that He may comfort you and give you joy as you walk through adversity.

For many years I kept a journal, recording my deepest thoughts, Scriptures, and prayers. However, the impact of our many trials is so etched on my memory that I can still "see," "hear," and "feel" these incidents as if they just occurred.

What you read in this book was born out of painful experiences such as the loss of our first three babies, two other very difficult pregnancies, and River's heart attack during my third pregnancy. With one disappointment after another, without the Lord we would never have survived. "Our soul waits for the Lord; He is our help and our shield. For our heart shall rejoice in Him, because we have trusted in His holy name. Let Your mercy, O Lord, be upon us, just as we hope in You" (Psalm 33:20-22, NKJV).

Some friends are not aware of all the unspeakable pain we have endured, and continue to endure. Because I have walked through—not around—adversity, I believe I am uniquely qualified to speak experientially. I can hold out the proverbial carrot called hope to you.

Jesus said, "The Spirit of the Lord is upon Me, because He has anointed Me to preach the Gospel to the poor; He has sent Me to heal the brokenhearted, to proclaim liberty to the captives and recovery of sight to the blind, to set at liberty those who are oppressed" (Luke 4:18, NKJV). I believe the Holy Spirit has anointed me to bring hope, comfort, and consolation because Jesus is the same yesterday, today and forever. However, I am convinced that obedience to God is not necessarily a prescription for blissful, pain-free living. If you feel the urge to give up or to give out, allow His strength to become perfect in your weakness.

"If thou faint in the day of adversity, thy strength is small" (Proverbs 24:10). This verse came to me with unmistakable power and certainty during an extended period of recuperation from a debilitating back injury. Would the faith I taught others sustain me when the "biggie" came my way? Read on!

CHAPTER 1

SO WHAT IS ADVERSITY?

What Adversity Is

Adversity is a condition of suffering, destitution or affliction, a calamitous or disastrous experience. I believe that affliction, tribulation and adversity are closely related. Affliction is grief or trouble, and tribulation is distress or suffering resulting from oppression or persecution; a trying experience.

The Apostle Paul encouraged the Christians in Lycaonia to continue in the faith stating, "That we must through much tribulation enter into the kingdom of God" (Acts 14:22). Drawing on his own experience, Paul asks the Roman Christians, whether tribulation, distress, persecution...could separate them from God's love. He emphatically affirms that we are more than conquerors and nothing can separate us from God's love.

Scripture is replete with references to suffering for Christ and the sufferings of Christ. Jesus said those who are persecuted for His sake are blessed. "Blessed are ye, when men shall revile you, and persecute you, and shall say all manner of evil against you falsely, for My sake. Rejoice, and be exceeding glad: for great is your reward in heaven: for so persecuted they the prophets which were before you" (Matthew 5:11, 12).

Paul warned his young protégé, Timothy, that he must "endure afflictions" and suffering for the sake of the Gospel. "If we suffer, we shall also reign with him" (II Timothy 2:12). But the joy of seeing the face of Jesus will be worth it all!

Am I suggesting that we be joyful in the midst of misery,

grief, and trouble? While I believe suffering adversity joy-fully is Biblical, many Christians don't want to hear any-thing about it. We entice potential believers with, "If you just accept Jesus as your Savior, everything will be alright." Would it not be better to teach them how to cope with life's many trials?

We are so afraid of scaring people away from church that we sometimes promote the idea that "our Jesus" answers every prayer without regard to His sovereign will. Unfortunately, we don't always tell them how to search out nuggets from the Scriptures that will build their faith when God does not answer their prayers quickly or in the way they expected. It is incumbent upon us to teach them to be like the Bereans. "...they received the Word with all readiness of mind, and searched the scriptures daily, whether those things were so" (Acts 17:11b).

You mean they checked up on what the Apostle Paul taught them? We must check after anyone who purports to be a teacher of the Word, no matter how big the name. To demonstrate my fallibility, one day I thought the Lord was telling me to read Galatians 7. I couldn't wait to get my spe-cial "word from the Lord." Since Galatians has only six chapters, I was mistaken, but I learned a valuable lesson.

What Adversity is NOT

The Apostle Peter says we are to "partake of Christ's suf-ferings." He says suffering reproach, or unjust accusation, for the name of Christ brings blessing and great reward in Heaven. However, he hastens to add that Christians should not "suffer as a murderer, a thief, an evildoer, or as a busy-body in other people's matters" (I Peter 4:15, NKJV). Adversity is not incurring the wrath of the IRS by failing to pay our taxes. It's not speeding down the freeway and get-ting a ticket. If we arrive at work late and the supervisor expects an explanation, we think we are being persecuted.

Adversity is not indulging in sex outside of marriage and getting pregnant.

I well remember a young Christian girl expressing her deep agony. "The devil is trying to tell me I'm pregnant!" she exclaimed. I shifted on my chair trying to hide my uneasiness. Would I indulge her or hold her accountable for her actions? After a few pleasantries, I asked whether she had indulged in intercourse? "No!" she replied emphatically.

Rapidly becoming frustrated, I searched for a way to help her accept responsibility and escape the victim mentality without crushing her completely. Finally, I blurted it out, "The devil is a bad boy, but even he can't make you believe you are pregnant if you haven't given him a reason." That was the defining moment for her.

Sin has consequences, but the world would have us believe we can sin with impunity. We have manufactured new definitions for sin to make it more palatable. Billy Graham used to say the new morality was nothing more than the old immorality. Sin hasn't changed much since the Garden of Eden, and couching sin in respectable terminology won't help. Did you ever have anyone try to manipulate your thinking, make you believe a lie, or play word games like this with you?

Abortion: A product of conception, a minor inconvenience. If we admit it is a baby, we have to admit that abortion is murder, and we are blithely killing millions. We accord more respect to a cat or a spotted owl than to the fruit of the human womb.

Fornication: Being sexually active, safe sex. The kids will do it anyway, so let's provide sex education and a condom. This teaches them to think they can escape sin's consequences—break God's law, but just don't get caught.

Shacking Up: Domestic partnership, significant other, lifetime companion. Such words now appear in obituaries.

Homosexual, effeminate, deviant: Alternative lifestyle,

partner, same-sex marriage.

Adultery, infidelity, unfaithfulness: An indiscretion or mistake. The philandering husband "fell into an adulterous relationship," which makes him a victim. One may fall into a ditch, but Christians who commit adultery, do so through a series of compromises and rationalizations.

Illegitimate or born-out-of-wedlock: Love child. I heard one woman say her "love child" was an answer to prayer, even though a married minister fathered it.

Genetic engineering: Trying to create human beings in ways other than what God designed.

Pride and arrogance: Independent spirit.

Lying and covering up: Error in judgment.

Getting caught committing a crime: Entrapment.

And the grandfather of them all, "that depends on what alone means," or "what is is."

On and on, ad infinitum and ad nauseam! God has not changed His definition of sin, and His moral absolutes still apply. But "the law" has become whatever we can get away with—just make up the rules as we go along. So adversity is not trying to get away with sin or using diversionary tactics to deflect the enemy.

Sources of Adversity

"What does adversity have to do with the adversary—the devil, the enemy of our souls?" I asked several friends, but failed to receive a substantive response. An adversary is one who contends with, opposes, or resists; it is an enemy; one who is hostile. Could we then conclude that adversity always comes from the devil?

God tests us in order to prove us; Satan tempts us in order to discourage us; and we bring trials on ourselves by our decisions and actions. We can expect some unpleasant result when we choose to ignore or deliberately disobey God. While Christians in some countries are persecuted and slaughtered for their faith, suffering for Christ is a foreign concept for most Americans. But the Apostle Paul warned that all who live Godly in Christ Jesus would suffer persecution. In Acts 9:16 the Lord forewarned a disciple named Ananias that Paul would suffer for the sake of the Gospel. "For I will show him how great things he must suffer for my name's sake".

Let's consider the devil as a source of adversity. Jesus told Peter that Satan wanted to sift him like wheat. Peter later described the devil as a roaring lion walking about seeking someone to devour, and advised us to resist him by faith.

When I asked a Bible study group how to stand against the devil, one participant blurted out, "We are to run from him!" James 4:7, NKJV: "Therefore submit to God. Resist the devil and he will flee from you." We must put on the whole armor of God in order to withstand him successfully. When we are full of the Word, the Holy Spirit can recall it to us in times of adversity.

I believe the devil authors adversity to tempt us to doubt God's love. When we pass God's test we become stronger Christians, while yielding to Satan's temptations depletes our strength and makes us weak. A test is hard; a temptation looks like fun, but leads to trouble. When God tests us, He already knows how we will respond, but sometimes we surprise ourselves.

According to Hebrews 12:1-11, God disciplines us because He loves us and is training us in the fruit of righteousness. How often we moan and groan, begging for deliverance, when God is attempting to teach us a valuable spiritual lesson.

The Psalmist said that God disciplined him with affliction upon his bed, but I don't know how that fits your theology. Also Psalm 30:6 says, "And in my prosperity I said, I should never be moved." Indeed, we have heard utterances such as, "Bless God, that would never happen to me!"

Sometimes when adversity strikes such a person, they fall apart because they have no framework for coping with what they thought could never happen.

Then there's God's pruning in John 15. The beautiful Shenandoah Valley produces luscious apples, but I know they prune the trees. The caretaker trims not only the dead stuff, but along with it some of the good branches.

When the Lord begins to prune us, He may purge some good things because His intensive pruning provides for maximum yield.

Inevitability of Adversity

No matter how often we are tempted or the depth of the temptation, we can have Joy in Adversity; however, the idea is antithetical to what many Christians have been taught. "Of course, all is well with my soul, but how about my life in general?" a Christian may wonder. It may seem the more they follow Jesus, the thicker the battle against the adversary becomes.

In a section titled, "Profiting From Trials," The Nelson Study Bible (NKJV) renders James 1:2-4 this way. "My brethren, count it all joy when you fall into various trials, knowing that the testing of your faith produces patience. But let patience have its perfect work, that you may be perfect and complete, lacking nothing."

Under "Loving God Under Trials," it continues, "Blessed is the man who endures temptation; for when he has been approved, he will receive the crown of life which the Lord has promised to those who love Him. Let no one say when he is tempted, 'I am tempted by God;' for God cannot be tempted by evil, nor does He Himself tempt anyone. But each one is tempted when he is drawn away by his own desires and enticed" (James 1:12-14, NKJV).

Satan is the author of seduction to evil, and our response to temptation is a true revelation of our moral character. If Satan can't get us to sin by any other means, he will assault our belief system with discouragement and despair. He wants us to be defeated; God wants us to be overcomers and conformed to the image of Jesus. The crown of life that awaits us in Heaven is sufficient incentive to keep us pressing on.

Believe Psalm 23, that when we walk through the valley of the shadow of death, we need not fear because He is present with us. He is using His rod to protect us and His staff to pull us up when our feet stray. Hallelujah!

Adversity is Normal for the Christian

In my travels, I have met a lot of saints; however, without exception, I learned they had to overcome adversity. I concluded that there is no such thing as instant sainthood, and everyone must at sometime learn to rise above adversity of some sort.

One of the most radical conclusions I reached through suffering is simply this: Obedience to God does not ensure immunity from adversity! To some this may sound faithless and heretical.

The Apostle Peter forewarned us to expect trials and suffering as a natural component of the Christian life. Through various trials, God shapes His character within us. Peter affirms that we are kept by the power of God and continues: "In this you greatly rejoice, though now for a little while, if need be, you have been grieved by various trials, that the genuineness of your faith, being much more precious than gold that perishes, though it is tested by fire, may be found to praise, honor, and glory at the revelation of Jesus Christ" (I Peter 1:6, 7, NKJV).

After a meeting I spoke briefly with the guest speaker I had just met. Reaching into his pocket he drew out a "gold nugget." Turning to me he said, "The Lord is telling me that when you are tried, you will come forth as pure gold."

Every Christian experiences trials and testing that produce pressure to question God. When Peter compares the
value of our faith with gold, faith triumphs. But the purity
of gold is brought out by intense heat; and we discover the
strength of our faith through the trials we overcome. But
faith that is not tested may not be faith at all! When we survive the heat of the furnace, our faith is validated and
authenticated.

Speaking to a persecuted church, Peter warns Christians
not to think it strange when fiery trials come. I think first
century believers, unlike contemporary believers, actually
expected to suffer and be martyred for their faith. Peter
writes to encourage them to remain steadfast despite the trials. He reminds us that Christ suffered for our sake, and he
parallels suffering and glory repeatedly. The more we suffer,
the more glory is to be expected when we reign with Jesus in
His kingdom. Hallelujah!

"Beloved, do not think it strange concerning the fiery
trial which is to try you, as though some strange thing happened to you; but rejoice to the extent that you partake of
Christ's sufferings, that when He is revealed, you may also
be glad with exceeding joy" (I Peter 4:12-13, NKJV).

Suffering proves our true character—anyone can have
vibrant faith when things are going well. However, I believe
we can expect suffering to be a part of our Christian experience as long as we live in this world. But Heaven will be a
different story.

No matter what adversity's source, its inevitability, or its
normalcy, when any type of pain comes into your life, you
look for relief. Jesus invites us to "yoke up" with Him
(Matthew 5:28-30). Even if our burdens endure for a while,
they become lighter because Jesus is carrying them for us. In
the passage, Jesus extends a three-fold invitation to each of
us. We can come for salvation, for discipleship, and for service with Him. When we accept His gracious invitation, His

response is at least three-fold. He will satisfy our spiritual, physical, and emotional needs.

If a trial persists for a season, Jesus will give us victory in the midst of it. We may still have the burden without feeling its weight, still be in the furnace without feeling the heat, or continue to walk through the waters without being drowned. Believe Jesus' words, "I will give you rest," and have Joy in Adversity!

Minor distractions brought on by the enemy can cause us to lose our focus; however, we can cast all our cares, or distractions, on Him because He cares for us. According to John 10, He is the Good Shepherd Who gave His life for the sheep. That's us!

If trials and suffering are normal for the Christian, of what possible value are they? At the very least, these disasters tend to define our values—what is most important to us. I have learned more through the school of suffering than at any other time. Through failed pregnancies, a back injury and several surgeries, as well as Rivers' job layoffs, I turned to God and His Word for strength.

Application Questions:
So What is Adversity?

Scriptures: Romans 8:35, Matthew 5:11, 12, Acts 9:16, James 4:7, Hebrews 12:1-11, James 1:2-4, 12-14, I Peter 1:6, 7, 4:12-14, 19.

1. Define adversity and how it relates to suffering for Christ.

2. Name three sources of adversity and discuss how to respond to each.

3. Do you believe all Christians suffer adversity? Why, or why not?

Rivers and Angie with Barth and Bert
following Silver Anniversary Celebration

Angie with siblings, Bert, Lois, Elvige, Eunice, and Elsie
at 25th Anniversary Celebration

CHAPTER 2

BIBLE HEROES AND ADVERSITY

In Scripture God brought deliverance in many ways. Sometimes He spoke through an angel, but He also spoke through a burning bush and a donkey. He spoke through circumstances, through prophets, and ordinary people like you and me. God's ways are beyond our comprehension, so we cannot second-guess Him.

Abraham and Sarah Await a Son

In Genesis 17 and 18 an angel told Abraham that he would have a son and become the father of many nations. Both Abraham and Sarah laughed because they were old, Sarah's menses had ceased, and having a child was out of the question. I would have expected to have that son in nine months, but they waited for some twenty-four years. God was taking too long according to their timetable, so they took a circuitous route to help Him out—produce a son through Hagar, Sarah's maid. We still suffer the repercussions of that misguided decision with the continuous fighting between the sons of Isaac and the sons of Ishmael. God made good on His promise and Isaac was born when Abraham was one hundred years old and Sarah was ninety.

When God tested Abraham's faith by asking him to sacrifice that long-awaited son upon an altar, he passed the test. He knew God was able to raise Isaac up, so he spoke faith-filled words when he affirmed to Isaac that God would provide a sacrifice.

Galatians 3:6-9,14, 29 proclaims that through Jesus we are

heirs to God's promises to Abraham. Some say, "I'm a daughter of Abraham, so it's mine!" If you want to claim Abraham's promise, are you ready to claim his waiting period?

Abraham is a very important figure in Bible history, and through his lineage the Messiah was born. Why is he listed as a hero of the faith in Hebrews 11:8-19? It's because he passed the faith test administered by God! Can't you tell when someone has endured nothing worse than a bad hair day or a failed golf game. Those who have never walked through the furnace or had their faith tested make flippant, presumptuous confessions and expect God to honor them. We must let God be God, the sovereign Lord of this universe!

Let us not forget that Abraham, this "friend of God" and "hero of the faith" had to wait on the Lord for an inordinate amount of time, and all he had was a promise. Do you suppose he ever entertained doubt about whether he had heard God correctly or why it was taking so long?

Joseph, From the Pit To the Palace

And what of Joseph, the dreamer? We know that Joseph was Papa Jacob's pet and that he made him a coat of many colors, an honor not bestowed on his older brothers. In Genesis 37 we read about Joseph's annunciation of his grandiose dreams. That braggadocio 17-year-old kid's dream inferred that his parents and brothers would some day bow down to him, and that earned him a place in an empty pit. But when Joseph's brothers loathed him; God loved him. While they provoked him, God was proving him. When they punished him, God promoted him. When they sold him, God sent him. They placed him in a pit, but God promoted him to a palace.

Once in the palace, Potiphar's wife told a lie that thrust him out of the palace and into prison? But God, Who could see beyond the prison to the palace again, used that very experience to mold Joseph into the powerful ruler he later became.

Joseph went from a prison sentence to a palace setting!

When Joseph's brothers were forced to negotiate for food with this mighty Egyptian ruler, they hadn't a clue that God was fulfilling the dreamer's dreams. Joseph extended the love of God to his brothers when, rather than getting even, he said, "But as for you, ye thought evil against me; but God meant it unto good, to bring to pass, as it is this day, to save much people alive" (Genesis 50:20).

Let's recap Joseph's journey. He went from Papa's pet, to the pit, to the palace, to the prison, back to the palace, to Prime Minister, and back to Papa's provider! He had to persevere through many trials while waiting on God to fulfill His promises. I can only surmise that Joseph was tempted to question whether those teenage dreams emanated from God.

Job Endures Under Pressure

I believe if anyone in Scripture could be held up as a model of enduring patiently under pressure, surely Job qualifies. But he has also been the subject of much misunderstanding. Have you ever heard someone preach that Job suffered because of fear and a negative confession? Job did say, "Though He slay me, yet will I trust Him" (Job 13:15, NKJV). Job was secure in God's love, even though he believed his severe trials were not a result of his sin. The Lord Himself describes Job as, "... blameless and upright, and one who feared God and shunned evil" (Job 1:1, NKJV).

We know that Satan used Job's friends and his wife to tempt him to stumble, but he confidently confesses, "For I know that my Redeemer lives; and He shall stand at last on the earth; and after my skin is destroyed, this I know, that in my flesh I shall see God, Whom I shall see for myself, and my eyes shall behold" (Job 19:25-27a, NKJV). What a confession of faith during the most unspeakable trials—not I think or I hope, but I know my Redeemer lives.

Job expresses his reliance and dependence on God as he

says, "But He knows the way that I take; when He has tested me, I shall come forth as gold. My foot has held fast to His steps; I have kept His way and not turned aside. I have not departed from the commandment of His lips; I have treasured the words of His mouth more than my necessary food" (Job 23:10-12, NKJV). Job recognizes all his trials as a test, and his strong faith is evident as he perseveres through the darkest adversity. Early in the Book of Job, he blesses the Lord and refuses to blame God for losing his wealth and his children.

In the New Testament Job is recognized along with the prophets for his patience in suffering. "My brethren, take the prophets, who spoke in the name of the Lord, as an example of suffering and patience. Indeed we count them blessed who endure. You have heard of the perseverance of Job and seen the end intended by the Lord—that the Lord is very compassionate and merciful" (James 5:10-11, NKJV).

But God, Who sees beyond the ash heap, had a plan. Not only did God restore his former health, but He greatly increased Job's wealth. Hallelujah!

It was spring 2002. The birds were singing, the flowers were in full bloom, and things were going relatively well. Rivers and I had our usual challenges, but no new diagnoses had emerged. I was scheduled to lead our life group in a study of Job, the master of suffer-through-it-and-keep-your-faith-in-God.

The week when that study was to begin, I was in the hospital facing a partial mastectomy for a malignant breast tumor. How would I handle such a test compared to the way Job handled his? I had one distinct advantage—I could read the end of the Book of Job, whereas Job could not. I knew that God had blessed Job tremendously after he walked through these horrific experiences. Job had no assurance of the outcome while in the midst of his trials, but he had that hang-in-there-until-God-answers type of faith.

The Bible says Job did not sin with his mouth or charge God falsely. Magnanimous! The Lord allowed Job to be tempted by the devil, but He put limitations on it. The devil was on a short leash, and could only go so far; he could not take Job's life.

When ministering to hurting people, let's not make it worse for them by giving pat answers off the top of our head. Sometimes we have to do more than make a faith command—we have to walk through the waters or the fire with them.

Ruth, An Outcast Redeemed

Ruth was a Moabite woman, a descendant from an incestuous relationship between Lot and his daughters. The Moabites were cursed because they refused food and provisions to the Israelites when they came up out of Egypt. Ruth knew the pain and grief of widowhood and the struggle to survive, but God eventually rewarded Ruth's faithfulness, and she married a wealthy man named Boaz. She was the grandmother of King David, which places her in the lineage of Jesus.

Daniel Survives the Lions' Den

Daniel was highly favored in the foreign land of Babylon, and King Nebuchadnezzar appointed him to a high position. When the boss likes you that much, beware. Some of his conniving, scheming contemporaries wanted to bring him down. Finding no way to besmirch his character, they hatched up a plan and got the king's approval that anyone praying to a god other than the king during the next thirty days would be cast into a lions' den. This must have appealed to the king's ego because he unwittingly signed on.

What was Daniel to do? I can imagine a little demon whispering to Daniel, "Why don't you just pray silently? Do you have to open that window, Daniel? God will understand."

But Daniel worshipped the true God, and he would not compromise. With the prospect of visiting a den full of hungry lions—I'm sure I would have been tempted to pray in secret.

But God, Who knew beforehand what Daniel would do, miraculously rescued him. Daniel's faith was vibrant and undeterred, as his enemies could see. The king, who was not a believer, made a faith statement. "Thy God Whom thou servest continually, He will deliver thee" (Daniel 6:16).

Daniel was taken up out of the lions' den unharmed because he dared to believe that God would deliver him. Why didn't God prevent his going into the lions' den? Sometimes He allows us to be placed in impossible situations where we have no option but to trust Him or sink. When God begins to work through us, even those who do not believe will have to acknowledge His power. Was Daniel tempted to doubt God?

Israel, God's Wandering People

The Old Testament contains great stories about God's dealings with the Israelites. Deuteronomy 6:23 says, "The Lord brought us out that He might bring us in, to give us the land which He swore unto our fathers." Sometimes they grumbled and longed for what they had left behind in Egypt. But God brought them out of Egypt in order to bring them into Canaan. But before they could claim the Promised Land, they had to cross the Red Sea, the wilderness, the Jordan River, the mountains, and to fight numerous battles with their many enemies, which required much effort on their part.

When the Israelites left Egypt, God assured them of His presence; but with the Red Sea before them and Pharaoh behind them, it looked like a no-win situation. God said through Moses, "Fear ye not, stand still, and see the salvation of the Lord, which He will shew to you today...The Lord shall fight for you, and ye shall hold your peace" (Exodus 14:13a, 14).

Psalms 105 and 106 briefly summarize Israel's history and reaffirm that God kept the covenant He had made with Abraham. We see their unfaithfulness and backsliding juxtaposed against God's faithfulness. The Israelites tempted God, but God tested them. The writer of Hebrews devotes much of chapter eleven to holding them up as examples of achieving great exploits through their persevering faith. We know the Israelites doubted God because we read about their rebellion, repentance, God's forgiveness and restoration...and the cycle repeats itself.

Did you ever beg God to deliver you out of a situation, and then discover that where you were was better than where you went? Did you ever thank God for not granting some ridiculous request?

David Overcomes the Giants in His Life

And what of David, the beloved shepherd boy and sweet psalmist of Israel? God called him, and the prophet Samuel anointed him as Israel's future king. The Bible says the Lord prospered David in everything he did. While not perfect, David was a man after God's own heart, and he communed with God while on the hillsides with his father's sheep. He affirmed in Psalm 138:7, "Though I walk in the midst of trouble, You preserve my life."

King Saul became very jealous of David and tried desperately to kill him, hunting him down like a wild animal. But David knew that God had anointed Saul to be king of Israel, and even though Saul was clearly displeasing God, David accorded him the respect due his position.

Perhaps David knew the battle does not always belong to the strong, nor do the swift always win the race. As God had allowed him to overcome a bear, a lion, and a gigantic Philistine warrior, surely God would give him victory over King Saul. When David had an opportunity to kill Saul, he said to him instead, "...as your life was valued much in my eyes, so let my life be valued much in the eyes of the Lord, and let Him deliver me out of all tribulation" (I Samuel 26:24 NKJV).

Did you ever hear someone say, "I don't get mad; I get even?" Unfortunately, some Christians fall prey to the ways of the world that say we must get the other person before they get us. Do you think David was tempted to doubt God while he waited to become king? Probably so, but David would not take matters into his own hands.

Peter and John, Jailbirds for Jesus

These apostles' obedience to Jesus' mandate to preach the Gospel was rewarded with incarceration, beatings, public ridicule and persecution. After they were filled with the Holy Spirit, Peter and John preached the Gospel boldly, and no jail could deter them.

Acts 5 records the story of an angel delivering Peter and John from prison. When questioned by the high priest, the Apostles' answer is forthright and unapologetic. "We ought to obey God rather than men" (Acts 5:29).

Peter's faith was thoroughly tried and tested. He had denied knowing Jesus not once, but three times. But Jesus did not forsake Peter because of his failure; rather the Holy Spirit emboldened him to preach the Gospel despite persecution.

How might you and I behave if our lives were in jeopardy because of our faith in Jesus? Like Peter, it is easy to boast when things are going well—and I believe he actually thought he was ready to die for Jesus—but he did not know what was in his heart.

Peter's words in his epistle bear much credibility when we recall how he suffered for the sake of the Gospel. He said the trial or testing of our faith is more precious than gold, and we should not think it strange when our faith is tested because he saw persecution as a normal component of the

Christian life.

I Peter 4:14, 19: "If ye be reproached for the name of Christ, happy are ye; for the spirit of glory and of God resteth upon you: on their part He is evil spoken of, but on your part He is glorified. Wherefore, let them that suffer according to the will of God commit the keeping of their souls to Him in well doing, as unto a faithful Creator".

When Peter talked about suffering wrong and taking it patiently for the name of Christ, he knew of what he spoke.

Raising Lazarus

Fearful and apprehensive, it must have been hard for Mary and Martha to understand why Jesus did not come immediately when they sent word that His beloved friend Lazarus was sick. Jesus waited for four days, allowing Lazarus to die, "that the Son of God might be glorified." The disciples did not understand Jesus' actions either; however, we know that illness, delays, and disappointments can be opportunities to glorify God. Through Lazarus' resurrection Jesus demonstrated His power over life and death and symbolized the act of salvation. It is also a precursor to build our faith that we too shall rise again and live with Jesus forever, as He affirmed to Martha, "I am the resurrection and the life" (John 11:25).

Stephen, Martyred For His Faith

Stephen was stoned for his faithfulness in preaching the Gospel. While we may never discover why God allowed such a thing, we know that one of the main advocates of his stoning was converted and became a mighty apostle and writer of the bulk of the New Testament.

Paul, Master at Overcoming Adversity

The Apostle Paul suffered mightily for the sake of the Gospel, and he declared that through much tribulation we must enter the Kingdom of God (Acts 14:22b). This man could speak with authority about adversity and persecution!

Paul also knew something about physical ailments, as the following passage confirms. "Ye know that because of physical infirmity I preached the Gospel to you at the first. And my trial which was in my flesh you did not despise or reject, but you received me as an angel of God, even as Christ Jesus. What then was the blessing you enjoyed? For I bear you witness that, if possible, you would have plucked out your own eyes and given them to me"(Galatians 4:13-15, NKJV).

In II Corinthians 4:7-11, Paul describes some of the severe trials he endured, such as being troubled, perplexed, persecuted, and delivered to death. After rehearsing some of the many adverse situations he overcame, Paul catches a glimpse of the eternal, and he admonishes us not to lose heart, because our light afflictions are all temporary.

Also in II Corinthians 11:23-30, he relates the many adversities he has walked through as a faithful minister of Christ. Five times he was beaten with thirty-nine stripes; he was imprisoned, shipwrecked, stoned and left for dead, robbed, hungry, thirsty, cold, attacked by false brethren...and on and on. Paul said the Macedonian Christians were suffering poverty and a "great trial of affliction." How could Paul proclaim, "I am filled with comfort, I am exceeding joyful in all our tribulation" (II Corinthians 7:4b)?

Despite persecution and hardships, his greatest passion was to know Jesus and make Him known. Philippians 3:10: "That I may know Him, and the power of His resurrection, and the fellowship of His sufferings..."

Can we expect persecution, tribulation or suffering to come our way? Paul said in II Timothy 3:12: "Yea and all that will live Godly in Christ Jesus shall suffer persecution." This verse does not say that some will suffer persecution, but all. When we're off on a speaking appointment, and they put us up in a home rather than in a four-star hotel, we think we're suffering for Jesus.

Paul withstood adversity joyfully and emerged as the victor. In Romans 8:31, Paul asks, "If God be for us, who can be against us?" We may never know the full purpose of Paul's suffering, but this we know—Paul's faith was a persevering one; and he demonstrated the ability to endure under extreme pressure. Did Paul suffer because he was out of the will of God or had made a negative confession? Absolutely not!

Jesus, Not Exempt From Adversity

The writer of the Hebrews, speaking of Jesus, the sinless One, our perfect example, says that He learned obedience by the things that He suffered (Hebrews 5:8). I don't claim to understand that fully. But Jesus suffered rejection, hatred, misunderstanding, lies, and incredible ingratitude from those to whom He ministered. He even had people who followed Him for what they could get—the loaves and fish. Imagine it!

But Jesus overcame every adversity, and the Bible tells us that He laid down His life for us. No one was able to take it from Him, even though they tried tenaciously many times. Only when the Father's plan was fulfilled did Jesus give His life. He was willing to be bound that we might go free; He was willing to die that we might live. Such love!

When Jesus was preparing His disciples for the time when He would no longer walk the earth with them, He did not promise exemption from pain and suffering. He did, however, promise that the Holy Spirit would be their Comforter and Guide. Jesus told His disciples that in Him there is peace, but He warned them that in the world tribulation would surely come.

Whatever our adversity here on earth, when viewed in perspective of eternity, it seems as nothing. Hebrews 12:1-3

(NKJV) seems to sum up what I have attempted to convey in this chapter. "Therefore we also, since we are surrounded by so great a cloud of witnesses, let us lay aside every weight, and the sin which so easily ensnares us, and let us run with endurance the race that is set before us, looking unto Jesus, the author and finisher of our faith, Who for the joy that was set before Him endured the cross, despising the shame, and has sat down at the right hand of the throne of God. For consider Him Who endured such hostility from sinners against Himself, lest you become weary and discouraged in your souls."

Let us not faint!

Application Questions:
Bible Heroes and Adversity

Scriptures: Galatians 3:6-9,14, 29, Hebrews 11:8-19, Genesis 50:20, Job 13:15, 19:25-27a, 23:10-12, James 5:10-11, Daniel 6:16, 21-23, Deuteronomy 6:23, Exodus 14:13a, 14, Psalm 105, I Samuel 26:23, 24, Acts 5:17-29, 40-42, I Peter 4:14, 19, Galatians 4:13-15, II Corinthians 11:23-30, 7:4b, II Timothy 3:11-12, Hebrews 5:8, John 16:33, Hebrews 12:1-3.

1. How did Bible saints handle adversity, and what can we learn from them?

    a. Abraham and Sarah
    b. Joseph
    c. Job
    d. Daniel
    e. The Israelites
    f. David
    g. Peter and John
    h. Paul

2. How did Jesus deal with His ever-present adversaries?

CHAPTER 3

PERILS OF PREGNANCY

Having always been a lover of children, I naturally assumed that after we were married, Rivers and I would have several. We both believed that God would give us a son. As promised in Psalm 127:3, "Lo, children are an heritage of the Lord: and the fruit of the womb is his reward." When I was unable to conceive we were referred to an obstetrician/gynecologist who specialized in problems of infertility. He assured us that I could become pregnant under the right conditions, and prescribed a series of exercises and coital positions.

During the time when we were trying to conceive a child and after I was pregnant, several well-meaning saints made me feel worse by their unkind and inconsiderate remarks. I had to pray to avoid becoming bitter over thoughtless statements, because the person was totally oblivious to the stabbing pain it caused me. "You just don't want to be pregnant, and that's why you're sick. I've had several babies, and I didn't curtail any of my activities." These and other equally insulting remarks came our way, but I knew the speaker had failed to understand what was going on in my body. Had I succumbed to my feelings, I could have justifiably stayed in bed all day.

First Pregnancy, Twins

Mine was a very complicated, painful, and uncertain pregnancy. Before missing a menstrual period I was already quite ill with vomiting and bloating. A team of three family practice physicians confirmed that I had appendicitis with a possible rupture. An appendectomy was imminent, dependent only on my pain level as a confirmation of its necessity. All my symptoms pointed to this diagnosis, and the stool darkened by the use of Pepto Bismol surely signaled internal bleeding, they reasoned.

Dissatisfied with the doctors' findings, Rivers took me to one of Washington, D. C.'s top gynecologists who had attended me in the past. As Dr. Paquin removed the speculum and turned off the light he smiled broadly and said, "Angie, you're four weeks pregnant, and you're going to have twins!"

Thinking he was teasing, I retorted, "You'd better not find any twins up there!" But then the idea began to appeal to me. "Lord, if You give us a set of twins, I won't ask for another baby," I prayed. At last we were joyfully "infanticipating."

Violent Vomiting Episodes

But something was drastically wrong. It seemed that, like Jacob and Esau in Rachel's womb, my babies were in active combat twenty-four hours a day, as my insides wretched and no prescription relieved the constant regurgitation that dominated my days and nights. Doctor Paquin had laboriously tried one drug after another, but I brought them up minutes later—the orange juice with which I swallowed them still cold. The crackers-twenty-minutes-before-rising routine left crumbs on our bed sheets and caused me to make a quick dash for the bathroom where I gagged and heaved so hard that I became incontinent. The doctor finally resorted to rectal suppositories. "You can't vomit these," he chided. The suppositories stopped the vomiting temporarily, but brought on an equally undesirable state of half-conscious stupor.

My weight, normally a little below average, dropped

rapidly. "If you don't quit this vomiting, we'll be forced to hospitalize you and feed you intravenously," the doctor threatened. Since my veins are very small and difficult to access, I tried doubly hard to retain my food. Patting me on the back, Doctor Paquin said, "This morning sickness won't go beyond the third month." I was relieved to know this was temporary and felt I could endure almost anything for three months. However, this "morning sickness" was a twenty-four-hour-a-day affair, and at the end of the third month it persisted. Nothing changed, and when I was not gagging, my mouth watered constantly. I remember racing out of church during benediction to get to the bathroom in time.

Fitted With an Orthopedic Brace

Backaches, which were the norm for me, became so intense that I could barely walk, so my obstetrician referred me to an orthopedic hospital where I was fitted with a brace from my shoulder blades to the base of my hips. What a contraption of fabric, metal, buckles and laces, resembling an antiquated corset. Adjusting this brace required assistance from my husband, as getting in and out of it was difficult. If keeping my back straight was the objective, it worked well, but did little to accommodate my frequent trips to the bathroom.

At the time, I was secretary-stenographer to the only forensic pathologist in the U. S. Navy and was employed by the Armed Forces Institute of Pathology in Washington. Doctor Charles J. Stahl and the other pathologists grew concerned about my tenuous condition. They questioned me regularly about the abnormalities of my pregnancy and my obstetrician's response. Although I was ill and uncertain about my troubled pregnancy, I felt loved and quite safe knowing I was surrounded by some of the world's top pathologists.

Losing Twin Sons

I moved into my fifth month, struggling to stay on my feet. It was a cold, snowy January morning when I entered my office building, the old Medical Museum on Independence Avenue. Having experienced a "bloody show," I headed for my office to call my physician. However, I fainted and crumpled to the floor just a few yards from my office door. Pathologists in white coats came to my aid quickly as they sprang from their second-floor offices.

What followed was a nightmare climaxing in a twenty-minute wait in the ambulance while they applied snow

Angie recuperating after losing twins

chains. Meanwhile, a certain fear gripped me because I could still feel what I thought was blood oozing from my body. Since snow strikes panic in the city, I tried to understand why the paramedics spent twenty minutes trying to fit the ambulance with snow chains. Would I hemorrhage while they nonchalantly did the unnecessary? Besides, the ambulance driver insisted on taking me to the nearest hospital, but my physician was waiting for me at Providence. After some insistence on Rivers' part they acquiesced and reluctantly delivered me to Providence Hospital's Emergency Room.

Assuming I would deliver my premature twins soon, the doctor placed me in the labor room with only a clock—no husband, no water, no food—just a clock that slowly ticked away the next twenty-six hours, one second at a time. I prayed a lot and longed for Rivers' strong arms to hold me and tell me it would be all right.

Doctor Paquin checked the position of my uterus again and gave me a disgusted look. "Your uterus is way up here," he said, gesturing in the direction of my slightly bulging upper abdomen. "And it has to drop for the babies to be delivered. This is the worst possible time in a pregnancy to lose a baby. Don't you ever do this again!" Half joking at a time like this—as if I had done it by design? "Nothing's going to happen now, so take her to the OB floor," he ordered after the twenty-six-hour ordeal.

They transferred me to a maternity ward that I shared with three mothers. Painfully, I listened to the happy sounds of communication between mother and child as they cuddled, cooed, and nursed their newborns several times a day. Not wishing to create any trouble, I never questioned the hospital staff out loud, but I said to myself, "This is downright cruel!"

The night prior to my hospital admission, Rivers and I had attended our first childbirth class taught by a priest and several nuns. Upon hearing that I was delivering out of term, the nuns dutifully came to visit me. "Come and see this little girl who is having twins," I heard one nun say to another.

And momentarily I felt like a small child on exhibit, remembering my past resentment when someone mistook me for a child and wondering when I would begin to look my age. Flashing my wedding rings, I replied, "I'm not a little girl; I'm 26 years old!"

"Complete bed rest," the doctor ordered, "And don't get up for anything!" Each time I changed my position in bed I could feel the amniotic fluid escape. I tried so hard to be good, refusing to drink much liquid to avoid frequent use of a bedpan. Each morning they came in to bathe me and to change my sheets by rolling me over in the bed. There was, however, a disgruntled nurse's aide who did not follow the doctor's protocol. She ordered me out of the bed, whereupon she changed the sheets and walked out leaving me sitting in a chair across the room.

I scooted the chair inch-by-inch in order to reach the

bedside. By the time I was back in bed, the exertion had brought on a violent vomiting episode. Hearing my heaving, the same aide hurried into the room, exclaiming, "Be a big girl!" Preferring to throw the bedpan at the offender, I suddenly felt like a helpless puppy and hot, salty tears spilled onto my pillow. Through my tears I was so tempted to report the aide to my physician, but being department head, I felt sure he would fire her immediately for messing over his patient. The Lord gave me empathy for the woman and I didn't want her to lose her job, so I just continued to cry.

Doctor Ivan Magal, an internist and friend from our church, grew very concerned about me. He examined my hospital chart to confirm that my treatment was appropriate. This gave me great comfort until he exclaimed, "You will just have a dry birth." Since he appeared unwilling to explain, I asked no further questions.

While hospitalized, it seemed that I became the object of every resident doctor's learning process. "At what age did you begin your menses? Did you have problematic menstrual periods? Have you been pregnant before? How many children did your mother have? Have any of your siblings had problem pregnancies?" On and on they fired questions in rapid succession like firecrackers on a moonlit Fourth of July night. Entering my room in teams—poking me, prying into my background, and taking prolific notes—I wondered whether my condition was rare and worth using for teaching purposes. Resenting the intrusive visits and frequent pelvic examinations, I fought back the tears and prayed they would leave me alone.

Complete Bed Rest at Home

After four days I was discharged from the hospital with firm orders to stay in bed for the duration of my pregnancy. Stay in bed for almost five months? And what of the amniotic fluid that kept escaping every time I moved? How could I deliver twins without that? "Let's just ride this thing out," Dr. Paquin said. "Take her temperature every two hours and call me if it rises. Antibiotics three times a day to ward off infection. Remember, complete bed rest, and don't you go cleaning the house or anything. I know you're a perfectionist; I can tell by your underwear!"

After I was discharged, I stayed home for one day while our pastor's wife, Kathryn Good, "baby-sat" me. I was allowed to make an occasional trip to the bathroom. Since I disliked feeling helpless and inadequate, I'd lie in bed and plot how I could change the towels or scrub the sink on one of those trips.

Henry and Edna Brunk, a loving Christian couple who had parented us since we were newlyweds, offered to take care of me. They moved into their guest room so we could have their first-floor master bedroom. My "complete bed rest" lasted for a few hours when chills and fever set in. Rivers called Doctor Paquin, who said, "Get her to the Emergency Room immediately!" Mom Brunk and Rivers cradled me for the seemingly interminable half-hour trip to the hospital. Dad Brunk tried to remain calm at the wheel, occasionally reaching back and giving me a little reassuring pat on the head. Then lovingly and helplessly, Rivers stood by my hospital bed praying.

The doctor arrived in the Emergency Room with a troubled look on his face. After examining me carefully and allowing us to hear the babies' heartbeats, he shook his head. "Angie, your babies are alive, and I'm sorry. I've done all I can." With that he turned on his heel to leave, but Rivers stopped him abruptly.

"Don't Let My Wife Die!"

"The babies can't live without her—please, don't let my wife die," he pled with the doctor. We had been married only three years, and I did not want to die. So many things were going through my mind—the shock of my sister's death on the delivery table only eighteen months earlier. How did my current problems relate to hers? Would I die also? We discussed this with Doctor Paquin, and he agreed to call her obstetrician to see if there were similarities between my case and hers.

As I endured the long, lonely night in Providence Hospital's Emergency Room, I would have done anything to have those babies, even though I knew my life was in jeopardy. Therapeutic abortion? No way! Neither the doctor nor we even considered such a procedure. Assuming that labor was imminent, in a weak and half-terrified voice I asked, "Doctor Paquin, how do labor pains feel?" He described the uterine contractions and low back pain.

I remember thinking I would consider jumping out of the window if Jesus had not given me hope. Two of Washington's top obstetricians were at wits end, having invested the best of their collective knowledge and experience in me. Both Rivers and I were aware of I Timothy 2:15 which says, "Notwithstanding she shall be saved in childbearing, if they continue in faith and charity and holiness with sobriety." We prayed that God would intervene. The Emergency Room nurse wrote my temperature on the bed sheet close to my head—103.4 degrees—as I drifted into a peaceful sleep, trusting God for the outcome.

Labor pains awakened me early the next morning, and because I knew that losing my babies was inevitable, I said to the doctor, "This is the best pain I have ever felt." Rivers and Pastor Kenneth Good were by my side, as the labor grew harder. The last thing I remembered was squeezing the pastor's hand. Two days later I awakened to learn what had happened.

"Mrs. Williams! Mrs. Williams!" I heard the nurse call through a thick fog. Completely disoriented, I opened my eyes, not having a clue what had transpired. Having been sedated with IV Nembutal on Thursday at noon, I had been "dead to the world" until late Saturday afternoon. They had tried unsuccessfully to arouse me, and my dear husband had wondered if he would ever see me alive again.

When the doctor came in to see me, I chided him, "Doctor, I told you to put me out completely, but I did not tell you to put me out permanently!"

Doctor Paquin replied, "Most women would have been up walking around after a few hours, but you were very weak. You have experienced an inevitable abortion. Because you were so ill, I delivered your babies in this private room," Doctor Paquin said. He had not moved me to the delivery room since there was no chance our twins could survive. "Your twin sons were born alive. You were asleep and your husband was not here, so I baptized them myself!" my Catholic doctor said proudly, knowing I was a Christian. Notice, the doctor called them babies and not products of conception.

After five days I was discharged from the hospital without having the customary dilatation and curettage (D&C) surgery performed after a miscarriage. "Because you're too far along, you'll just have to slough it off as if you had delivered full-term," the doctor said.

The lengthy recuperation process was slow but progressive. Mom Brunk lovingly nursed me back to health. Not once did I hear Rivers complain about our not having that set of twins we wanted so much. With fresh memories of my sister's death in the delivery room, he was just grateful to have his young wife alive and on the mend.

When people tried to pity me I would say, "It could have been worse." Observing a pensive look on Diane's face, I continued, "Let's think positively. I lived through it; we did not have to name them or have a funeral; we had no baby furniture or clothing; we did not take them home and then have them snatched away..." Looking at me incredulously, I could tell Diane was wondering how I could feel that way. I continued, "What if we had had a set of twins with some terrible abnormalities? Yes, it could have been a lot worse!" As I enumerated the positives surrounding this episode, it was easy to see that they far outnumbered the negatives.

Second Pregnancy of Short Duration
In less than a year we lost another baby in the first six weeks of pregnancy. While I was hospitalized for a D&C, one of the nurse's aides consoled me with, "Honey, you're young. You can get pregnant again."

However, wincing through my pain I muttered, "What good is it to get pregnant if I don't have a baby?"

Doctor Paquin said he would try to discover why I had difficulty getting pregnant and staying pregnant. He later told me that his two-hour probe in the operating room had not yielded the answer. "Whatever it is, it's elusive," he admitted sadly. I was thinking, that's a nice way of saying, "I really don't know."

During my six-week check-up Doctor Paquin said, "If you so much as think you are pregnant again, come immediately and I will prescribe a hormone for you."

Third Pregnancy, a Son at Last!
When the time came, he kept his word. Knowing that medications increased my nausea, I asked, "What are the contraindications of this drug?" as I accepted his latest prescription.

"I'd hoped you wouldn't ask. You're already sick, and these pills will make you feel worse. But mind you, you can't lose your baby if you take them as prescribed."

"Are you sure?" I queried.

"Yes," he replied.

Obediently, I began to take the ten milligrams of Enovid per day—a hormone to prevent pregnancy, usually prescribed in one-milligram doses at that time. True to the doctor's word, I became more ill than ever—back and leg problems, and pernicious vomiting around the clock. I became very thin and anemic, weighing barely one hundred pounds.

The doctor ordered me to begin wearing the orthopedic contraption for my back that was prescribed for my first pregnancy. At the time, I was employed at the Smithsonian Institution as a secretary-stenographer. In order to cope with my physical problems, I would arrive at work an hour early. Sometimes I had to lie on the floor for a few minutes before the staff arrived in order to garner the strength for my day. I would get up and put on a pot of coffee for them, and by the time they arrived, I was perched at my desk smiling happily as if all was well.

Some mornings when I arrived at work, I headed straight for the bathroom where I heaved and vomited for a few minutes. Then I would lie on the bed in the women's room and rest before I emerged smiling to everyone. I remember the day when a guard stopped me to ask whether I was so happy because I was pregnant, or was I that happy all the time. Little did he know that many times I actually wondered if I would live to see the day end. On a wing and a prayer, I kept coming to work day after day.

My director had come to rely on me heavily, especially when he traveled abroad. Unlike some of my colleagues, I was always there early and giving my best. Finally, I said to him, "I'm not much good to you, so I might as well quit so you can hire someone else."

Giving me one of his rarely seen caring glances, Mr. Durant replied, "You do more work sick than anyone here who is well. You're the best secretary I've had in my whole career, so just keep coming in as long as you can." I pushed myself almost mercilessly to work up to the eighth month, excusing this abuse by, "If I stay at home, I will feel worse."

I had been scheduled for an epidural so I could watch

my baby's birth. After several painful attempts to insert the needle without success, Dr. Paquin said apologetically, "You don't have anywhere to put it,"—whatever that means. "I'm sorry, Angie, but I'll have to put you to sleep." By then I was panting and ready to deliver, and not much else mattered.

After this very difficult eight-month pregnancy, miraculously, I gave birth to five-pound-eight-ounce Barth, who went promptly into an isolette. We could watch the little red bundle through the window, but were not permitted to hold him. I had been anesthetized and neither Rivers nor I had watched the birth, but that was fine. While this pregnancy had been dominated by constant nausea and vomiting right up to the labor room, along with severe back and leg problems, when I finally held our firstborn in my arms, the suffering seemed minimal.

John 16:21 says, "A woman when she is in travail hath sorrow, because her hour is come: but as soon as she is delivered of the child, she remembereth no more the anguish, for joy that a man is born into the world."

The life that God had created was precious, and I would never take it for granted. The empty crib syndrome would plague me no longer because we had a baby we could cradle. On Sunday evening, September 22, 1968, I was in love with the whole world, and as the anesthesia was wearing off I continued to repeat a little refrain to my husband and physician. Later, when Barth turned twenty-one, I described my feelings in poetry, some of which I have included below.

"Ode To K. Barth Williams"
'Twas a warm Sunday evening
In Washington, D.C.,
September 22, 1968,
When in Providence Hospital
A happy mother lay panting,
Giving birth to a champion, lightweight.

'Twas at seven-forty-eight,
Not a moment too late,
When Barth Williams entered this planet.
Weighing in at five pounds, eight,
Nineteen inches in length.
Why, his birth was never taken for granted.

A little wisp of a woman,
Mom now skinny and frail,
Had grown weaker day by day.
Trying to nourish babe in womb;
To remain on her feet,
The physician's strict orders to obey.

But today she understood—
Quite clearly, in fact,
What John 16:21 really means.
That a woman soon forgets
Travail, labor and such,
When a beloved child arrives on the scene.

What an occasion it should be,
Time for merriment and glee,
For family, friends and all those who knew.
God had blessed with a son,
But the blessing had only begun.
Why the whole world should be elated too!

Dad in his red shirt,
Tall, handsome and alert,
Was grinning from one ear to the other.
But the happiest person
In the whole wide world,
Was Barth Williams' worn-out mother.

Yes, this miracle birth
Was a time of great mirth.
For Mom, Dad and Dr. Paquin too.
They had waited five years,
And prayed through many tears,
For this son to make his debut.

Three babies they had lost
For no readily apparent cause.
And Mom had suffered piteously.
But their faith did not bend;
They persevered right to the end,
'Til their faith was rewarded with victory!

Barth was anxious to depart
The cramped quarters he was in
For his mother's body held him very tight.
So at the end of month eight,
He made his grand escape,
Thinking the timing was exactly right.

Mom, groggy from medications,
Saw her husband standing by.
Was talking clearly "out of her head."
She exclaimed, "I love my husband;
I love my baby; I love my doctor;
But isn't my baby ugly and red?"

Dad patted her gently,
Trying desperately to quiet her,
His embarrassment now clearly showing.
But the slurred words came out,
With such rhythmic repetition,
For today her little heart was overflowing.

When to diaper him, he was laid
On his back—he should have stayed.
But instead, he quickly flipped to his right side.
As in his bed he tossed and turned,
His startled parents were concerned,
How a five-pound preemie could be so alive!

When his arms and legs were unbent,
Back to fetal position he quickly went.
For he missed the cozy quarters of the past.
But his pediatrician did explain,
That these actions would not remain,
Once he reached full-term he would not move so fast.

September 1989

When Barth was three days old, Doctor Paquin surprised us with some good news. Now we could hold him for the first time and I could nurse him. He was five pounds-one-and-one-half ounces, barely over the minimum weight required for discharge. If all went well, both he and I could go home soon.

What a homecoming it was! But this precious bundle was not without his problems, not the least of which was a severe case of colic and allergy to milk products. Because of his size he had to be fed a small amount sometimes every half hour. Since I could not nurse him that often, we supplemented with a bottle. It seemed that as soon as I got him to ingest a little, changed his diaper and put him down for a nap, he would awaken and we would repeat the cycle.

As a newborn he would stiffen his legs and back, turn red, and throw back his head and scream. When I lay him on his back to change him, he immediately flipped to his right side. When left in his cradle, he traveled to the other end and turned across the bed, placing his head against the rails. I had never seen a newborn behave this way, so I asked the pediatrician, "How did I get a baby with such a temper?"

Examining Barth carefully, Doctor McDonald smiled and said, "This isn't temper; this baby is sick! He has colic."

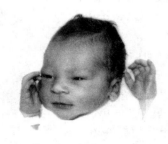

K. Barth Williams as a newborn

He changed the formula to soy, prescribed some medication, and gave me instructions on how to keep Barth as comfortable as possible.

I was so elated to be a mother after all we had been through, but Barth required twenty-four-hour-a-day attention. The colic persisted for over four months, and during that time he never slept through the night. This began to take its toll on me physically, and my already frail body showed it. I had gained only a few pounds during my pregnancy, and now I was losing weight again. The doctor pumped me full of iron and other supplements to build me up. Finally at five months,

Grandma and Grandpa Brunk
admire Barth

Barth's colic subsided and I could get a good night's sleep at last.

To our amazement, five years later God gave us a second son, a mere four months after my husband suffered a myocardial infarction. I was physically ill during this pregnancy also, exaggerated by the additional stress of Rivers' heart attack. But God is always faithful to His promises, and a second son was immeasurably more than we could ask or think.

Application Questions:
Perils of Pregnancy

Scriptures: Genesis 30:1, Psalm 127:3-5, I Timothy 2:15, Psalm 106:37, 38, Micah 6:7b, Luke 1:5-45.

1. How would you have kept your faith vibrant while coping with failed pregnancies and the empty crib syndrome?

2. Describe ways to deal with mothers who don't understand the plight of childless women.

3. Would it have been appropriate to consider an abortion given the fact that the author's life may have been in jeopardy? Why, or why not?

Ministry in Florida

First assignment at Christian Retreat, interviewing
Tim and Beverly LaHaye for Blessing Magazine

Donna Spence, June Carter Cash, and Angie
at June's autographing party

Angie, as Publicity Director,
prepares poster for celebration with June Carter Cash

CHAPTER 4

THE MOST DIFFICULT TIME
OF MY LIFE

Rivers and I had walked through some deep waters and difficult circumstances in the loss of our beloved babies. However, the summer of 1973 brought a challenge we had not imagined in our worst nightmares, and it certainly ranks among the most trying things we have ever faced.

Rivers' Debilitating Heart Attack

How can a healthy, robust, athletic young man with no propensity toward heart abnormalities or family history of such, suddenly have a heart attack? In the normal scheme of things, that is just not supposed to happen. When we are sure that we have obeyed God, how can cruel adversity grab us in its all-encompassing grip and nearly overcome us?

Rivers and I had followed God's call to resign our government positions in Washington, and to relocate to the Shenandoah Valley of Virginia where Rivers would enroll as a full-time student at Eastern Mennonite College (now Eastern Mennonite University). I accepted a position as Administrative Associate, while Rivers worked part-time. It was a very happy time for us and for our two-year-old Barth, who enjoyed much attention from the students. And so it went for two full years until...life seemed to unravel suddenly, and we were stripped of much that we held dear. But who ever said that following the Lord's leading would guarantee a trouble-free life?

With the faith of a child, four-year-old Barth began praying for a baby. I tried to encourage him, but knowing my history, did not expect anything to happen. We decided that because hormones had made me so ill in the past, we would not resort to that. If God wanted to give us a baby, He could do so without medical intervention. We just went about our busy lives filled with work, school, and the business of raising our young son.

In January of 1973 I accepted the nomination as Vice-President of our denominational Women's Missionary and Service Commission. Surprisingly, in April I became pregnant. Some who knew what the next nine months held for me questioned whether I might wish to resign. I replied, "We've prayed a lot about this, and the Lord knew we would have this baby when I accepted the nomination, so I will continue." At five months pregnant, I was elected during Mennonite General Assembly in August. My prayer and earnest desire was to get beyond my fifth month since this was the time when we had lost our twins during my first pregnancy.

Because of complications, Doctor Nipe ordered me to resign from my position, stay off my feet, and rest as much as possible. Having no intention of leaving my job so early because of financial necessity, I would trudge up the steps to my office each morning, arriving sick, but determined to forge ahead.

On a hot August morning, only twelve days after being elected as Vice-President, I was about to face one of the most difficult tests of my life. I was seated at my desk at the college although I was not feeling well. Operating under the assumption that "if you can walk, you can work," I felt I had to earn some income at any cost, especially since Rivers was now a student in his senior year at Eastern Mennonite.

Rivers had called me from home that Tuesday morning—how could I ever forget the day? "I was working in the garden, and I've pulled some muscles in my chest," he said. "I'm on my way to see Doctor Brunk now. I'll call you later." That call never came.

Instead, the next word I heard came from Clayton

Shenk, my kindly office director who was a devoted Christian. He stood in my office door with a furrowed brow. Shocked by the grim look, I asked, "What's wrong?"

He replied hesitantly, "Doctor Brunk just called and said that Rivers has been taken to the hospital with a heart attack! Come, I will take you to the hospital to see him." Doctor Brunk, the attending physician, knew I was pregnant and not well, so he called Clayton and asked him to break the news to me.

Remembering Rivers' earlier call, I faintly replied, "Well, he is young and healthy, so it can't be very serious." Collecting my belongings quickly, I remember meekly following him down the hall. It seemed that my mind was swirling around like a buzzing bee. Never in my worst nightmare had I ever associated the words heart attack with Rivers. How could it be that my thirty-three-year-old husband, who was not overweight, had never smoked or ingested alcohol, had low cholesterol levels, and was quite athletic, had a heart attack? After all, he had a relatively well balanced diet, exercised regularly, and for the first time was working in the sizeable garden he had planted. At his last thorough physical examination, his Watergate-based internist had affirmed, "You have the heart of an athlete!" Furthermore, he was a Christian since childhood, and this certainly was not his due. Or was it?

My thoughts were interrupted by Clayton's, "Ok, Angie, let's go in." I was beginning to feel quite nauseated as we rode the elevator to the third floor. We walked into a waiting room full of grim faces. Some cried softly while others just stared into space, and still others buried their faces behind well-worn magazines.

I was ill prepared for what I saw next. Looking over my right shoulder, I saw a sign that sent chills rushing down my spine. It read simply, "Intensive Care/Coronary Care Unit." I asked Clayton, "What is he doing in there?" He did not reply, but my worst fears were soon to be realized.

Clayton notified the nurse that I had arrived and she invited me in. Remembering that even though it was difficult to keep my food down, if I did not eat, I was assured a case of dry heaves, I said to Clayton, "It's lunch time, and I must have a bite to eat. Would you please get a sandwich for me?"

I had never been into an Intensive Care Unit before, so I did not know what to expect. The walk down the long aisle between patient beds seemed one of the longest I had ever taken. It was lined with bed after bed of very sick men. One of the first things I noticed was that they were all gray-haired except for Rivers.

Words cannot adequately describe the shock of seeing my husband, hospitalized for the first time in our ten-year marriage. Tubes, oxygen mask, electrode patches, intra-venous needles, and other paraphernalia surrounded his youthful body. A middle-aged nurse sat nearby at a work-station monitoring his every move. The kind doctor explained to me that Rivers had suffered an acute antero-lateral myocardial infarction, a heart attack resulting from stress. I was later to learn that some eighty-seven percent of young men suffering such an attack die instantly or live for only a short while.

What happened next as I stood beside my husband's bed defies description. Right there in the Intensive Care Unit, God did a special miracle. He gave me supernatural strength that I cannot explain. I, who cry over sad components of the evening news, while not understanding all the why's of our situation, felt no urge to break down and have a good cry. Leaning over Rivers' hospital bed, I made him a promise. "Just rest, listen to the doctor, and take care of yourself. I'll take care of myself, Barth, and the baby I'm carrying." Knowing that I became quite ill if I allowed myself to get too hungry, he did not stop until he extracted a promise that I would eat well even if I was not able to keep it down.

So began an eight-day cycle that consisted of daily trips to the hospital Intensive Care Unit, five precious minutes with Rivers followed by another one-hour wait. As I glanced around the unit, I noticed no chairs by the patients' beds, a clear indication of no provision for extended visits. Knowing this was best for Rivers, I would plan the topic of discussion since every moment had to count. He always wanted to know how four-year-old Barth was coping with life without his Dad. Carefully shielding him from anything I thought might upset him, I bravely tried to put on a good front. But it really was not an act, because God gave me the ability to endure and to be joyful despite our circumstances.

Because of Rivers' delicate condition, I carefully concealed the unfavorable information my obstetrician had just given me about a problematic hernia I had. Not expecting to lean on him for strength, I would just have to bear any bad news alone. Savoring every second of that five-minute visit, I filled it with messages from well-wishers and quotes of funny things Barth was saying and his special prayers for Daddy to get well. The precious moments passed too quickly and I rejoined other relatives of heart attack victims in the waiting room. They always inquired about Rivers' condition and we shared any shred of encouragement and good news we could. Observing their pain, I prayed with several of them.

I was becoming quite weary, and the August heat was a contributing factor. Observing the frantic pace I was forced to keep, Clayton came to my rescue by writing a letter to every student, staff and faculty member at the college. He described what had happened and expressed appreciation for their outpouring of love; however, he suggested they not contact me directly. "Don't go to the hospital, and don't go to their home," he said. While I thought it sounded ungrateful, I knew it was necessary. He further advised everyone, "If you want to help the Williams family, stay at home and pray." But Clayton did not leave them in the dark, as he agreed to become a liaison between the college and us, keeping them apprised of Rivers' condition.

Setback in Intensive Care

After the first few days, I became less apprehensive that Rivers might not survive even though his condition was still guarded. Prayers were being answered, and I was so grateful that he was making such good progress. And then it happened.

Rivers had been taken off the monitor and would soon be transferred from ICU to a private room. But one day eight different ministers called on him. None of them stayed very long—they read Scripture, had a prayer and a few encouraging words, and left. But eight in one day was a bit much, so Doctor Brunk said to me, "They nearly preached the man to death!" Things had to change, so he excluded everyone except Pastor Owen Burkholder, College President Myron Augsburger, and Academic Dean Dan Yutzy.

Doctor Brunk had a sign printed in bold red letters and placed on the door that read, "No visitors except wife. All others must check at desk. This includes ministers."

The monitor was reconnected to Rivers, and again they watched his every move a while longer. After eight days he was moved to a private room where he remained for another thirteen days. During his entire hospital stay, never once did I hear him complain about his lot or question God in any way. We both continued to rest in God's supernatural peace and the faith that He would take care of us.

During Rivers' confinement to Intensive Care, I began writing an article for Gospel Herald magazine expressing my feelings. Since this article resulted from an intense time of prayer and waiting, holding on when sheer faith was all I had, I felt it would encourage others during their trying times.

Experiencing God in the Little Things

With limited physical strength because of my pregnancy,

it was difficult to walk even one block. As I approached the hospital each day, I would begin to pray for a parking space, and without exception, God answered that prayer. One day I had to drive around the hospital three times, and that tested my faith. By the third time around, God spoke to someone to move their car that was parked along the back wall of the hospital, the closest entrance to Rivers' room. Praise the Lord, God cares about the little things we need.

I had never experienced God's presence in such a practical manner. Well-meaning Christians suggested that I ask my obstetrician for sleep-inducing medication. My reply was, "I've loved the Lord as long as I can remember; if He will not help me now, I will not need Him when things are going well." God never failed me!

Each night I went to bed quoting Philippians 4:6, 7 from the Living Bible. "Don't worry about anything; instead, pray about everything. Tell God your needs, and don't forget to thank Him for the answers. If you do this, you will experience God's peace, which is far more wonderful than the human mind can understand. His peace will keep your heart quiet and at rest as you trust in Christ Jesus."

I surmised that refusing to worry about anything included heart attacks. Praying about everything included pleading to God for Rivers' healing. Tell God your needs included strength for coping, physical endurance, baby-sitters for Barth, among other things. Thank Him for the answers meant that, by faith, I could begin to give thanks before I saw the answer. The result of putting this Scripture to the test was what blessed me the most. "If you do this, you will experience God's peace."

The peace that I experienced cannot be explained apart from God's grace. How could I have peace when I knew that at any moment I could receive a call that my husband had expired, leaving me with a young son and another child in the womb?

No Guarantee of a Trial-Free Life

Who would have guessed that only two years after he entered Eastern Mennonite College Rivers would suffer a debilitating heart attack and be hospitalized for three weeks? At the time, this made no sense to me at all.

Since his myocardial infarction resulted from stress, it later became clear why Rivers was a candidate for a heart attack after all. We had both held pressure-laden positions with the federal government, but we had given up our professions to return to college. God worked things out in such a miraculous way that we never doubted this decision. But does that ensure we will face no trials because we have followed Jesus? Hardly! Jesus never said that obeying Him would guarantee a trial-free, blissful existence.

Rivers had worked at the Federal Bureau of Investigation (FBI) when J. Edgar Hoover was the "reigning monarch." Their every action was carefully monitored—from weight to the color of their shirts. Rivers, naturally tall and slender, came home one day with lunch bag in hand. "Why didn't you eat your lunch?" I inquired. "Because they weighed me today, and I'm two pounds overweight!" he said. "I won't get my promotion until I lose the two pounds."

He worked in the Fingerprinting Division during the early to mid-sixties when rebellion was the order of the day. The hippie movement had begun, and this meant an inordinate number of arrests with the attendant fingerprinting, manual searching, and identification. So he worked long hours and was sometimes on call when he was at home. Out of this background, he had become a full-time college student, which produces its own special stress.

As I look back on that traumatic day in the humid Virginia August heat of 1973, I can still see my young husband attached to a myriad of tubes, monitors, and other devices, surrounded by nurses in the open area known as

Intensive Care/Coronary Care Unit in Rockingham Memorial Hospital. Also etched in my memory is the seemingly interminable aisle that led to his bed that I walked once each hour to be by his side.

The best memory of all is of God's constant loving care over us. He gave me wisdom beyond my years and forbearance that I cannot describe. I take no credit for it, as it was God's gift to me.

Now, don't go off on a guilt trip if you have not been able to bear up under adversity. If you had a good cry, I suspect it was

Rivers and Angie just prior to River's heart attack

very therapeutic. If you needed Valium to help you sleep, that's all right too. But, I do know it is easy to proclaim our faith when the family is well and the bank account is bulging.

Did we consider it normal for a young, healthy man to suffer a sudden heart attack? Statistically, it was quite rare at that time, and that in itself was cause for grave concern. As I spent many hours both literally and figuratively "in the waiting room," I had a lot of time to ponder why God saw fit to spare Rivers' life and why his prognosis included the doctor's optimism that there would be no long-term residual effects. Whether or not God reveals His reasons to us, we count life as precious.

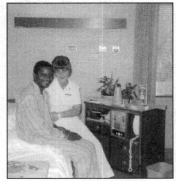

Rivers with a nurse readies for discharge after myocardial infarction

As you will discover elsewhere in this book, the myocardial infarction was like the tip of the iceberg—only one instance of our waiting on the Lord and walking through adversity. My sister Eunice and her family were the only relatives close by, but brothers and sisters in Christ were always on hand to assist us. We would soon discover the importance of allowing God to answer prayer through His people and how humbling this can be.

Application Questions:
The Most Difficult Time Of My Life

Scriptures: Philippians 4:6, 7, I Peter 4:12, 13, John 11.
1. Describe the most difficult thing you have had to deal with and how you reacted to it.
2. How would you have handled an unexpected serious illness of a loved one?
3. How have you experienced God working in the most difficult time of your life?

CHAPTER 5

SUPER SAINTS AND MISERABLE COMFORTERS

As is usually the case, when Rivers was hospitalized we had our share of well-wishers daily. Since we were attached to a Christian college and seminary, the word spread rapidly when the students and faculty returned in the fall. It was difficult to find time even to bathe because of the constant stream of people ringing our doorbell or our telephone. From early morning to late night it continued while Rivers was hospitalized. People meant well and no one knew how many others had called or visited.

I became so weary that Clayton and Dorothy Shenk allowed me to come to their home and crawl in bed for a few hours on a Sunday afternoon just to escape the traffic in our home. On another occasion I asked a student to "hide" our car at the college so it would appear that I was not at home. That was a bit dishonest, but my health was in jeopardy, and this was how I thought Barth and I could get some rest.

Miserable Comforters

One thing that did not boost my faith was that during Rivers' hospitalization we heard about several young men who suffered a myocardial infarction and died immediately. They keeled over and died while riding a bicycle, playing basketball, or taking exercise. Also, some whom I soon labeled as "miserable comforters," told me of everyone they knew who had died of various forms of heart disease. It was just what I needed to build my faith that Rivers would be healed. I already knew the statistics, and the devil saw to it that I did not forget his slim chance of survival by reminding me often.

I was bombarded with all sorts of questions that kept me rehearsing the grim details and experiencing the pain repeatedly. The most unbelievable came from a minister who asked, "Can your husband function sexually?" But for every person who expressed negativism, God supplied several who spoke encouragement.

Rivers' Unusual Trip to the Hospital

One such encouraging person was his Christian internist, Doctor Brunk. While Rivers was in the hospital, he related the story to me of how he actually got there. When he went to Dr. Brunk's office complaining of chest pain, they immediately gave him an electrocardiogram. Observing some irregularities and not wishing to take any chances, Doctor Brunk left another patient on the examining table and took Rivers to the hospital in his private car. He also maneuvered the wheelchair through the corridors over the objections of orderlies and nurses who wanted to assist, and never let go until Rivers was properly medicated and resting in the Intensive Care Unit.

Thinking that a pair of his own pajamas would make him feel better and preserve his dignity, one day I dutifully carted them in. As I struggled to help him slide into his fresh pajamas, the monitor at the nursing station registered a problem. The nurse, who let nothing escape her notice, was instantly on her feet. His every move showed up on that monitor, and I felt confident that everything within the realm of medical science was at his disposal.

Those ICU nurses and physicians were so kind and treated Rivers like a celebrity, and I kept wondering if it was because of his youth. The royal treatment continued throughout his stay and later earned them one of my home baked cakes and the following poem.

Thanks, Nurses and Orderlies

You fourth floor nurses are so very sweet;
Your bedside manners are really hard to beat.
You prod him; you poke him and give him a shot.
He smiles and says, "Thank you," when thankful he's not!
You monitor his vitals along with his diet.
He'd like some cheesecake—just one teeny bite.
But since you know what is best for him,
He tries to cooperate and keep his body slim.
Now orderlies, my friends, don't you feel left out.
You too are proficient—of that there's no doubt.
How could nurses survive without your strong backs;
To help them get ornery male patients on track?
So thank you, our friends, for all that you do.
Keep up the good work, and may God bless you.

August 1973

Home At Last!

"Mr. Williams is being discharged today," the nurse said cheerfully. A flood of emotions engulfed me. After three long weeks of staring at the ceiling in a hospital room, Rivers was actually coming home. Quickly gathering up some clothes for him and getting a sitter for Barth, I was soon on my way.

It was not unusual for me to cry with someone over his or her problems; however, during the three weeks of Rivers' hospitalization, I had not succumbed to self-pity or shed a tear. But on the way to the hospital my emotions spilled over like a waterfall after a heavy rain, as I cried, laughed, and prayed all the way. God had spared my husband, and it was a joyous time for me. I felt I had to be strong for Rivers, and too much emotional upheaval could affect an already unstable pregnancy and perhaps Rivers' ability to get well.

Being home from the hospital, however, did not mean

that Rivers was well. He was unable to do any work, and my capacity was also limited by complications of pregnancy. Rivers' medications left him sedated or groggy, so I needed to care for him a lot. We joked about getting a taste of what it must be like to grow old and be dependent on others.

Help Him Live!

When I accepted the fact that Rivers was not completely whole and his recuperation process would take many months, I knew that without God's constant care I could not endure the pressure. I remember thinking that my support was an important key to Rivers regaining his health. The Lord dropped a thought into my mind, "You can help him live, or you can help him die." What an awesome responsibility I felt and how sobering was the thought. It seemed a burden too heavy to bear, but I made up my mind to help him live. I would do everything in my power to support him medically, nutritionally, and spiritually and to relieve our home of stress and negative influences.

When other adverse things started to occur, I began to think we were under a satanic attack. One day as I was praying through the house, I walked to the front door, opened it and told the devil he was not welcome in our home, and he had to leave. Then I symbolically closed the door leaving him on the outside.

Catastrophes can cause a young couple's savings to dwindle quickly, and soon all of our savings had been exhausted and we were in need. Rivers' out patient medical expenses were exorbitant, and now we were struggling to pay them along with our living expenses. Entering my fifth month of pregnancy, I knew I would not be able to work much longer, and I did not want Rivers to have additional stress brought on by financial problems.

The Scripture from II Corinthians 1:8-10 (TLB) where Paul describes the difficulties he faced while preaching in Asia sounded as if it had been written for us. "We were really crushed and overwhelmed, and feared we would never live through it...we saw how powerless we were to help ourselves; but that was good, for then we put everything into the hands of God, Who alone could save us...And He did help us...and we expect Him to do it again and again..."

As we prayed, we knew the Lord would take care of us, but would our pride and self-sufficiency stand in the way of receiving God's answers delivered by a Christian brother or sister?

Super Saints

We appreciated the wonderful friends and neighbors who expressed concern in many ways and assured us of their prayers. But in my physical condition and with the added stress of a sick husband, sometimes I felt as if people would "love me to death."

Evangelist Steve Wingfield, then a student at Eastern Mennonite, took upon himself to become our liaison to the student body. Functioning as "president of the labor union," he called me each morning to ascertain our needs, then dutifully assigned a student to meet the need. What a joy and blessing that was.

One student had heard President Augsburger speak of our situation in class. He called and said, "God has been talking to me. Do you have any floors needing to be scrubbed? I just love to scrub! It's worship for me."

I replied, "God has surely been talking to you, because we haven't seen you for over a year. How could you know that during dinner last night I stared at our kitchen floor in disgust and exclaimed to Rivers, 'This floor is so dirty, but who is going to clean it for us?'"

Our floor scrubber was a singer who had just released a record album. Ken Parsons provided a Gospel concert while he scrubbed and waxed the floor on his knees weekly for the next several months. "Now, Lord, this is in the category of more than we could ask or think," I reasoned.

To show our gratitude, after we both recovered, we had a dinner party for the many students who had ministered to us. Often my feelings are best expressed in poetry, so I wrote the following poem of thanks to these super saints, which was published in the college newspaper.

Thanks to Super Saints

How can we tell you; what can we say,
Concerning the help that has come our way?
But may God clearly this day to you reveal
The sentiments that the Williams Trio feels.

Regarding your continuing concern for us,
You have helped us greatly, as in Him we trust.
He has no hands but yours to do His work.
You listened to His Spirit, and no task you have shirked.

You've mowed our lawn; you've scrubbed our floors.
You've emptied our trash, and done much more.
We've wondered how soon your energy will wear out,
But this is what serving our Master is all about.

You have followed His command to help those in need.
May He grant you His blessings as His Word you heed.
Heretofore it's been easy for us to do our part,
But accepting help from others really does come hard.

So thank you, our friends, for your love and care.
For many of you have done much more than your share.
We could never have faced these crises alone.
With prayers, gifts and muscles our burdens you have borne.

Yet we've not asked God why this should come our way;
For His cleansing by fire is only for today.

But as we emerge, we shall be as pure gold.
Through this whole experience, His will can unfold.

He has much to teach us that we have not yet learned;
He has grace enough for us that we have not earned.
Continue to pray with us, as faith is our only hope.
We must keep our eyes on Jesus, or be consumed by the smoke.

November 1973

Monetary Gifts, Meals, and More

Many neighbors, friends and relatives showed the love of Jesus to us in more ways than I could imagine. We experienced the Lord's exceeding abundance through His people, because when we prayed for a specific need, God sent it by a human being. Knowing this was even more difficult for Rivers than for me, I chided him one day, "When the Lord answers our prayers, He does not drop it out of Heaven, but He sends it by a person, and we will have to swallow our pride and accept it."

The hardest thing to accept from others was cold cash. After all, it had been only two short years since we were living in our "dream home" just outside of Washington and commanding two adequate government salaries. Accepting charity was not a part of what we had bargained for when we moved to Harrisonburg.

Nevertheless, the gifts began to arrive from other states and local people when word got around about our plight. That was really hard, and my pride began to suggest, "What will they think when they look at us?"

One professor at the college gave us a check for an odd amount of money. He explained to me this way. "The Lord spoke to me to give you this amount, but I am not sure why. I wonder how I would have responded if He had asked me to add more zeroes to it." I knew immediately that he had heard from God because, not coincidentally, it was the exact amount we needed for our electric bill.

One evening Pastor Harold Eshleman called to see if we had any unmet needs. Did we ever! By now we had exhausted all our savings and neither of us could work. We stared at the stack of bills and tried to decide what we would say to the pastor. Before he arrived, we found a surprise in our campus mailbox—an envelope with enough cash to cover our house payment. The note read simply, "We love you." We never learned the source of that money, but because of our pride we were happy to be spared the embarrassment of accepting charity from our church.

From mowing the lawn, washing windows, bringing meals, doing laundry, grocery shopping, ironing, baby sitting Barth, picking and canning vegetables from Rivers' garden, cleaning, and more, the kindnesses continued. Sometimes our needs were met before we uttered the prayer. The Lord knew our situation, and He sent someone to provide what we needed.

Sometimes people brought too much food, so a church friend volunteered to serve as a sort of food patrol, tracking and assigning daily meal preparation. Since diet was so important, I was always happy when someone inquired before preparing a meal.

I well remember the evening when we were served hamburger casserole for the third consecutive day. Friends were so generous in bringing meals, we would not dare complain, but I knew I could not ingest oily foods. "What I wouldn't do for a little piece of chicken right now!" I exclaimed to Rivers while staring into the hamburger casserole. Nothing further was said.

The following evening when Glenda came with our dinner, she said, "I don't know why, but I had the strongest urge to make chicken breasts for you today." Again we saw the hand of God supplying not only our needs, but the desires of our heart.

Recuperation from a heart attack is slow and arduous. One day I exclaimed to Rivers, "This is long-term, and these people will get tired of waiting on us!" But they never seemed to tire as days stretched into weeks, and weeks into months. Fall arrived and our situation had improved some, but we still had to depend on others for many things.

Lessons Learned

During this time I learned some very valuable lessons that would have evaded me apart from such a crisis. The Lord taught me how to accept His answers sent in His way, at His time, and not mine.

Friends have often heard me exclaim, "God has called me to be a servant!" It is so comfortable for me to rush to someone's side to pray and give a monetary or other gift. However, accepting gifts from others did not come easy, and my pride was seriously trampled on. Since I had always been a giver, I did not realize how our gifts could ingratiate others to us until the shoe was on my foot.

I also learned not to follow my emotions when responding to crises—our many challenges have changed the way I view and respond to hardships. When the first inclination is to dash right over, I stop to consider what is best for the patient and the family. I pray for and attempt to minister to the caregiver as well as to the patient, knowing their life can be very stressful, and their needs may be overlooked.

In an article published in Gospel Herald following Rivers' heart attack, I enumerated some of the lessons we had learned through that difficult situation.

1. The meaning of faith, such as praying for parking spaces at the hospital and being granted them.
2. Catastrophes can happen to anyone, including us!
3. How to empathize and show love to others who hurt.
4. Never to feel sorry for ourselves.

5. How to trust God's love and care when we don't understand.
6. How to gain spiritual strength from our adverse circumstances and to strengthen others.
7. How to depend on God through other Christians, and to accept their good will.

"If a member of a church is suffering and their needs are not being met, it's because the saints are not listening to God," I told Rivers. "God has not prepared a meal, mowed the lawn, or scrubbed a single floor for us," I said, "but He has used the hands of His people." Repeatedly we experienced the Scripture, "Bear ye one another's burdens, and so fulfill the law of Christ" (Galatians 6:2).

We still marvel at how God supplied every need through His special people. While some greeted me with "Poor little Angie," others can best be described as super saints and good Samaritans who saw us "bleeding by the roadside" and came to our rescue. To God be the glory!

Application Questions:
Super Saints and Miserable Comforters

Scriptures: II Corinthians 1:8-10, Galatians 6:2. Also review Appendix B, "Tips for Assisting Those Who Hurt."

1. What is the most effective way to handle well-meaning friend(s) who fit the description of miserable comforter(s)?
2. How can you help a seriously ill loved one live by the behavior you exhibit?
3. Describe the response of a "super saint" and why you appreciated them.
4. Why is it just as important to learn the grace of receiving as the grace of giving?
5. What important lessons have you learned on how to minister to hurting persons effectively?

CHAPTER 6

UNEXPECTED BLESSING,
A SON

Although Rivers and I had wanted to have five children, after Barth's birth we had resigned ourselves to the idea that we may not be able to have more children. We were not sure that I could conceive a child, so we began adoption proceedings only to abandon them when Rivers decided to return to college. We were to learn years later that I was allergic to the very drugs given me in mega doses to keep me pregnant! If God chose to give us a child, He could do so by natural means, we concluded.

Fourth Pregnancy, Another Difficult One

Surprisingly, we conceived a child without hormones and their attendant risks and complications. We concluded that the Lord had been merciful and answered Barth's prayer for a baby. The three of us were so grateful and joyous for God's gracious gift I now carried.

We were anxiously awaiting the birth of our second child, for more than one reason, not the least of which was my delicate physical condition. I did not look forward to the twenty-four-hour-a-day "morning sickness" that continued even in the labor room. Once I delivered, the frequent regurgitation and incessant mouth-watering stopped abruptly. Other unexplainable problems had kept me visiting the obstetrician's office with a degree of frequency not required in normal pregnancies. We often mused that we were glad they charged a flat rate, and we sure got our money's worth.

Having lost our twins at the beginning of the fifth month, and another baby in the first trimester, we were ecstatic over the prospect of having a full-term baby. But this pregnancy was not without its problems—I still had to deal with the constant nausea that left me weak and mal-nourished. Then there was the excruciatingly painful sciat-ica in my right hip that radiated down my leg and some-times caused me to lose my balance and collapse. Doctor Nipe had assured me, "You may break your leg, but don't worry, you won't hurt your baby."

To complicate matters further, it was during my fourth month of pregnancy when Rivers succumbed to the heart attack, detailed in chapter four. Since he was still recuper-ating and unable to work, I was trying to remain on the job over my physician's objections.

By my fifth month of pregnancy, my condition had worsened and I was eventually forced to tender my resigna-tion. I well remember the day when I kept an appointment with College President Myron S. Augsburger. A little embar-rassed to announce my resignation outright, I devised a lighthearted way to get my point across. I prepared a small announcement that showed a musical score on the front. Three whole notes in descending order formed a chord. Tucked inside the second whole note was a small quarter note. Immediately deciphering my message, Doctor Augsburger leaned back in his chair and laughed heartily, as he accepted it good-naturedly.

Soon I could not sit, stand, or lie for very long because of the condition of my back and my under-sized pelvis. For the remainder of my pregnancy I would need to change my position often, never very comfortable in any position. At night, it was difficult to sleep for more than two or three hours before having to get up and walk around for a while. So I never felt completely rested.

Many an evening I would prepare for bed and then head

off to a reflexologist who lovingly massaged my back, neck, legs, and feet. This helped me immensely, and I came to depend on Delphia Rhodes to keep me mobile. I encouraged myself while joking to Rivers, "The longest this thing can last is nine months, and having a baby will more than compensate for anything I have to endure." I was often reminded of Jesus' analogy of the disciples' weeping and mourning over His going away and then becoming joyful, with a woman's labor and subsequent joy of giving birth to a child.

Sometimes Rivers, Barth and I were all feeling sick for different reasons, so we sometimes shared the same bed. Whoever was able to do so waited on the others when no one else was around.

Barth's Asthma Attacks

When fall arrived and the trees began to shed their leaves, Barth, who was allergic to mold and dust, began to experience breathing problems. Once after he had played outside, he became quite ill after midnight. He started to vomit and cough, which culminated in severe wheezing and gasping for breath. I saw no way to avoid a trip to the Emergency Room.

But neither Rivers nor I could lift him, and Rivers' medication had him so sedated that I knew I could not awaken him. How would I get help for our sick child? Most of the neighbors were older people, and I could not bring myself to ask them.

As I prayed, the Lord reminded me of Sam and Sara Weaver, whose son Michael and Barth were the best of friends. Hesitantly, I called and Sam graciously agreed to help me. He carefully lifted Barth from his bed, drove us to the hospital and waited for his treatment. Then he brought us home and placed Barth back in his bed. Rivers never awakened, but this is another example of God supplying our need by using one of His children.

God Supplies a Layette

Since our funds were severely limited, I prepared a list of bare essentials for the baby. Having come down with a strep throat, I tucked the list into my coat pocket and left it there.

It was the week of Thanksgiving, and a Christian couple we barely knew invited us to share their special meal. Aldeen Wenger is quite the homemaker, and her home was always impeccable. Admiringly, I said to myself, "Now this is a woman after my own heart." She and Eugene were very gracious, and we enjoyed wonderful fellowship with them and their little daughter Jennifer.

After the meal, Aldeen led me into a spare bedroom. "Do you need some things for the baby?" she asked.

Ashamed to admit it to a newfound friend, I responded, "Yes, I do." To my amazement, she began to lay out diapers, undershirts, sleepers, diaper pins, and other things in the exact numbers on my list. I shared my list with Aldeen, and we rejoiced together that God had laid it on her heart to meet the need. How loved I felt as I again saw God's miracle-working power on our behalf.

One thing Aldeen did not have were the rubber pants we used with cloth diapers. God used another friend to supply them. Ruth Ann Burkholder, who was baby sitting Barth, asked, "Do you need any rubber pants for the baby?" Now I was really excited because God was supplying the baby's layette, and I had done no shopping.

Brief Labor and a Bouncing Baby Boy

My due date was January 3, 1974, but some of my colleagues at Eastern Mennonite gave me a surprise card shower on December 11th. We laughed so much that I joked, "Now, don't you guys cause me to go into labor."

Early the next morning, I knew that labor was imminent.

Today our Bertram Don Williams would be born! Since it was a mere four months after Rivers had suffered a heart attack, I was very concerned about how the stress of my delivery might affect him. "Lord, please take care of Rivers, and don't let my labor last too long," I prayed, not knowing how God might answer me.

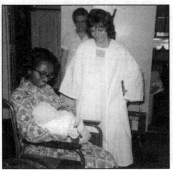

Leaving the Maternity Ward with Bert after seven days

By now Rivers could drive the car, so he took me to the hospital, as the labor became more intense. We arrived at twelve o'clock noon, and it was time for Rivers' medication. I said, "Just go and get a sandwich and take your medication. I'll be fine."

By the time Rivers finished his lunch and returned to the waiting area, the nurse appeared and said, "Mr. Williams, you have a son!" This was exactly fifty-four minutes after I walked into the hospital. I was reminded afresh that God cares about the things that concern us, and I kept thanking Him.

I was hospitalized for a week, but it never became a hardship because our friends, Dwight and Fanny Heatwole, offered to keep five-year-old Barth on their dairy farm. This was a special treat for Barth because we had visited in one another's homes often, and he loved them. He was fascinated by the animals and the sounds, but most of all he enjoyed Fannie's excellent food that included homemade doughnuts, pizza, and potato chips. Also, the Heatwoles had four children. Edwin, the youngest, was Barth's favorite, since he bathed him in the evening and played with him a lot.

A Special Christmas
Bert was born just thirteen days before Christmas, and

with our mounting medical expenses, we knew it would have to be a very quiet affair. We purchased a couple of small gifts for Barth, and as Christmas approached we were just happy to be alive and on the mend, and gifts seemed unimportant.

Barth clutching a gift and his 13-day-old brother

The last four months had been filled with one miracle after another, and Rivers and I were both grateful. Although people had continued to show us love, I thought Christmas was a different matter. I said to Rivers, "Christmas is a family holiday, and I know no one will want to be bothered with us. We'll just eat whatever we can get." My faith was so small, but I was wrong.

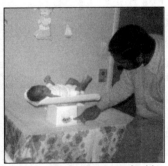

Daddy weighs three-week-old Bert

The outpouring of love continued. On Christmas day, Sara Weaver brought a wonderful home-cooked meal with all the trimmings, while other friends such as Harold and Ruth Lehman, and Orval and Dorothy Shank brought gifts for Barth. Isn't it great that God is not limited by my imagination or weak faith!

Strep Throat and a Nursing Infant

After Bert's birth, I underwent major surgery. The pregnancy and other stresses on my body had left me somewhat run-down. I soon became hoarse and began to have problems with my throat. While I recognized the symptoms because of a recent bout, the doctor diagnosed it—strep throat! "Get the baby out of the house!" he ordered.

"But Doctor," I protested, "I'm nursing him, and he's only two months old. You can't take him from me!"

"I don't want you breathing on that baby," he countered. The doctor won, and dejectedly I accepted his decision as what was best for Bert.

Almost at the breaking point, I started to wonder what more could happen to us during this traumatic period. Again, it was Fanny to the rescue. She offered to care for Bert, so Rivers packed up his bed and other items and entrusted Bert to the loving care of the Heatwole family for a full week.

This was yet another instance when God provided beyond what we could ask, think, or imagine. Someone has said you don't know Jesus is all you need until Jesus is all you have. Just when we didn't know where to turn, He sent one of his super saints to help us. God is so good!

Juggling My Executive Duties

The fall of 1973 had brought another set of challenges, just before Bert was born. Some friends, Orval and Dorothy offered to care for Rivers and Barth in their home so I could attend my first meeting as Vice-President of the Women's Missionary and Service Commission to be held in October in Elkhart, Indiana, some six hundred miles away. I would need to take three flights to get there and then sit through the meetings.

I was anxious to make a good impression on the Executive Committee members, so I did not consider saying I was too sick to travel. I had just met these women from different parts of the country and was also the "baby" of the group. Already intimidated by their knowledge and experience, I felt somewhat humiliated to be at less than my best.

Shifting from one side to the other, I tried so hard to endure the elongated meetings. No matter how hard I tried,

I would get sick and they would take me back to my room. Most of these ladies were mothers, but I felt they would not

Leaving after an
Executive Session
I had attended with
Bert

understand. Finally, one of the ladies suggested they get a cot and place it beside the conference table. I spent the remainder of the three-day executive sessions on that cot where they cared for me royally.

By the time the spring meeting rolled around, I was still nursing three-month-old Bert and needed to take him along. Balancing a fifteen-pound baby on a bony hip as I hurried through the airport to board the three flights, while carrying a diaper bag and purse was quite a feat.

Our meetings usually began right after breakfast and culminated in a night session after dinner. This was difficult because I had to take time out to nurse Bert or to feed him a bottle every few hours. I never doubted God's faithfulness, and I knew Bert and I would manage in Indiana while Rivers and Barth were in the loving care of the Shanks in Virginia.

Back to Work, Reluctantly

I had certainly waltzed into the President's office of Eastern Mennonite to turn in my resignation a few months earlier. Now I had to eat my words because I needed a job, at least until Rivers was able to return to work.

Upon hearing that I would go to work, a well-meaning, but unenlightened friend said to me, "I just couldn't leave my baby like that."

"I don't want to leave mine either, but I have to do what I have to do," I responded indignantly.

Another friend almost succeeded in placing a guilt trip on me by saying, "If you would just live by faith, you would not have to go back to work."

"If I live by faith, then you will have to work to take care of me," I said. It was hard enough to leave my baby and return to the office, but such encounters made it even more difficult.

Rivers, still on heavy medications, could not be counted on to hear the baby cry or to be awake when he needed attention. He felt awful about this because we could ill afford to take both children to a sitter. Our savings had been depleted and we needed funds for day-to-day expenses and numerous prescriptions, and this weighed heavily on both of us.

Then I remembered what the Lord had put upon my heart months earlier about helping him live. I said, "Thank you, Lord, that I have skills I can put to use." With that I joyfully accepted working as the best thing for the family. But to preserve his dignity as head of our home, I would make excuses to ask him to deposit my paychecks in the bank.

Application Question:
Unexpected Blessing, a Son

Scriptures: Genesis 3:16, John 16:21, Psalm 40:1-3, Hebrews 6:13-15, 10:36.

1. How have you experienced the pain of childbirth turning to joy at the birth of a child?
2. How would you cope with being away from your nursing baby if this became necessary because of illness?
3. How do you feel about a mother returning to work when it means leaving an infant in someone's care?

CHAPTER 7

SURPRISED BY A HYSTERECTOMY

During Rivers' lengthy recuperation period, God had taught me to live in victory by meditating on His Word. I continued to draw strength from scriptures that had served me well in the past, the main one being Philippians 4:6-7.

Rivers' strength returned slowly, and eventually the doctor said he was able to return to work. How joyful we were, but our joy was short-lived because of the painful experiences he suffered of one rejection after another. "You had a heart attack, didn't you? We can't take a chance on you." Rivers had worked so hard to secure a part-time position at Safeway, but had worked only one evening before he suffered the heart attack. Because of their fear of liability, they would not allow him to return to work. The burden became quite heavy for him, as he was barely over thirty and desired so much to provide for his young family.

Meanwhile, some friends provided us registration to a marriage retreat, and that weekend the floodgates opened as Rivers dropped his guard. In a rare moment he shared how it made him feel to be rejected by employers and treated like a criminal. "I could not help having a heart attack," he sobbed as we embraced. The group ministered to us and prayed the Lord would provide a job. Shortly thereafter, Rivers was offered a position as bookstore manager at Eastern Mennonite.

Life for our family returned to normal for about three years with no major catastrophes. I left the college and went to work at Mennonite Broadcasts, a division of Mennonite

Board of Missions, and had an active speaking schedule. We moved into a larger home, and the little brothers played together happily. All was well, but then it happened.

Suspected Appendicitis

From my teenage years, I had always had abnormal menstrual periods that incapacitated me for a couple of days. I would develop a high fever that cracked my lips, severe abdominal cramping, diarrhea, frequent vomiting, and fainting spells. When my mother gave me the prescription pills, they came back quickly, the orange juice still cold. It was doubly embarrassing to have to explain to a male supervisor that this monthly menace sometimes interfered with my employment.

The "custom of women," as the menses are referred to in Scripture, controlled too much of my life—it was either on the way, it was there doubling me over in pain, or I was ovulating. I had only one week out of the month when I was free from its grasp. I tried to clear my calendar to accommodate my cycle with its excruciating vice-like grip, knowing it would debilitate me completely. It had interrupted and wreaked havoc with my entire life, and caused untold embarrassment as I had collapsed and fallen in some interesting places.

When someone called for a ministry appointment a year or more in advance, I literally kept them hanging on the telephone while I tried to figure out when my time-of-the-month might begin. Most of the time I avoided the crisis, but a few times I miscalculated. Such was the case as I traveled to Cleveland one afternoon and became ill during the first flight. When I arrived in Washington, I was trying hard to handle my luggage and praying for help when a young man "right out of the blue" came by and exclaimed, "Lady, if you can carry my newspaper, I can carry your suitcase."

"Praise the Lord, thank you, Jesus," I said under my

breath as I quickly yielded to his request.

Over time my condition improved some—I still became ill each month, and the doctor was not able to find anything to alleviate the problem completely. I could not understand why I was still suffering this way well into my thirties.

But now I began to have a different kind of abdominal pain daily—unlike anything I had ever felt. It felt as if a sharp knife was being inserted into my side and then twisted. Sometimes when it hit me suddenly, I would gasp. But then my abdomen began to bulge and I said to Rivers, "I look as if I'm pregnant!" When the doctor examined me I said, "Doctor, this is not normal for me. My abdomen has the same shape it had when I was pregnant."

He replied, "My wife has that problem too. She tends to gain weight around her waist." Rather than providing some satisfaction, this annoyed me because my condition had nothing to do with his wife and I considered his answer unprofessional.

While returning from a trip, the pain became so intense that we begged the Lord for relief. When the pain continued, we changed our prayer to, "Lord, just let us get home, please." Once home, I called my doctor who ordered me to go straight to the Emergency Room. From my description of the pain, he felt sure I must have appendicitis.

A surgeon was waiting to perform an emergency appendectomy late that Sunday evening. So the myriad of tests began, along with probing, prodding, and poking until I felt I could hardly bear it. When the results of the tests came, it was not appendicitis. The surgeon confided to me, "That uterus is not doing you any good, but at your age, if I remove it and it is not diseased, I could be in trouble." With that he discharged me the next morning and sent me home with prescription drugs to alleviate the pain.

The surgeon's solution was clearly not working and the pain had become more intense. After sharing my dilemma with a friend who was a nurse, she said, "I think you need a hysterectomy, and I know just the doctor you should see. Now, Doctor X is not knife happy, but if you need surgery, that's what you will get," Eileen said.

Fibroid Tumors and a Ruptured Adhesive Band

Another good friend agreed to take me to the doctor some forty miles away. Before going into the office Donna

Three-year-old Bert gives Mom a gift after her seven-day hospitalization for a hysterectomy and adhesive band repair

Suter and I sat in the car and prayed together. "Lord, please give the doctor wisdom." With that I decided to accept the doctor's decision. The last menstrual period had been so severe that I had prayed then, "Lord, if I never see this again, I will be so happy."

The gynecologist gave me a grim look as he said, "You have fibroid tumors that need to come out." Stretching out his fourth and middle fingers, he poked into my navel area. "Your adhesive band is ruptured and needs repair. I can get two fingers down through it, and that's why your belly is bulging. How attached are you to this belly button?"

Sounded like a strange question to me, but I replied, "Well, I don't know."

He said, "I may just have to remove it when I repair the adhesive band. You need a hysterectomy, and we usually remove the appendix at the same time."

"When?" I asked.

"Well, don't you have to think about it—talk to your husband?"

"Doctor, there is nothing to talk about. We've already

prayed about this, and if this is what I need, the sooner the better."

Casting one of those incredulous looks my way, he picked up the telephone and booked the surgery for April 20, 1977, a mere two weeks away. A sense of gratitude overwhelmed me, because finally I would have some relief. It never occurred to me to feel sorry for myself; although a few miserable comforters came my way to tell me what a mistake it was to have a hysterectomy at my age. Two women related horror tales about their surgeries, but I

The family attends Mennonite General Assembly in Estes Park, Colorado, five weeks after Mom's hysterectomy

immediately rejected the notion that theirs had anything to do with me.

To keep my faith strong, I kept meditating on the Scriptures as I had in the past. If God could get me through Rivers' heart attack while I was pregnant, then surely His grace was sufficient now as well. But how was I to explain this to our children? By now Barth was eight years old, but explaining it to three-year-old Bert was a different matter. I began with, "Mommy's body is sick and I must go to the hospital for the doctor to make it well."

Immediately Bert interjected, "Is the doctor going to operate you?" I had no idea where he had heard the word or whether he knew it's meaning, but this made the announcement easier.

"I'm a Student of the Master"

The surgery went well and my friend, Donna waited along with Rivers. Then they lovingly sat by my bed and moistened my lips with a damp cloth to aid in my comfort.

After a week I was discharged with some pretty strict orders. Because of the need to repair the adhesive band, I had a long "railroad track" down the full length of my abdomen, and it would take time to heal. However, with the surgeon's approval, I traveled from Virginia to Colorado for speaking appointments six weeks later. This was very difficult, and at times I questioned the wisdom of having come, but the family enjoyed traveling together and living out of our camper for three weeks.

The Lord is so good! His healing power prevailed, and my strength returned in time. However, as I reflected on the surgery, I began to wonder what lessons I might learn. To express deep emotions, as usual I wrote a poem that was published in our church paper.

The family "steps back in time" in Central City,
Colorado following General Assembly

I'm a Student of the Master

I'm enrolled in the school of the Master again,
The institution of suffering, patience, and trust.
As I aspire to be more and more like Christ,
Matriculation in this school is a must!

Well, I thought I had graduated three years ago,
But my kind Master Teacher says, "No."
"My child, I have many more lessons for you,
So back to class you must go."

I protest, "But, Lord, have I not learned well
All the lessons You taught me before?
Must I continue to suffer again like this?
I earned 'A' in this course years ago!"

"And, Lord, You made this frail body of mine,
So You know what is wrong with me.
Can't You heal me just this once, dear Lord?
And the praise will all go to Thee."

But God's way seemed not my way in this.
I must needs submit to His will.
So off to a Christian surgeon I go,
While His peace my spirit stills.

At this point my prayer did change its tune,
As I focused on the doctor and his tests.
"Lord, give him discernment as he studies my case;
Help him know how to treat me best."

So after ten minutes and a careful check,
The kind doctor looked at me.
He pronounced the verdict on what he had found,
And advised I submit to surgery.

"Well, the sooner the better," I thought to myself,
For I'm tired of the pain that I bear."
So the date was set for my hospital stay,
As I entrusted myself to his care.

O, such joy and peace that my Savior gave,
As I gently was put to sleep.
For I knew that even in the operating room,
A constant vigil the Great Physician would keep.

And God was faithful throughout the time
When my body was racked with pain.
For He sent His servants to minister to me,
Meeting my needs again and again.

He sustained my family during this time too,
And their love for me never failed.
I said, "Don't think of how sick I am,
But how soon I am going to be well!"

When trials come your way, don't moan or fret,
Or enlist sympathy from your friends.
But rather, relax and let the Spirit work
While your physical body mends.

Endeavor to learn what the Master would teach,
While you're faced with this painful test.
The sinless Son of God learned through suffering on the cross,
So can His children expect any less?

Yes, I'm in the school of the Master again,
And I'm learning new lessons each day.
Lesson one is patience; lesson two is trust;
But the greatest is learn to obey!

As you can see, I thought we had paid our dues, and were all set for a season of smooth sailing. We felt we had endured more adversity than most people our age, so how could anything else possibly happen to us? We learned that it could, and it did.

Application Questions:
Surprised By a Hysterectomy

Scriptures: Philippians 4:6-7, James 5:13-16, Psalm 37:7.
1. How can you believe God for healing and yet accept medical intervention?
2. What lessons have you learned through suffering?

CHAPTER 8

BACK OUT OF WHACK

When we are certain we have followed the Lord's leading, does that ensure a trouble free life? The answer is an obvious no. When a person obeys Jesus, this may be the very time when the devil deploys his best weapons and initiates a major assault.

Rivers and I have found our strength in the Word of God and prayer as we have walked through trials we did not understand and could not appreciate. Because we were firmly rooted in our Christian faith, by the grace of God, our trials have not swallowed us up. Such was the case in the summer of 1982.

New Business, New Challenges

We felt it was time for a change in our lives, and we were seeking the Lord for direction. When I felt sure the Lord had spoken, I said to Rivers, "I don't know how God could make it any clearer unless He writes it in the sky." He was in full agreement, so I took a risky step and resigned an excellent position to begin a home-based writing and editing business. I wanted to be available to our boys, and from my office I could look across the lower deck and watch them play in the back yard. Ideal, or so I thought.

We purchased a personal computer and set up an office. I submitted my resignation to the Mission Board, but had not left the office yet.

As I dashed off one morning to a breakfast meeting, I bent over to open the garage door as usual. This was a two-car garage with windowpanes across one section, and was quite heavy. I had opened this door many times in the last four years, but this time was different—I heard something snap in my back and I could not straighten up. From the master bedroom on the other end of the house, Rivers heard a noise coming from the garage and came running. There he found me hanging onto the back of the car unable to move.

Behaving Like a Superwoman

Most sane people would have called the ambulance, but not me. Superwoman that I tried to be, I said, "Just get me back into the house and put some flat shoes on me. I can attend my meeting." Rivers complied.

At the meeting I was in such pain that the tears began to stream down my face. Completely embarrassed, I told them I had injured my back. They prayed, we finished the meeting, and I headed for my office. I had sprained muscles before, so I figured I would not let this get me down.

At the office I told Sue Pennington, the bookkeeper, "If you will be my legs today, I can work." But the pain became so excruciating that I began to cry. Over the objections of my colleagues, I drove the car home, and Rivers took me to the doctor's office. He treated me, and even prayed with me, but Rivers virtually carried me out. On a subsequent visit, when I attempted to leave, I was in such pain that the doctor came out and put me into the car.

I learned that I had wiped out a lower disk and my recuperation period could be a long one. During the first few weeks, the pain was so intense that I could not read because focusing my eyes nauseated me. Rivers brought the tape recorder in, and I would lie there hour after hour listening to Scripture. I could not get off the bed alone, nor could I bend enough to put on my underwear or to shave my legs. Every movement caused sharp, stabbing pains to my lower back. If I coughed, sneezed, or even laughed, the pain only increased. I was virtually helpless, which is hard for some-one who was accustomed to going at such a frenetic pace.

My Boys "Baby-sit" Me

Rivers took as much time from work as he dared and then returned. This meant that thirteen-year-old Barth and eight-year-old Bert had to "mommy-sit" me for the next two months. How humbling it was to rely on them for every glass of water. They played in our back yard or family room with other children or swam in the neighbors' pools, but came in about every half-hour to see if I needed a visit to the bathroom, medications, food, water or juice.

Barth and Bert did not know much about cooking, but they dutifully fed me cold cereal for breakfast, and hot dogs, hamburgers, or canned spaghetti for lunch. Rivers was on hand to prepare the evening meal when friends did not supply it.

Remember, those who like to give don't especially enjoy receiving. I know of nothing to cure this malady better than a case of helplessness and dependence on others, and whether I liked it or not, I was at the mercy of others. I thought this would last for a couple of weeks since I had a lot of people praying for me, and I was doing the most spir-itual thing I knew to do. After I was able to read without nausea, I took my Bible and confessed every Scripture on healing I could find through my concordance. But days stretched into weeks, and weeks into months as the pain mercilessly pummeled my body.

Condemnation Heaped On

Rivers and I were associating with some people who believed strongly in Divine healing, and so did we. However, I well remember the one who prayed for me this way, "Lord, we will not put up with this!" I was trying my best not to put up with it, but it persisted.

After confessing all the healing Scriptures a second time without any obvious results, I began to search my heart for hidden sin and to confess anything that came to mind, no matter how small. To make matters worse, some well-meaning friends suggested sin could be the problem.

One person attempted to put condemnation on me with, "I don't allow any sickness to exist in my body!" That did it—this man must think he is sinless, and my injury means I am hiding some unconfessed sin.

Soon, I told Rivers, "I don't want to be around him anymore, because the last thing I need is the ministry of condemnation and judgment." I knew that despite the pain, God loved me and would bring some good out of it, though my finite mind could not comprehend how.

I believe Adam and Eve's sin brought sickness and death on the human race, but I don't believe we can trace every illness to the individual sufferer's transgressions. Jesus taught through the example of the man born blind that we cannot directly attribute sin to the sick person. When asked whether the man's blindness was a result of his or his parents' sin, Jesus replied, "Neither this man nor his parents sinned, but that the works of God should be revealed in him" (John 9:3). Jesus clearly demonstrated the healing power of God over blind eyes.

When a Christian has repented of every sin the Lord reveals, why should we begin our ministry by accusing them of hidden sin? Such automatic assumptions are presumptuous and arrogant, if not downright cruel. While we know that some sins have adverse physical consequences and that sometimes folks need to repent, we cannot conclude this is always the case.

During the many months of suffering from the back injury, I realized I had always considered myself unselfish, thinking of the needs of others before my own. Now every action would be measured by how it affected me. If I move this way it will intensify the pain; if I read it will nauseate me; if I laugh or cough the jabbing pains will shoot through my back... Soon I understood why pain causes some people to become self-centered—it almost forces one to think constantly of self. It offers strong temptation to become depressed about what we have lost rather than focusing on what we still have.

Another painful reality was that some friends seemed not to want to be in my presence. Finally, I said to Rivers, "They don't know what to do with a sick Angie." Admittedly, it hurt to feel unloved by some who had loved me before. The devil began to suggest that people loved me for what they could get, and for a while I agreed. But this season was short-lived as the Lord loved me through others, and taught me things I probably would not hear apart from this trial. I did not know why I was suffering, but God's presence was comfort enough to sustain me.

Pain is Pain!

During this time of forced bed rest, God taught me valuable lessons about patience and Joy in Adversity, and trusting Him in situations I did not understand. God burned into my consciousness a phrase that I have cherished since, "Pain is pain." This changed the whole tone of my ministry in relating to hurting persons. I had encountered people who requested prayer for problems that were not a part of my experience. When they spoke of abuse, drunkenness, or marital infidelity, I tried to empathize, but had no frame of reference for it. When the Lord showed me that pain is pain regardless of its source, pain took on a whole new meaning. Someone's pain may have been emotional or psychological, but because of the inordinate number of physical things we had endured, I could begin to enter into their pain.

If You Faint In Adversity

Several weeks after my accident, the Lord brought a verse to my mind that I had not noticed before. Proverbs 24:10: "If thou faint in the day of adversity, thy strength is small." You mean when adversity or hard times come into my life this is a test of my strength? I would lie on the bed hour after hour and ponder this Scripture, turning it over and over in my mind. Then I began to re-phrase it—"if you faint when adversity comes into your life, your faith is anemic...your faith is small...your faith doesn't amount to much..." "If you can't believe God under adverse circumstances, your faith is weak." "If you buckle and fold up when things go wrong, your faith is puny and limited."

I would continue, "Conversely, if we believe God in the heat of the furnace, our faith is strong." "If we can hope against hope, our faith is dynamic." This helped me to remain joyful.

The Prophet Jeremiah experienced such grief and sorrow of heart over the destruction of Jerusalem, and he poured out his anguish of soul in the Book of Lamentations. By chapter three, however, he recalls God's mercies, His compassions, and His goodness and expresses hope in the face of adversity. Jeremiah said in Lamentations 3:25,26 (NKJV), "The Lord is good to those who wait for Him, to the soul who seeks Him. It is good that one should hope and wait quietly for the salvation of the Lord."

Physical suffering forces us to abandon our plans and take time out to get well, and gives us a lot of time to pray and read the Bible. I found encouragement in reading Biblical examples of suffering such as Job, Daniel, and Joseph. I read the outcome of the story and how God delivered them, but while they were in the midst of the trial they had only tenacious faith and a promise from God.

Through these stories the Lord revealed new truths

about perseverance and waiting. I realized that sometimes when God made a promise, He attached a long waiting period to it—promises were not necessarily fulfilled immediately. Waiting in faith was a part of how God tested someone's faith.

In looking at some of God's dealings with the Israelites one day, I asked Him out loud, "Lord, why did You have to continue telling them the same things over and over?"

The answer came immediately, "Because they were so soon to forget, like you."

Ouch! God told them not to forget how He had led them through the Red Sea on dry land, had fed them in the wilderness with manna, and so on. And they did not own a leather-bound Bible in every version known to man. What an encouragement it was to my own faith to hold on to God's promises whether or not I understood His timing.

The Lord brought a new concept to my mind that has helped me on numerous occasions since, "We are what we are in adversity!" Walking through adversity and waiting for my healing was not my choice, but He taught me that I could choose how I waited. I began to see how easy it is to trust God when everything is going well, but our best testimonies grow out of the tests. The word test is the root word of testimony. Without the test, there is no real testimony to God's miraculous power to deliver!

While some may not agree with such theology, I believe this to be true. My whole attitude toward suffering was tempered by this revelation, and I began to think that God must really love me to entrust me with such tests. I would trust the One Who knows all things, and endeavor to learn how the Holy Spirit would build up my spirit while my physical body was mending.

My back injury had occurred in July, and now the fall foliage was at its peak. Summer had ended and the children had returned to school. By then I could get up on my own if I maneuvered my body just right. However, when I was alone in the house, anything I dropped on the floor had to remain until someone came to pick it up.

Attached to My "Umbilical Cord"

The moist heating pad had become my constant companion as I moved it from one site to another. Morning, noon, and night, it was never very far away. I asked Rivers to bring in a heavy-duty electrical cord we had used in camping. With this "umbilical cord" attached to my trusty heating pad, I could walk around a bit in the house.

One day when I was walking around, meditating and praying, the Lord brought a phrase to my mind. "Recall God's acts in the past to build faith for your present situation!" What a revelation this was to me. I began to see the Old Testament as a rehearsal of God's dealings with the Israelites, and the example it provides for us. "Now these things happened to them as an example, and they were written for our instruction"(I Corinthians 10:11a, NASB).

The Lord disciplined the Israelites because of their disobedience and grumbling. He had done miraculous acts among them, but when they faced another test, they seemed to forget His power to deliver. Since no one can sin with impunity, God corrected and disciplined them in order to teach them. I was determined to learn from them and not fall prey to their mistakes.

Rivers and I had prayed together and stepped out on sheer faith to start the business. Now what were we to do with the new computer equipment downstairs in the office when I was unable to negotiate the steps and learn how to operate it?

Praise and Thanksgiving

During late summer, more invitations to speak out of town arrived, and I grieved at not being able to answer the letters. Along with those requests came one that actually provoked me because it came from someone who knew my physical state. Would I please write an article on praise and thanksgiving for a Christian women's magazine? Temporarily forgetting about my determination not to grumble, I began to complain to Rivers, "Why are they asking me to write for them when they know I'm not well? Aren't there many other women who could do this article? To make it worse, we need money, and this one is gratis!" And for a while the devil must have been jumping up and down with glee over my response.

The Lord began to deal with me that now was the time to write such an article when I didn't feel like it. Since I could not lie, sit, or stand for very long, I vacillated among those positions as I penned the words, all the while attached to my umbilical cord. First on my left side, then on my right, I scribbled on a pad. In a straight chair propped on pillows, then walking through the house with pad in hand, I continued to persevere.

The article was published in the November issue of Voice, and a few months later I received a letter from Sister Kniss, who was wintering in Florida. The dear old saintly lady thanked me for the article, stating that her daughter-in-law in India had been so encouraged by it because she too was recuperating from a back injury. Hoping I had passed the test, I figured that if nothing else good cane out of the back injury, this would have been worth it all. Thank God, I was obedient despite the way I felt.

Rivers' Strange Illness

Christmas was approaching, and our boys, now fourteen and nine, had a few ideas about gifts they wanted. Rivers was working as a department manager in a retail store. Our medical expenses were considerable, and I was still unable to do office work or accept speaking appointments, so our finances were suffering.

To make matters worse, Rivers began to show signs of some strange illness. He lost weight rapidly until his shirts began to hang off his shoulders. His skin became ashen-col-

ored; he slept a lot, and barely communicated with the family. Although his appetite was voracious, the weight loss continued until one day to my chagrin, I noticed his rib cage pro-truding under a thin layer of skin. I realized that something was drastically wrong and he needed help.

Eight-year-old Bert administers treatment to Mom's back

Rivers was under his physician's care, and although quite ill, he remained on the job, sometimes working long hours. One day the nurse called me, "Mrs. Williams, the doctor says Mr. Williams' blood sugar level is way out of line, and something must be done about it. Bring him to the hospital today!"

Relieved that he was about to get some help, but fearing Rivers would not agree to desert his post, I called Pastor Jim Delp for prayer and headed off to explain to Rivers in person. The store manager was quite unhappy with this announcement. He screwed

Christmas 1982 during Rivers' eight-day hospitalization for diabetes

up his face into a slightly maniacal frown, as he asked, "Can't this wait? It's five days before Christmas!"

"But the doctor says he must be admitted to the hospital today!" I said emphatically. Too sick to resist, Rivers apologized and left the store filled with impatient Christmas shoppers.

Rivers heaved a sigh of relief as he entered the hospital that afternoon. Within a few hours he began to look like a different man. His skin color, as well as his energy level, began to return. He was suffering from adult onset of diabetes, and once the insulin was administered, relief came quickly.

For the next eight days, I trudged back and forth to the hospital while nursing my back injury. Rivers remained in the hospital over Christmas, yet we all survived without our customary family celebrations. The dozens of cookies I usually baked, the fat roasted turkey with dressing and all the trimmings, the decorated tree, and the many houseguests would all have to wait for another time. It's amazing how unimportant these things become in light of medical catastrophes.

I could not help but think about the time some nine years earlier when we were both ill at the same time. Exercising my new lesson revealed by the Holy Spirit, I walked through the house rehearsing out loud how the Lord had brought us through. This built my faith that He would do no less now.

Application Questions:
Back out of Whack

Scriptures: Acts 7:54-60, Psalm 107:20, John 9:3,4, Proverbs 24:10, Lamentations 3:25,26, I Corinthians 10:11a.

1. Have you ever been sure of God's leading, and then run into difficult circumstances? If so, how did you cope?
2. Do you try to be a superwoman/man? If so, how can you maintain balance in your life?
3. How do you deal with condemnation from Christians

when you are already hurting?

4. Discuss the phrase, "Pain is Pain" and how understanding this will enable you to be empathetic with others who hurt.

5. What does it mean to faint when adversity comes into your life?

6. How have you increased your faith by recalling God's past acts and building faith for your present crisis?

Bert examines ashes remaining from a
three-pound steak after a kitchen fire

Rebuilding the chimney after
second fire

CHAPTER 9

MY ORDEAL WITH TMJ, "THE MONEY JAW"

You heard about the failed pregnancies and the loss of our first three babies, Rivers having a heart attack during my pregnancy, the hysterectomy in my thirties, a serious back injury and Rivers' eight-day hospitalization at the same time. I did not begin to mention all the adverse things such as the two house fires. Could anything more possibly happen to us? It could, and it did! It seemed as if our struggles had only begun.

Don't Claim It!

While I was still recuperating from a back injury, I began to notice certain symptoms that had been around for a long time, but had become more pronounced. I couldn't explain exactly how I felt, but I was miserable all over. Being the superwoman I thought I was, I continued to function as normally as possible, traveling and speaking, and writing from our home office.

Rivers and I associated with some people who were heavily involved in the "name it and claim it" teaching. I did not dare confess to having physical problems if I could avoid it because if you said it, you had brought it on yourself, some of them taught. Speaker that I was, I certainly did not want anyone to think I was so unspiritual as to make a negative confession. Besides, I felt I lived in a glass house, and people would scrutinize my behavior anyway.

Lest you misunderstand, I believe in confessing the promises of God, but I am not one to pretend nothing is wrong when I'm suffering. If I request prayer, I will tell the individual I have a need. When I discovered my diagnosis, I knew I had never confessed such a disease because I did not know I had a temporomandibular joint. This blew that theory out of the water.

But my symptoms started to compound, and I went to my internist searching for answers. Wanting to check my throat for an infection, Dr. Brunk extended the tongue blade and said, "Angie, open your mouth." As I opened it, crack!

He chuckled and said good-naturedly, "Your jaw has too much play in it." Little did I know this was a very serious condition and not a laughing matter, or about the chain of events about to be set in motion.

Long-Standing Problems

Looking back, I can trace the onset of these symptoms to 1969. When Barth was a baby, I started to experience debilitating headaches that occurred intermittently. The pain was so intense that over-the-counter medications did not alleviate it. My internist assumed the headaches to be stress-induced and prescribed painkillers and bed rest.

I did not feel my stress level was high in the federal office where I worked, and could not pinpoint any connection between stress and the occurrence of the incapacitating headaches that left my scalp tender to the touch, my eyes red and swollen, and my body feeling weak. I would resort to lying in a dark room with a moist heating pad over my face, sometimes with tears slipping softly down my cheeks.

I remembered that the symptoms had grown worse about ten years earlier, to include unexplained piercing earaches, frequent sore throats, eyes sensitive to sunlight, and a feeling of general weakness. "Why do I have earaches as an adult when I did not have them as a child?" I asked Doctor Brunk.

Finding no infection, he had tried washing out my ears

but determined they had never developed to adult size and his instruments were too large. Finally, I asked our children's pediatrician and he irrigated my ears.

Symptoms Grow Worse

Normally an energetic individual who moved quickly, I had to push myself to get out of bed. Frequent migraine headaches, low energy level, ear, nose and throat pain without attendant infection or elevated temperature, and a feeling of general weakness characterized my condition.

Then I noticed my jaw made cracking, grating sounds whenever I chewed, opened my mouth or yawned, so I would lower my chin to my chest to squelch a yawn. Shoulder and neck pain, as well as tingling and numbness in my upper and lower extremities started to plague me. Feelings of "unreality" began to occur with increased frequency, and it became difficult to concentrate. When prescriptions for sinusitis did not relieve the pain in the bones of my face and my eyes' sensitivity to sunlight, my internist referred me to an ear, nose, and throat specialist, as well as an ophthalmologist, neither of whom could pinpoint its etiology.

I began to experience what felt like "non-specific toothaches"—I could not determine which tooth was aching. Sometimes the shooting pain was in a spot where I had the tooth extracted several years earlier. I became self-conscious about restaurant dining because when I chewed, my jaw joints made a popping sound that could be heard across the room. My ears began to ring with such intensity that it sounded as if a thousand bees were playing a symphony. This buzzing was constant and annoying, before I became so accustomed to it that I only noticed it when the room was quiet.

Dr. Zunka, My Panacea

By April 1983 when I met Dr. Craig A. Zunka, an oral

surgeon specializing in TMJ dysfunction, I had been examined by an internist, an ophthalmologist, and ear, nose and throat specialist, an osteopath, a general practitioner and a chiropractor, all to no avail. After numerous tests, exercises, and x-rays, Dr. Zunka's diagnosis was "internal derangement and arthritic changes of right and left temporomandibular." "On a scale of one to five, I would say you are in stage five already," he said. "TMJ involving arthritic degeneration is the most difficult type to treat," he continued.

As he went down the list of questions to determine the extent of my problems, he smiled and said, "Yours reads like a textbook case." I had nearly every symptom that could be expected from TMJ dysfunction. Dr. Zunka was most reassuring, and this kindled strong hope until I read on the narrative report, "prognosis after treatment: fair." Could I afford to embark upon a six to eighteen month treatment that would thrust us deeply into debt on the premise that the outcome would be only fair? It was worth a try.

Doctor Zunka said he would carry out the "conservative treatment" which consisted of wearing an acrylic splint at all times except when I ate, equilibration of the teeth, cranial adjustments, and a program of vitamin therapy and nutritional supplements. He placed me on a soft diet and asked me not to chew gum, ever again. This seemed like a small sacrifice, because I just knew I had found the answer to my multi-faceted problems.

My special friend, Linda Wilt, who had introduced me to Dr. Zunka was faithfully wearing her splint and having some positive results. On the day when I was fitted with mine, she and I attended a service at our church where we would watch a Joyce Landorf film. While I don't remember anything else about the film, I remember Joyce describing the serious problems she had with her jaw joints. As she talked about this complicated health issue and her quest for solutions, it sounded like a carbon copy of what I was going through. Linda and I both cried throughout the film.

My maximal mouth opening was 50mm at the time I first visited Dr. Zunka. I felt as if the pressure in my head would cause it to explode, and the only medication that would relieve it was the Fiorinal Dr. Zunka prescribed. Not wishing to become addicted, I used it judiciously—only when I could bear the pain no longer—Fiorinal with moist heat applied to my face. I would lie as still as possible and ask Rivers and the boys not to jar the bed in any way.

During the seventeen months when I was under Dr. Zunka's care, he instructed me to receive chiropractic adjustments on the same day as my appointment with him. At the beginning I sometimes had to see him daily for splint adjustments. Then the office visits ranged from one to three times a week. These two-doctors-a-day episodes took their toll on our already slim wallets. Some days when I dragged into the kitchen to prepare a meal, I found myself missing some ingredient for whatever dish I wanted to prepare, and going to the store was not an option. Soon we had to spend money we did not have, and we began to incur debt. One day I said, "Rivers, we are eating our home one room at a time."

He chuckled and said, "I'm naming it 'the money jaw' because of how much it costs."

Since no one in our hometown specialized in TMJ dysfunction, I felt I had no choice but to continue the trips back and forth to Front Royal. Including the chiropractic visits, each trip put 143 miles on our car and cost $97 for the day, plus money for any medications. That was a lot of money in 1983, and how could we possibly sustain it? Since Linda was suffering from the same disease, we often shared rides and provided a lot of spiritual support for one another.

TMJ dysfunction was somewhat unknown at that time, so a newspaper reporter interviewed me for a feature article. Through the article a lot of patients came forward who had the same symptoms but did not know they added up to a specific disease. One lady said she thought she was insane, because no one had been able to pinpoint the source of her problems.

It became necessary for me to cut back on an extensive travel and public speaking schedule since these occasions fostered headaches, ear pain and unexplained sore throats. Also my ability to sing high notes became increasingly limited, and undue fatigue resulted from laughing, singing and public speaking. Eventually I developed chest pains from these activities as my ability to open my mouth became more and more restricted. After the seventeen months of treatment I was feeling much better, but the symptoms did not completely disappear.

Ministry in Florida

Meanwhile, in 1985, we accepted a call to join Gospel Crusade, a ministry in Bradenton, Florida. The doctor said the warmer climate would probably be better for me than the frigid winter Virginia temperatures.

Accepting that call was not without its difficulties. Even though we felt sure the Lord had opened the door, a pastor was adamant that it was not "of the Lord." He attempted to browbeat us, finally exclaiming, "I'll just pray that you can't sell your home!" He had no idea what we were going through—we still looked quite prosperous, living in an almost new home, driving two cars, and wearing very nice clothes. Our pride led us to conceal our problems from our family and friends. Outwardly, we were quite happy without the slightest hint of the pain we covered by the facade of smiles, never divulging to the church that Rivers was laid off and we were in dire financial straits.

Several other friends also expressed their dismay over our plan to move away. I heard numerous variations of the phrase, "I don't know why you have to leave." Then the person would begin to enumerate some of the assistance I had provided them. Finally, I complained to Rivers, "They don't care about what's good for us. The underlying message is that I am meeting a need they have, and if we leave, who will meet that need?"

Normally, I am very outgoing and enjoy people, but the constant exclamations of why we should not leave began to wear on us, so I devised a plan for avoiding people. I grocery shopped when I thought most people were having dinner. When I needed something from the mall, I asked Rivers to drop me off at the nearest entrance to my destination. One day after we had entered the back door of a department store, I saw what I described to Rivers as two "little old biddies" come in, so I ducked behind the bra rack until they passed.

Eventually, we scaled down our belongings about sixty percent and headed south. The whole family enjoyed basking in the Florida sunshine. At Christian Retreat Rivers worked in the computing center and I served as editorial assistant and publicity director for the Blessings magazine and taught in their Kingdom Living Institute.

Some people mistakenly think that when they obey the Lord no trouble will come. We have found that when we have stepped out on faith, it seemed evil forces were unleashed on us. One aggravation after another bombarded us in Florida, and we often discussed the importance of being certain of God's call in order to overcome hindrances to ministry.

* * *

In the school of ministry I had become quite comfortable with the students' affirmation and encouragement. The first time they rated their instructors, I received the top marks. However, an African student had arrived unannounced expecting a scholarship, and had behaved inappropriately during the first few days. It became apparent to me that he was not there to become an "able minister" as our completion certificate would attest. After I informed him that I would not graduate him, his roommate decided to take me on.

My office had no exit door, and as I sat behind my desk this large American man came storming in making demands on behalf of his roommate. Completely undeterred, I explained my reasons and held my ground. In utter frustration, he banged on my desk and growled, "You're a pretty little petite woman, but you're behaving like a heavy handed foreman!" A sudden fear gripped me when I saw the anger in his eyes and momentarily, I thought he might assault me.

Little did I know that the secretary had notified Rivers, who stood outside the door, conveniently out of sight, ready to intervene if necessary. Isn't that so like God Who stands ready to intervene in our affairs when the time is right?

* * *

Squish, squish, squish, the sound emitted from the watery underfoot cushion as I bounded out of bed to shower and dress for my morning class in the Tabernacle. "This place is flooded!" I exclaimed to my half-awake husband. "This has never happened to us before, but why today?" I asked. Ironically, my topic that day had to do with being joyful in adversity. One of the verses I planned to use was from Isaiah 43:2, "When you walk through the waters, I will be with you."

During class I relayed the story to the students and we all laughed about the incredible timing of flooding in our home. Sometimes during the day I found myself singing a song that reminded me to do what comes spiritually, not what comes naturally, "Count it all joy."

* * *

Overall, life in Florida was good, but something was drastically wrong. On my next trip north, I returned to Dr. Zunka, who checked me over carefully. Since the symptoms had begun to intensify, he said, "Surgery is a last resort!" However, he assured me that Dr. Joe Reitman was the best and I would "feel so much better." By now, it was worth a shot.

When Dr. Reitman, an oral and maxillofacial surgeon, made special effort to see me quickly and called in another specialist, I just knew my problems would soon be over. And the skilled surgeon was most optimistic about his ability to alleviate my problems. His diagnosis was "degenerative osteoarthritis with internal derangement (pathology of the meniscus)." After a very painful arthrogram in which they poked dye-filled needles into my sore and swollen jaw joints, Dr. Reitman announced, "I may need to insert plastic joints, but I won't know until the joints are incised." I had cried throughout the horrible procedure, and by now my head was throbbing. Dr. Reitman proposed a "bilateral temporomandibular arthroplasty," and arranged for my surgery in August 1986.

Prayer and More Prayer

When we returned to Florida, I felt optimistic that at last my problems would be over, but I also knew the Lord could heal me without surgery. When I announced my dilemma, the saints petitioned God for my healing at the early-morning prayer meetings. Also, many others prayed over me during that time. I fully expected to be healed without further medical intervention; however, that is not the way it turned out.

Painfully, Rivers and I decided to keep the appointment for surgery, fully expecting that God would work through it. I had had a dream in which I saw myself in a hospital bed surrounded by a bright light. So I began to ask God to calm my fears and to use this in some way if I had to go through with it.

That warm August Saturday, I spoke to a Women's Aglow group and stayed around for ministry for a long time. I remember telling them jokingly that my husband was the only man in Bradenton, Florida who was praying for his wife to be able to open her mouth! We left later that afternoon to head for Maryland, driving all night.

We were all in good spirits when we arrived at Montgomery General Hospital in Olney, Maryland. The family followed me through the various departments as they performed the many outpatient tests. Then off to Mom and Dad Brunk's for the night we went. Early the next morning we joined hands and prayed before leaving for the surgery.

Indescribable Surgery and Unbearable Pain

When the phlebotomist finally located my tiny vein, the delayed surgery began. It lasted five-and-one-quarter-hours and included: Eminectomy—recontouring of long projection anterior aspect of joint to relieve interference with meniscus and condylar head; High Condylectomy—shaving down head of lower jaw and recontouring to a smooth convex shape; and Meniscoplasty—repair and reattachment of cartilage. After surgery, Dr. Reitman reported that he did not need to insert implants, and he was pleased to be able to use my own cartilage to make the repairs.

I awakened from surgery to an indescribable nightmare—regurgitation, face, head and neck pain, and a stabbing backache. I had also developed a secondary infection brought on by antibiotics to which I was allergic. My entire head was swollen and distorted, and my hair had been shaved in an arch two inches above the ear and extended to the nape of the neck on both sides. Most of my head was covered with bandages, and puncture wounds were on both jaws. (When I inquired later, Dr. Reitman told me the puncture wounds resulted from their having used a vice like wrench to hold my mouth open during surgery.) The pain was so intense that nothing relieved it, and I was too dizzy to be on my feet.

Touched By An Angel?

Some remarkable things happened following my surgery. A beautiful, well-dressed lady came into my room. She smiled happily, and in her hand she carried a nicely wrapped gift. Handing it to me she said, "I just came to see how you are and to give you this gift." We embraced, and she left shortly. Opening the gift, I saw it was a bottle of German perfume.

Later, reflecting on her visit, I thought she was a lady we had seen in the hospital with her husband two days before. I thought she had said he was coming in for cataract surgery, so on the following day when Rivers took me for a walk I searched the surgical floor for them to no avail. Two things baffled me—how did she find me in such a large hospital without my name, and why did she want to give me a gift? Sometime later we went to the Admissions Office and inquired about such a patient. We never located him or her, so whether she was an angel or not, the Lord used her to bless me, and to this day, I keep that bottle of 4711 as a reminder of God's goodness.

Also, my anesthesiologist, who had no professional reason to visit me after surgery, came by to talk each day. He showed a genuine interest and concern for me, and I thought that was unusual.

Because of the surgery I could not open my mouth and

could barely speak in a whisper. Nonetheless, my IV therapist said to me, "You have a glow about you!" Then I
remembered my dream in Florida. And I decided that
whether or not we know it, we are attractive to people sometimes, not because of us, but because of Jesus in us.

Mom Brunk took care of me royally, grinding in the
blender a portion of whatever she prepared for the others
and setting it before me. For more than a week, it hurt so
much to open my mouth enough to insert even the tip of a
teaspoon that I would sit and cry. She'd say, "You have to
keep up your strength."

Since Rivers and Barth needed to get back to work, Bert
and I remained with Mom and Dad Brunk a few more days.
Bert accompanied me on the difficult flight back to Florida
because I was not well enough to travel alone. During the
flight I was so dizzy, and when we arrived I was escorted off
the aircraft in a wheelchair.

I continued to recuperate very slowly, and for several
weeks I could find no comfortable position for sleeping on
either side. With a deep incision on each side in front of the
ears and a puncture in each jaw, that was not an option, and
when I lay on my back it put pressure on both sides.
Normally, I am a person who takes minimal medication and
am very easily anesthetized; however, the intensity of the
pain was such that five milligrams of Valium would not
keep me sleeping. Spasms would jerk my mouth open as the
pain radiated through my head.

God used the people at Palma Sola Bay Baptist Church
and others to encourage us and assist with meals. When I
opened the envelope Carol, our Sunday school teacher, handed me, three crisp twenty-dollar bills and a loving note fell out.
Marcus had mowed lawns in the Florida summer sun to earn
that money. Deeply moved by his kindness, without thinking
I asked out loud through my tears, "Lord, did you have to supply our needs by taking it from a sixteen-year-old?"

A New Emotion, Hopelessness

Although I had endured TMJ problems for seventeen years without depression, twelve months after surgery I experienced a feeling of hopelessness for the first time. Had I undergone this expensive nightmare only to discover that my condition was not improved? Furthermore, I noticed that my right eyelid continued to droop, and I had less vertical and lateral mobility of my jaws than before the surgery. My face was somewhat distorted, and my lips did not come together properly.

One night when I was home alone, I spoke with a new friend in the northeast who had been forced to retire because of TMJ problems. What she shared sounded so hopeless, so beyond medical science, that I temporarily took my eyes off Jesus and for the first time began to despair. It was unusual for me to cry much, but this was no soft weeping—it was great body wracking, heaving sobs. After that I sometimes cried myself to sleep when it seemed that no amount of prayer or prescription drugs alleviated the pain.

As a public speaker, I became painfully aware that my articulatory muscles did not seem to function as they had prior to the surgery. I could not always form my words properly, and it appeared that my mouth could not keep pace with my brain.

Of necessity, I underwent a personality change in order to accommodate the disease. From a bubbly, effervescent, laughing, singing person, I became more serious. I tried to avoid crying because it hurt my face so much. I remember excessive laughing at a social function and the resultant sore throat, lightheadedness and headache. I began to dread family reunions and other gatherings because of the residual effects of sore throat and chest pain that required additional medication and bed rest.

Family Split Apart

Even though we knew without a doubt that God had sent us to Florida to affiliate with Gospel Crusade ministry, we suffered many trials. Within a year, I had undergone two surgeries, and the insurance company the ministry contracted refused to pay for either. As the bills began to mount, well-meaning friends at the ministry began to ask us how much we owed. We refused to total all the medical bills for fear it would overwhelm us, so we prayed and cried, and looked for solutions. When it became apparent that our expenses far outweighed our income, we knew that honesty dictated we find a way to repay our bills. Painfully, we made a decision—we would move back to Maryland. However, this solution was fraught with problems.

We had been very close as a family and had always enjoyed doing a lot of things together. If we left Florida, would we leave Barth there as a college student? And what about Bert, now a freshman at Bradenton Christian School? Would we tear him away from his friends and take him to Maryland? Every solution for one problem seemed to create another. Clearly, our backs were against the wall.

The Lord answered our prayers in the form of two special friends from Virginia, Lawrence and Linda Wilt, who came for a visit. Seeing our dilemma, they not only helped us financially, but also offered to become surrogate parents to Bert and enroll him in Eastern Mennonite High School for his last semester in ninth grade. Praise the Lord, this was more than we could ask or think!

That February day when we left Florida was one of the saddest days of our lives, as it seemed our hearts were ripped apart. Nineteen-year-old Barth would remain in our home, we would take Bert to Virginia to live with the Wilt family, and Rivers and I would move into Mom and Dad Brunk's guest room temporarily. From a happy foursome, overnight we had become a family of two accepting the generosity of our adopted parents, with our sons each in a different state. How humbling the whole experience was, but their love and care for us was consistent and unfailing.

One important lesson I learned again was that God sends the answers to our prayers through His people. It would be a lot easier if God would drift those miracles down from Heaven and no one would have to know our circumstances. Accepting favors from gracious friends is difficult for the best of us, and it comes with its own set of stresses and feelings of helplessness.

"Dental Cripple!"

The stresses of being away from our children and finding employment in Washington took their toll, and my jaw joints, already diseased, took a beating. It became evident that something must be done about my recurring TMJ problems. After returning to Maryland, I visited the oral and maxillofacial surgeon who had performed the triple bilateral arthroplasty. Completing an extensive examination, he said, "I might as well tell you in my typical, blunt fashion. The surgery did not work, and it will have to be done again. Angie, accept the fact that you will be a dental cripple the rest of your life!"

I was so traumatized by his crude, insensitive statements that I don't remember anything else he said except that he proposed to repeat the surgery. My only response was to weep uncontrollably, which seemed to shock him, since I had always been so upbeat in the past.

For days, Dr. Reitman's words rang in my ears and I cried a lot. One day when the tears started to come as I was walking to my car, I suddenly heard the Lord's words in my spirit, "He is only a doctor; he is not God!"

I quickly agreed as I repeated out loud, "That's right, Lord, he is not God. He is not God." With that I began to laugh and praise God fervently.

Lord, No More Surgery, Please!

Remembering the surgical nightmare three years earlier, I could not face another surgery now. I looked for ways to alleviate the pain without drugs or surgery, such as moist heat and avoiding situations that might induce a headache. I sliced and peeled my apples and avoided chewing anything that required much grinding. When the pain became incapacitating, I took Fiorinal. My symptoms gradually grew worse.

I had ceased going for regular dental check-ups and prophylaxis because of my limited mouth opening. In 1990, I lost a large filling in a right molar that had been intact for many years. Since I was unable to open my mouth properly, the oral surgeon did panoramic x-rays, used wing bites to x-ray the molars, and consulted with his associate. He said he would have to determine how to handle my TMJ problem before he could crown the tooth, so he prescribed a four-view CT-Scan.

Expecting an x-ray of sorts, I was ill prepared for the excruciatingly painful tests they administered. They pried and propped my mouth open and held it there for fifteen minutes for each view in four different positions. I felt fine when I came, but by the time this was over, I had cried many tears, and I stumbled out and into my husband's loving arms. It took several days for me to recover from the problems generated by these CT scans, and I was infuriated to learn later that they were not medically indicated.

After all of this trauma, I was never able to get an interpretation of the tests from Dr. Ross, and he had his receptionist call and cancel all three appointments I had for him to crown my molar. What was I to do with this gaping hole in my tooth if I could not count on him to help me? I felt as if I was against a brick wall with little recourse—but God reminded me of an old friend who is an oral surgeon. I called Dr. Marvin Nolt and told him my dilemma. He agreed to crown the tooth, but we had to travel to Pennsylvania to have it done.

Suicide Not An Option!

For several years after returning to Maryland, I looked for a study on TMJ conducted by the National Institutes of Health. The opportunity arose in April 1992, so I signed up for a study in Bethesda, Maryland. I knew for sure that if medical science held any answers, this is where they might be found and my prayers were answered at last.

I was admitted after very thorough questioning by telephone and a lengthy application process. During my first visit I received the first let down. As the nurse perused my file, she gave me that startled look and said, "You are excluded because you have had surgery. We can't take anyone who has had surgery." She must have read the disappointment in my face, so she continued. "Oh well, you're here now, so you might as well see the doctors."

What followed was a one-hour consultation with two physicians, who asked many questions and took prolific notes. Only one question troubled me, and they asked it twice during that hour. "Have you tried to take your life because of the pain?"

My immediate response was, "No! Suicide is not an option for me. My husband and I are Christians, so we just pray about it," I asserted without apology. When I was asked the second time, I gave the same answer and the matter was dropped.

So although the study was not designed for post-operative patients, the team of physicians did extensive consultations, performed tests to check my mobility, and ordered MRI's and x-rays. They referred me to a private practice physician, Dr. John W. Mizukawa, indicating he was the best oral and maxillofacial surgeon they knew.

Silastic Implants and Another Nightmare

Dr. Mizukawa's initial consultation was in July 1992. My maximal mouth opening was only 23mm, and I had almost no horizontal mobility. Dr. Mizukawa proposed bilateral revision surgery and carefully explained with diagrams. He would insert silastic implants that would remain for three months while my tissue formed around them, and then be removed. Despite his very kind and understanding manner, I refused to consider another surgery.

By the time I met Dr. Mizukawa, I could not use an adult toothbrush, could barely poke my tongue out, and gagged when he inserted a tongue blade. No one had been able to look down my throat for six years because of my limited opening. I could barely sing, and laughing left me hoarse and gasping for breath. As much as possible, I avoided being outside in cold or damp weather because my ears had become so sensitive. My scalp was tender to the touch, and I carried Fiorinal in my purse at all times, since I could not predict the onset of a severe headache with regurgitation and dizziness. The intermittent headaches and other symptoms had persisted for so long that it seemed almost natural, and I didn't remember what it was like to feel well.

After describing the nightmare I suffered from the 1986 surgery, Dr. Mizukawa remained optimistic that he could alleviate the pain and achieve a 35-40mm opening through revision surgery. Every adverse effect I mentioned from my prior surgery was answered to my satisfaction. Yet my skepticism did not allow me to share his enthusiastic optimism.

The previous surgery had left me with severely limited range of motion, a drooping right eyelid, two incisions that remained tender and not supple after six years, a sunken area in front of my right ear, and a somewhat twisted mouth. Why risk another presumed nightmare with dubious outcome? I even entertained the idea that my condition might worsen. All I had ever heard about TMJ surgery were horror tales, and not one success story!

Doctor Mizukawa understood my dilemma and did not pressure me. It took a full two years and further degeneration in my condition before I was willing to undergo surgery. As I continued to be reticent about it, Dr. Mizukawa introduced me to two of his patients who had experienced a surgical nightmare with the same doctor. Mary Ann, formerly a nurse who underwent TMJ surgery two weeks after mine, had lost sight in her right eye and could not close her eyelid. After seeing her limitations, I became grateful that my outcome was not worse. However, both patients had excellent results following Dr. Mizukawa's corrective surgery, so I agreed to bilateral revision surgery scheduled for August 1994.

I was confident and happy as they prepared me for surgery until no one could locate my tiny vein. Then the nightmare began that culminated in the anesthesiologist concluding, "We'll just have to put her to sleep and locate the vein in the operating room." With that I said goodbye to my husband and Pastor Dave Eshleman as they wheeled me off for the inevitable.

In my mind I can still see Room 508, bed two of Holy Cross Hospital in Silver Spring, Maryland where I was placed after surgery. The next day Dr. Mizukawa gave me the good news that all had gone well and he was pleased with the outcome. I was joyfully on my way to having permanent relief from that which had plagued me for some twenty-five years. I was discharged with extensive instructions on how to perform the exercises that would aid in my healing.

Although the experience was a lot better this time, it was still quite painful. But I was determined to cooperate fully with the physicians. So I faithfully performed the five sets of exercises five times a day, recording my progress regularly. It hurt so much that I said to Rivers, "I cannot do this to myself unless you pray the whole time." So as I inserted the tongue blades one at a time, he prayed. What a sight I was

walking around with the tongue blades protruding out of
my mouth and a moist heating pad pressed against my face.

By day four following surgery, I could already open my
mouth 23mm. By day 22 during my first post-operative
examination, Dr. Larry Bryant inserted 19 tongue blades
into my mouth. I continued to increase them and to record
my progress. By day 81 I could insert 27 tongue blades and
leave them in for 10 minutes. Moist heat and a generous
amount of prayer and perseverance kept me steadfast when
I was tempted to give up.

After three months, it was time to remove the silastic
implants, and again, I became somewhat apprehensive. I
called the office the day before my appointment and asked,
"Do I need someone to drive me home? Should I plan to
take a few days off from work?" The nurse assured me it was
a simple procedure, I would be just fine, and I needed no
one to accompany me. Thankfully, I did not believe her, and
asked Rivers to go with me.

That November day stands out in my memory as another nightmare! Uneasy because the doctor had told me very
little, I did a most unusual thing. I decided not to sit in the
chair until he explained exactly what he planned to do. "Oh,
I will make a small incision here," he said, touching my right
cheek, "and I'll pull the implants out."

"Do you plan to give me any anesthesia?" I asked Dr.
Bryant. He assured me that I needed none, but if I insisted
he would give me "a little something to relax you." With
that I sat and he injected me with some Valium. I was fully
awake as he began.

He incised the area in front of the left ear and began
what sounded like grinding or drilling. The noise alone was
unnerving, but the pain was unbearable. All I could do was
to cry and pray while he repeated the same on the right side.
About an hour later, I stumbled out of the office and Rivers
had to help me to the car.

I recuperated at home until the big black stitches protruding out in front of both ears were removed. With the implants removed, I pursued a modified version of the previous self-administered therapy until I could insert 27 tongue blades without undue pain, which represents a 45mm opening. The recuperation process required a monumental amount of discipline to persist with the tongue blades and exercises. But after all, I would be well now, and any sacrifice would be worth the effort, or so I thought. Doctor Bryant admitted to me later that I was the only patient he knew who had done those exercises as prescribed.

Still Not Well, But Deeply in Debt

I had been through so much at such tremendous expense, that we had been plunged into deep debt that would take many years to liquidate. Our situation was tenuous when we moved back to Maryland, but now we had added two more surgeries. However, we were willing to pay any price for better health; but as time went on, I could see no appreciable difference in my condition.

My jaws continued to crack upon opening or yawning, and biting and chewing raw fruits and vegetables was difficult. Since my face and ears remained very sensitive, I had to protect them from cold or damp weather. It was still difficult to sing, too much laughing was problematic, and crying really caused pain. I simply adjusted my behavior—put a lid on my emotions. I was greatly disappointed with the doctors' optimism that this nightmarish revision surgery would provide a cure. How wrong they were!

While we did not understand my situation, Rivers and I stood in faith. I continued to reflect on a promise the Lord had given to me and then confirmed it through my pastor and three other persons over a four-year period. "I waited patiently for the Lord; and He inclined to me, and heard my cry. He also brought me up out of a horrible pit, out of the miry clay, and set my feet upon a rock, and established my steps. He has put a new song in my mouth—praise to our God" (Psalm 40:1-3a, NKJV).

Since I have no option but to wait, by God's grace I choose to wait patiently. But Lord, how long? Some fifteen years later I am still waiting for the complete fulfillment of those promises, but isn't that what faith is all about?

The following poems only scratch the surface of my true feelings and summarize the content of this chapter. Though I am seldom at a loss for words, these were such horrific and painful experiences that I cannot find words to describe them adequately. I started the first poem a few months after the 1986 surgery, but the memories were so raw that it was too painful to continue. With vivid recollection of almost feeling the pain over again, I completed the first section in 1990. After the last two surgeries, I started to write the sequel "It Still Hurts to Smile," and completed it along with this manuscript. As I said to some friends, "Hold your jaws and read on!"

It Hurts To Smile
My energy level had become almost nil.
I could not describe just how I did feel.
It's somewhat nebulous; it's somewhat vague.
To put it into words, I was almost afraid.

The pain in my head was driving me wild.
It ranged from throbbing numbness to somewhat mild.
The top of my head was constantly tender,
And had been that way too long to remember.

The earaches and sore throat plagued me year after year.
I was losing my singing voice, which caused me to fear...
That something was wrong that the tests did not show.
And my competent internist was hard pressed to know...

What was causing the pain in my shoulders and neck.
So he ordered some x-rays and did a thorough check.
Meanwhile, my arms tingled and my fingers grew numb.
When I used my hands my fingers were all thumbs.

Furthermore, my thoughts became muddled and my memory bad.
Until I began to wonder what disease I really had.
My sinuses appeared clogged but never showed on tests,
So the pain in my head must be induced by stress.

For the internist's light showed my sinuses were clear;
All the antihistamines had made my symptoms disappear...
Though only for a season, and then they'd return,
To plague and buffet me until I would yearn...

For someone to get to the root of my pain,
And to do something permanent at least to restrain
My jaw joint from popping and cracking so loud,
That I hated to eat in a restaurant crowd.

For it grated and cracked, and made such a sound,
That it could be heard by other diners around.
The non-specific toothache that almost drove me mad,
Why, which tooth was aching—all the teeth that I had?

I can't pin it down; this pain that's so intense.
Now it's here; now it's there; but it's always immense.
The ringing in my ears, the pain in my back,
All added up to something being really out of whack.

Are they related; can one doctor diagnose?
Can he confirm for me what I only now suppose?
Some doctors treated my symptoms and tried to relieve
The pain from which I found little or no reprieve.

Ophthalmologist, ENT, osteopath, chiropractor...
Our wallets grew thinner just from the diagnostic factors.
The pain was pounding and pulsating in my ear,
And down my cheek there trickled a tiny tear.

My head was throbbing and my senses grew dim,
When I finally decided I should go to see him.
Dr. Craig A. Zunka came onto the scene.
His kind manner was impressive, his countenance serene.

He never seemed hurried, or frazzled, or frayed.
"But, Lord, give him wisdom," I constantly prayed.
"I can't tell you how long this has been your plight,
But your temporomandibular joints are the problem alright."

I nodded my head, smiled and pretended to perceive,
But the words he spoke, I could hardly believe.
TMJ sounds so serious—the word intimidates.
Your diagnosis astounds me and leaves me quite blank.

Temporomandibular dysfunction—what's that all about?
Just the sound of the words caused me to doubt...
That I could be heir to this awful disease.
"Why, doctor, have you made a mistake? Please!"

"You do have TMJ," the kind doctor said.
"The problem is not in your mind, but in your head...
Though it manifests itself in many strange things;
You'd be amazed at which symptoms a case of TMJ brings."

"How's the strength in your arms—first try the right.
Resist my tug on your arm as you firmly bite.
How wide can you open your arthritic jaws?
How is your digestion when you eat vegetables raw?"

"Can you chew carrots and crunch a lettuce leaf?
Does your bite seem unnatural when you close your teeth?
Do your ears hurt, your eyes burn, your head ache so much?
Do your back and neck hurt; your scalp tender to the touch?"

"Does your energy level ever seem to be up to par?
How does your back feel when you ride in a car?
Can you bend over now and touch your toes?
Is there pain in your sinuses or dripping from your nose?"

"When you do public speaking or start to sing,
Have you noticed what type of fatigue such activity brings?
Does the pressure in your head build up more and more?
After a migraine headache, does it leave your face sore?"

"Do your upper extremities ever have a numb feel?
Yes, Angie, your symptoms are all very real.
In sunlight, are your eyes so sensitive you can hardly see?"
It sounded as if the questions were all tailor made for me!

"Do your jaws pop, crack, grind and sometimes grate?
All indications are toward TMJ, but it's not too late.
TMJ dysfunction with arthritic degeneration;
The worst case I've seen in my travels through this nation."

"I'll build an acrylic splint, made especially for you.
You must wear it at all times except when you chew.
This splint will move your jaw joint back in line.
You'll feel better soon; it's just a matter of time."

"Then occlusal equilibration, slowly little by little.
To put it crudely, your teeth I'll have to whittle.
Now, take these natural vitamins seven every four hours;
Refrain from eating white sugar and also white flour."

"The healing process is slow, but will surely be there.
Just follow my instructions, and do not despair."
So for seventeen months the man gazed into my mouth.
I took that arduous journey from my home in the south.

But Linda, a great friend, kept my company each time,
We encouraged one another and prayed it would be fine.
And it was for a few months—yes, everything was cool,
If I watched my eating habits and lived by the rules.

Then at last the time came when it flared up again.
By now I was in Florida and did not know when
I could take the trip to Virginia again for to see
The doctor who would tell me what the trouble could be.

"I've done all I can," Dr. Zunka sadly said.
"But Dr. Reitman can fix the problem you have in your head.
Why, surgery is the last resort for patients of mine;
But with Reitman at your side, you will be just fine."

Then another trip that lasted a full eleven hundred miles.
An arthrogram and counseling that made the trip worthwhile.
At last a date was set for my indescribable surgery.
"Report to Montgomery General Hospital and then we will see."

"We may replace the jaw joints, depending on the damage there.
Or maybe we will salvage it by some extensive repair.
This surgery could be lengthy, lasting seven hours or four,
Then the recovery period could be a full six weeks or more."

"So don't plan to work hard; concentrate on getting well.
Whether you need a joint replacement now, only God can tell."
With facial puncture wounds and trauma of finding my tiny vein;
Yet with God's enduring mercy, I joyfully endured the pain.

Then a short trip into a fully staffed operating suite,
Where doctors and nurses waited my surgery to complete.
Five hours in OR and several in the recovery process,
Regurgitation, pain and injections are what I remember best.

When at last in the mirror I beheld my rotund face,
What I saw resembled a creature just in from outer space.
With bandages and ice pack and swelling galore;
My whole body tingled and my head did ache so.

But my gentle husband sat for many hours by my side,
Praying, loving and comforting his twenty-three-year bride.
And Barth and Bert prayed and loved and showed much care.
I could endure the greatest pain as long as my family was there.

Family, friends, IV therapist, and anesthesiologist too,
All made me feel quite special, though little they could do...
To alleviate the excruciating pain I now endured.
But I could be victorious because of Jesus Christ, my Lord.

For God gave me comfort beyond what man can ever give.
He provided me the hope that in His strength I could live.
The flowers, the friends, and my beautiful family,
All helped to soothe my spirits and to keep my sanity.

Now a second nightmare—surgery—for the first one did not work.
"Your jaw is not translating—little wonder that it hurts!"
"No! No! I can't take more," my hurting heart now cries,
Then hopelessness engulfs me, and tears fill my eyes.

"Dental cripple!" says the doctor, "for which there is no cure."
Had I not known Jesus, I would have panicked for sure.
But still, the hot tears rolled slowly down my cheeks,
A choking sensation engulfed me as I tried so hard to speak.

Triple, bilateral arthroplasty—words I now greatly feared.
And down my hot, flushed cheeks rolled floods of salty tears.
"Dental cripple, dental cripple!" the post-op surgeon said.
And his words reverberated in my ears and in my head.

His words were so brutal; they were so very hard;
'Til my Heavenly Father whispered, "Remember, he is not God!"
I have a plan for your life now, you'll soon see, My child,
Let My joy be your strength, even when it hurts to smile!"

September 1990

"It Still Hurts to Smile"

Then some years later my pain was still bad.
The headaches were among the worst I'd ever had.
So what shall I do, since my wallet is now flat?
But my mobility is limited, and I can't afford that.

My mouth opening registers at millimeters 23,
And to look down my throat is an impossibility.
The pain is recurring more often than before;
My ears are ringing and my jaw joints are sore.

I can't bite into an apple or a plump juicy steak;
And if I try to do it, oh the trouble it does make.
My popcorn eating habits must come to an end,
The result is two days for my jaw joints to mend.

Since NIH had done TMJ studies in the past,
I just knew that I had my answer at last.
With physician's recommendation now firmly in hand,
We set the appointment and joyfully made our plans.

When the doctors saw the pain that I had endured,

They thought I'd attempted suicide for sure.
After asking me the same question not once, but twice,
I said, "Doctor, it's not an option for me to take my life!"

"We just pray and put our faith and trust in our God
Even though intense pain sometimes makes it very hard."
With many tests and x-rays, and MRI's and such,
My face became more sore and tender to the touch.

"But you'll be a new woman," my friend Mary Ann said,
As I could feel the pain now numbing my head.
When I consented to revisit our dear Doctor M.,
And I knew immediately that I could trust him...

To repair the damage that had before been done,
And my road to recovery I thought had now begun.
Would my mouth finally open so I could freely sing?
What kind of relief would this surgery bring?

The doctor was pleased; he had done his best.
The silastic implants should take care of the rest.
So I exercised my jaw through tears and much pain,
Since I wanted the optimum mobility to gain.

And I said to Rivers, "Please stand by and pray,
To do these exercises that's the only way."
As day after day I did one hundred twenty-five,
With prayers and moist heat is how I survived.

As always, the Lord has brought me safely through,
We trusted in Him; what else could we do?
And to this day, I'm praying my jaw will be healed,
Let it be, precious Jesus, according to Your will.

February 2003

Application Questions:
My Ordeal With TMJ, "The Money Jaw"

Scriptures: Isaiah 43:2, Psalm 40:1-3a, Psalm 91:16, Deuteronomy 30:19.

1. What is the difference in "claiming" an illness and admitting you have a problem?
2. What do you do when you request prayer and your symptoms grow worse?
3. Have you ever felt hopelessness because of some adversity you faced? If so, how did you overcome it?
4. Has a medical professional pronounced a negative prognosis over you? If so, how did you continue to believe God in spite of it?
5. Do you consider suicide an option for a Christian as a way out of their pain? Discuss.

Angie exposing incision and shaved area after 1986 triple bilateral TMJ surgery

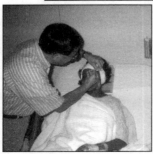

Dr. Mizukawa removes bandages after 1994 TMJ revision surgery

Dr. Bryant removes silastic implants three months after surgery

CHAPTER 10

FORCED TO RETIRE

Rivers and I had both worked for the federal government long enough to be tenured, but had spent several years working for Christian organizations. Now as we began to think of retirement, we prayed for the Lord's leading, sensing it was time to return to the Washington area. "Working in ministry has its rewards in Heaven, but we need some we can spend down here," I said convincingly to Rivers.

Readjusting to City Life

At the time we moved back to Maryland in 1988, Rivers and I had incurred many medical debts that we couldn't possibly pay on our ministry salaries. He and I found jobs at Providence Hospital in Washington. I liked my position, but my colleagues were mostly lesbians whose conversations were vulgar and quite offensive. Although they knew my husband, one of them invited me to a gay bar. Diversity had come to the work place for sure, and with it came also perversity. I used to sit in my office and pray for them.

One woman who was particularly vulgar frequently used the Lord's name in vain, but He gave me an idea. I asked, "Janice [not her real name], what's your dad's name?"

She replied, "Richard."

The very next time she hollered, "O God," I responded with, "O, Richard!"

"What?" she inquired.

"If you can call my Father's name in vain, I can call yours in vain," I said. Never again did I hear her say "O God."

One day Janice, who suffered from manic depression,

turned on me. She became furious over my cool response to her lesbian lover who had attempted to hug me. By the time the swearing tirade was over, I felt as if I had been raped.

Janice's voice rose to an uncalled for crescendo as she spat out the words staccato fashion with an unwritten exclamation point after each word. "This is the lifestyle I've chosen for myself!" Although I had never told the women I was praying for them, in anger Janice continued, "Don't even pray for me to change because I don't want to change!" I saw her exclamation as an expression of confidence in my prayers. If I prayed, she reasoned, the Lord might change her life, and she didn't want that.

I replied to my irate colleague, "Janice, God won't make you change. He'll allow you to destroy yourself if that's what you choose to do."

Remembering the story in the Book of Numbers about Balak sending for Balaam to curse God's people, I knew that even though the devil is persistent, he cannot out persist God. When Satan's emissaries come against us we know it is doomed for failure because, "No one can curse whom God has blessed."

Silver Wedding Anniversary

In June of 1988, Rivers and I celebrated our twenty-fifth anniversary. We asked Pastor Nelson Burkholder, who had married us, to preside over a reaffirmation of our vows. I donned my wedding dress and marched down the aisle at Warwick River Mennonite Church, escorted by our sons, Barth and Bert. I wrote the following poem as a surprise gift to Rivers, and my sister, Eunice read it while the audience watched Rivers blush. It summarizes portions of our life together, some joyous and some painful.

Our 25 Years Together
June 22, 1963 – June 22, 1988

'Twas at a Christmas party
Two young lovers chanced to meet.
He noticed her; she noticed him,
But the two did barely speak.
As she eyed that handsome man,
In her heart she heaved a sigh.
"Can any good and holy thing
Come out of Carver High?"

Yes, it's possible that it could,
She finally decreed.
And from that time forward
Their relationship did proceed.
Now Rivers sought with diligence
To win the lady of his dreams,
But she was playing hard to get;
His efforts were futile it seemed.

Next Sunday, Rivers and two friends
Came calling at the Bass household.
Of the four single girls greeting them there,
He chose Angie to have and to hold.
So to win her hand, he immediately began
His arduous journey to pursue her love.
'Twas a difficult task until he convinced her
It was the will of the Father above.

But there were those who opposed them;
Who sought daily to expose them.
To prove why this relationship was all wrong.
For how could a Mennonite gal
And a Church of God guy,
Ever in marriage hope to get along?

Well, together as they prayed,

Listening to what the Lord said,
They determined exactly what to do.
As the Lord made it clear,
They were engaged later that year,
Which was October 20, 1962.

Then in March came the ring,
As the maiden's heart did sing;
With delight she displayed it to all.
As she rubbed her face with glee,
Adjusting her specs constantly,
Daydreaming of her Rivers strong and tall.

Some of his church folks did not like it,
And with fervor they did fight it.
As this young man was first choice for their daughter.
But the more those folks objected,
The more he did protect her,
And their love won out despite the way they fought her.

For while the saints engaged in strife,
He determined to make Angie his wife,
As for "until death" he pledged to be her man.
So while they fussed and fought her,
He went promptly out and bought her
A ring and placed it on her little hand.

On June twenty-second, nineteen sixty-three,
The happy couple did wed most joyfully.
A simple ceremony, without pomp and circumstance.
Pastor Burkholder hitched them together,
And despite much inclement weather,
Their marriage has lasted with romance.

They saved their love for each other,

As neither of them knew another.
Purity and fidelity have characterized their marriage.
So impenetrable has been this bond,
That they've fought many battles and won,
For the word "divorce" was not in their vocabulary.

Together they've walked through the fire,
Through the floods, and through the mire.
Through wind, rain, and early morning dew.
But the Lord was at their side,
The Holy Spirit was their Guide.
As their prayers went up to God, not a few.

For you see their love has lasted,
Though storms and stresses have overcast it.
And many illnesses and hard times have beset it.
For they took the hand of God,
As He became their staff and rod.
And they've never had a reason to regret it.

They lost babies—one, two, three,
For no real reason the doctor could see.
And through it all they experienced some upset.
But after five years Barth came to join them,
And with his love he did warm them.
In five years Bert rounded out the Williams Quartet.

Now in harmony they all do sing,
As to one another they do bring
Much joy, much love, and much pleasure.
For in all their tribulation,
God brought peace and jubilation.
And His love has been poured out beyond all measure.

They're still trusting in the Lord,

Walking in the Spirit in one accord.
As before God and these witnesses they stand together,
Reaffirming their vows in year twenty-five,
Testifying that their marriage is still alive,
And that God is able to outlast any stormy weather.

So they thank you for your love,
For your prayers, and your example.
For you have helped to make their marriage strong.
As Father God has been their Source,
They've never considered a divorce,
And to Jesus Christ the glory does belong!

A Nasty Fall on the National Mall

Rivers and I had returned to Maryland determined to work hard, maintain good health, and get out of debt. The Lord had blessed us with the tenacity to hang on, even when we couldn't foresee a positive outcome.

In July 1989, I went to work for the Federal Aviation Administration. I realized that life in a federal agency was fraught with competitiveness; however, the FAA Christian Fellowship was a great source for prayer and encouragement. The Lord continually provided the strength to work long hours under the intense pressure I had to endure in the office of a high-ranking FAA official. He was known to be "impossible" as a supervisor, but that posed a special challenge to me, and I'd sit at my desk and shoot up little prayers like arrows.

Mr. Gray was a very brilliant man who could be quite intimidating to his colleagues as well as his subordinates. However, he respected my Christian convictions, and while he didn't agree, he enjoyed discussing spiritual things with me. We got along quite well because he expected a lot and I often put my needs on hold to ensure his needs were met. He liked my work ethic, commended me often, and gave me special achievement awards.

But one day something happened that would change my life permanently. Rushing across the office, I did not notice a trash can in the aisle. I hit it with full force and it catapulted me across the room. Completely embarrassed, I pretended to be just fine as Mr. Gray helped me up. But this had been a serious fall that would transform my life.

My internist sent me to a physiatrist, a doctor of physical medicine, who diagnosed me with myofacitis with a prognosis of fair. He put me through extensive therapies and modalities, painkillers, a neck brace, injections, nerve conduction tests that I found quite painful. The Pro-TENS (transcutaneous electrical nerve stimulation) unit prescribed for home use had four electrodes that I attached to various sites to deliver shocks to the nerve endings. I used them faithfully, but the pain persisted. Twice when I headed home from work, I became so ill in the car that I regurgitated.

Seeing that I had done permanent damage to my back, Dr. Gooding urged me to retire. "No way!" By God's grace, I would beat this one too. Many a day I awakened in severe pain, administered my home therapy, and then went to work. Some days I rested in the Health Unit at lunchtime. The office staff would compliment me on my cheerful personality, not knowing the depth of my pain.

I walked rapidly from place to place, and often used the steps in lieu of the elevator, pushing myself ridiculously hard. Determined not to give in to the recurrent stabbing pain in my back and the sciatica that caused radiating pain down my legs, I pressed on. One day, a guard stopped me and threatened me with, "If you don't slow down, I'm going to give you a ticket for walking too fast in the building." Little did he know how difficult it was just to keep putting one foot before the other. When asked why I walked so fast, I would reply that it made me feel no better to walk slowly. If I slowed down, people would think I was sick, and we couldn't have that!

After a second fall five years later, I still held on hoping for the best annuity. Doctor Gooding scolded me repeatedly, "Don't be so stoic!"

I'd reply, "Pain is my friend. When I bend the wrong way it tells me to straighten up." Numerous medications he prescribed made me light headed and nauseated. For three years I steadfastly refused the nerve blocks the doctor recommended. When I could no longer ignore the pain or neglect my health, Dr. Gooding wrote an order, and my supervisors, Lauraline Gregory and Bill Bradford, graciously allowed me to work part time to accommodate my multiple health challenges.

Overnight in Cardiac Care

One hot June day I became quite ill during my train ride home. Praying under my breath, I so wanted to get to Greenbelt where Rivers was waiting for me. When it became inevitable, I bailed out as the train pulled into the Columbia Heights station in Washington. "Lord, please protect me," I prayed, strongly suspecting this was a crime-infested neighborhood.

The nightmare that followed included a violent vomiting episode, an ambulance ride accompanied by two attending paramedics, treatment in Washington Hospital Center's emergency room, and admission to the cardiac care unit. I felt so vulnerable, so alone, so at-their-mercy. Upon my insistence, the train station manager located Rivers in Maryland, and he came immediately.

I remained in the unit through a very long and pain-filled night of poking, probing and blood draws, followed by a nuclear stress test that included two twenty-minute sessions with the nuclear medicine camera. By the next evening, I felt even sicker, but they released me with thirteen electrodes still attached to my chest. I had not suffered a heart attack, for which I was grateful.

Rivers' Declining Health

While we were dealing with my physical problems, Rivers had his own set of concerns, including thyroid problems and high blood pressure. He underwent surgery for prostate cancer at a time when he was getting over a viral infection. On a cold, rainy January day Rivers was discharged from the hospital. A few hours after we arrived home, a severe ice storm swept through, bringing sub-freezing temperatures and wiping out our electricity. With a total electric home, it became increasingly difficult to keep him warm, fed, and medicated. My "little sis" Tricia Brunk brought hot tomato soup, and we survived. I never thought I could thank God for a catheter, but that day I did because it kept Rivers under the covers and possibly from a case of pneumonia.

On two occasions his blood sugar plummeted to very dangerous levels that left him in a semi-conscious state and required paramedics to revive him. One morning Rivers awakened not feeling well. Trying hard to cooperate with his desire for independence, against my better judgment, I went to work but called him several times. When I returned home he was quite ill. Looking around the bedroom, I noticed he had not eaten the snacks I had left for him. Lying very still on his back with his eyes closed, ashen colored and barely speaking, Rivers looked like a case for the emergency room to me. However, he insisted that he needed no medical inter-vention, so I set out to get some nourishment into him. He had lost the bit of food he ingested in the morning and I knew that by this time food was life to him. Bert helped me to feed him a few bites, and he seemed to improve a little.

Without my knowledge he got up and took his evening insulin, but then lost what little food he had eaten. That meant having two insulin injections in his system and no food. Around midnight I felt a slight nudge, and I believe the Lord must have awakened me. I held Rivers' hand and prayed. Then I realized Rivers was trying to tell me something but could not talk. He continued trying to speak until I understood one thing, "Kiss me."

Observing his ashen color, I reasoned, "He's dying, and he wants to kiss me goodbye." I cannot describe what else was going on in my head as I tried to awaken him. I asked Bert to hold Dad's hand and pray with him while I went to call his physician, the paramedics, and Pastor Dave.

Our home was close to the fire department, so they arrived promptly, but unbelievably, could not revive him. Although when I called I had explained that he was diabetic, had suffered a heart attack in the past, and had high blood pressure, they sent two inexperienced paramedics. They summoned a second team of two, and with four of them in our bedroom, set about to revive Rivers. Oxygen, injections, orange juice laced with sugar... After Rivers was aroused and alert, I wanted to take him to Providence Hospital where he was employed because they would give "Mr. Rivers," as he was affectionately called, the best possible treatment.

After I signed a release, the paramedics helped Rivers into our car. Several inches of snow and ice lay on the ground. Assuring Bert that I could drive Dad the nine miles to the hospital we set out.

About seven miles from home I heard a thud and knew immediately it meant a flat tire. It was two-thirty in the morning, we were in a very undesirable section of Washington, and the temperature was a frigid twenty-two degrees. Unable to get help at the gas station, we huddled in the car and waited for Bert to come and transport us.

Later in the emergency room when I shared with Bert about thinking Rivers was dying, I learned that he too had such a moment. While Bert was praying with his Dad, his body began to twitch and his legs to jerk involuntarily. Bert continued to pray, as a calm settled over his Dad and a slight smile came to his face. Bert thought he was about to go to Heaven and was happy about it. He said, "I sat on that bed and processed my Dad's death." This affected Bert profoundly, and for days he was broken up about it.

The emergency room staff took care of Rivers immediately, but the triage nurse said, "Mr. Rivers, you would have died if you had been alone." It was a long night interspersed with short visits to Rivers' bedside. The next morning he was discharged, and we were again reminded that life is fragile, and must not be taken for granted.

Pain, Pills and PT

I continued to battle the physical pain, spending my evenings at home strapped to a moist heating pad. In a journal called "Pain, Pills and PT," I kept track of my condition. Attempting to remain on the job as long as possible, I brought a padded mat, a small pillow, and a coverlet in. At lunchtime I would eat a bite, take my pain medications and nap on the floor. Behind my locked office door, I felt secure—I could take the stress off my back for a few minutes and gain the strength to work through the afternoon. Then one day Margaret discovered me lying on the floor, and I knew it was a secret no longer.

As the problems compounded and the pain grew progressively worse, it was difficult to maintain my customary facade of masking my feelings with a smiley face. The chronic pain began to play with my emotions—when forced to talk about it, I would tear up. Sometimes I avoided business meetings because I could not sit for extended periods. One day I told my supervisor, "If anyone tries to pity me today, I will burst into tears."

Forced to Retire

The amount of my monthly annuity became secondary to my health, as I knew the stresses of the office only added to my misery. Even though they tried to accommodate me, I began to make plans to retire. "Life is too short to spend it this way," I told my friend, Malinda. "I'm going to listen to what the doctor has been telling me for years, and retire soon."

After much prayer, I began to look forward to retiring. Having had a strong testimony in the FAA building for twelve years, I knew my send-off had to be synonymous with the way I lived. The elaborate luncheon on December 21, 2000, at the Fort Myer Officers Club in Arlington, Virginia near the Pentagon, must honor the Lord in some way. While the program would contain some elements of surprise for me, I interjected an invocation by Pastor Dave, a solo by our son Barth, and a special impromptu rendition of "Praise God From Whom All Blessings Flow," sung a cappella by all of us Mennonites.

Most of the people who responded to "open mike" time mentioned my Christian faith. Jack Jackson authored a special slide presentation based on "The Virtuous Woman" from Proverbs thirty-one, and Mike Packard wrote beautiful poetry that attested to my faith. My manager, Lauraline, mentioned the times I prayed with her in her office.

How blessed I was to have close friends Nelson and Donna Suter and Lawrence and Linda Wilt from the Shenandoah Valley, and Bessie Sellaway from Petersburg, who sacrificed to fight the Beltway pre-Christmas traffic and support me. What an outpouring of love, and what a grand finale to a long career.

Since some considered me as FAA's poet in laureate, I thought it only fitting that my farewell address and response to all the congratulatory remarks be set in poetry.

Ode to Myself As I Retire
It was July third, nineteen eighty-nine,
When I entered the FAA just in time,
For to reinstate my government career.

International Aviation first claimed me,
Then the Office of Training gained me,
And Information Technology followed near.

My life was now forever changed,
As my schedule I then rearranged,
To accommodate the work I had to do.
Employment at the FAA,
Caused for me many a hectic day,
And my overtime hours numbered quite a few.

Then to Business Management I came,
And I've never been the same.
For I took upon myself new tasks at hand.
Pressure cooker notwithstanding,
And supervisors being demanding,
With God's help the new job I soon began.

Analyst, Admin. Officer, Awards Coordinator,
Training Specialist, and Ethics Program persuader—
These and many other hats I had to wear.
But with patience and love I took them;
In hard times I never forsook them,
For with encouragement I could forbear.

Thanks for all you've done to mold me,
As within your arms you hold me.
I've been loved and at times treated like a queen.
When my back hurts you protect me.
But then sometimes you upset me,
When you inadvertently treat me mean.

But when "fun lunch" you do serve me,
Or with long meetings you unnerve me,
I try my best my interest to keep.

But long discussions, they do fret me,
And indecision does upset me,
As I fight so hard not to go to sleep.

"Sweet Little Angie," you have named me,
And with loving kindness claimed me.
You have showered me with compliments for sure.
For when business pressures mounted,
On one another we have counted.
And we've worked together this stress to endure.

Thanks for the lessons you have taught me,
And experiences you have brought me.
From this place I take away more than I should.
But if you'll be sure to read my lips,
You'll learn the excess is on my hips.
For you've added all the pounds you possibly could.

Now you may have your Beltway pile-ups,
Snow, sleet, rain, and temper flare-ups;
Management Team meetings you can fight.
For promotions you may try out,
But just leave me with my bailout.
I'd rather stay home and my poems write.

And I'll write the book within me.
To the Lord's work He will send me,
As I'll do all my service with a smile.
But if hard times do beset me,
And temptation starts to fret me,
With God's help I can still go the extra mile.

Folks, I'm not lame, old, or decrepit;
I'm just smart enough to accept it.
I know how to leave when I'm still on fire.

I'll depart while I'm still liked,
Rather than be told to take a hike.
So, leave me be, and just let me retire!

Having launched my retirement, I could now devote time to writing the book God had placed on my heart to encourage others in their times of adversity.

Carpal Tunnel Syndrome

I was still under the doctor's care and receiving therapy for my back when I noticed that my wrists and arms hurt a lot. I attributed this to two previous falls when I had spontaneously tried to soften the blow by extending my hands. But now it had become difficult to grip a pen, brush my teeth manually, open containers in the kitchen, and even to grip the wheel enough to drive. Picking up my Bible sent severe pain through my wrists.

During a visit with my physiatrist, I described the problem, and he performed a nerve conduction test. "Carpal tunnel syndrome!" he announced. "Now Ang, we will try to treat your condition without surgery." Wear braces to protect my wrists and avoid extensive typing was the mandate. "You can type fifteen minutes a day."

"I'm writing a book," I protested, "And I can't write that way!" The doctor was unimpressed, and he fitted me with the braces and ordered me to wear them around the clock. I complied, but after many months saw no improvement. My arms and wrists ached with the slightest activity, and I added them to sites where I applied the moist heat, along with the lower back, upper back, neck, and face.

Sensing my dilemma, well-meaning friends had wonderful solutions—just dictate the book and have someone else type it, or use a voice-activated computer program. My response was always, "Talking and writing are not the same thing. I have greater creativity when I use a keyboard."

Tendonitis, Osteoporosis, and Other Maladies

Right on the heels of the carpal tunnel diagnosis was that of tendonitis, which explained why my arms ached so much. While I felt sure both were a result of the extensive writing by computer on the job, I was no longer working for the government.

I joined a double blind study at the Women's Health Research Center on the effects of certain hormones on the body. One requirement was a bone density test, whereupon they discovered osteoporosis.

One aggravation after another came my way, to include rushing out of church one Sunday and ending up in the hospital with acute gastrointestinal distress or food poisoning. Hadn't I followed the Lord's leading in retiring and trying to give priority to writing a book on Joy in Adversity?

Yet, in my first year of retirement, many physical challenges had interfered with my ability to concentrate on the manuscript. How much adversity did I have to endure before I could share about God's overcoming power? But the granddaddy of them all was yet to come.

Application Questions:
Early Retirement

Scriptures: Proverbs 20:30, Psalm 27:14; 31:1-3, 15a, Isaiah 26:3, Matthew 6:25-34, Hebrews 6:13-15; 12:1-3.

1. In what ways do you need to adjust to changing situations in your life?
2. How would you cope with an unexpected accident?
3. If you have not yet retired, what plans should you begin to make now?
4. How well do you deal with emergencies such as a spouse's declining health?
5. How do you deal with disappointments when you feel certain you have followed God's leading?

Rivers and Angie attend "I Still Do"
Conference in Washington, DC,
39th Anniversary

Rivers and Angie
40th Anniversary, 2003

Rivers and Angie with sons and
grandsons, Bert, Barth, Garrett
and Parker

Barth, Angie, Garrett (9) and
Parker (5), Christmas 2002

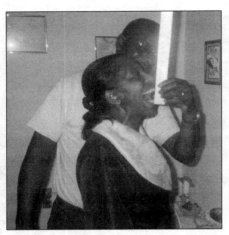

Rivers measures Angie's mouth opening
after the second TMJ surgury to insert the
silastic implants

Rivers with Bert following his
prostate cancer surgery,
January 1998

Rivers and Angie at her retirement from FAA, December,
2000

Mennonites performing impromptu
"Praise God From Whom All Blessings Flow" at
Angie's retirement celebration

CHAPTER 11

DIAGNOSIS: BREAST CANCER!

My annual mammogram was overdue and I thought I felt some thickening in the right breast. Since it was almost time for a physical check-up, I decided to wait and inform the doctor during that visit. On a cold February day, I stood before the x-ray machine as usual, but the results would be like none in the past.

Calcifications of the Breast

The radiologist read the x-rays while I waited, and with a concerned look, he pronounced the diagnosis—calcification formations in the right breast. He assured me, however, that I need not be alarmed because until I returned for x-ray magnifications of the abnormalities, it was not possible to determine whether they were benign or malignant.

Not desiring to upset Rivers and Bert with what I hoped was a false alarm, I went home and began to pray, but not alone. I called my sisters, a few close friends, and the 700 Club and requested prayer for the calcifications, carpal tunnel syndrome, and tendonitis. We agreed together in prayer and believed God for healing.

March 14, 2002 was a chilly day, and I pulled my jacket tightly to keep out the fierce wind, wishing I had worn warmer clothing. This was the day when I returned to Dr. Branda for follow-up on the mammograms he had taken two weeks earlier. Fully assured that it was only a routine visit, I had not asked Rivers to accompany me.

After taking two views of the right breast, the technician

suggested, "Get dressed and wait here for the doctor." However, a few minutes later, she reappeared and said, "The doctor wants me to take two more views." Reluctantly, I disrobed the second time and tried to remain calm.

This time while I waited for the doctor to come and explain his findings, I became a little anxious, as the devil began to bring negative thoughts to my mind. As usual, I turned to prayer, daring to believe that whatever the diagnosis, God would take care of me.

I was reminded of how the Lord had cared for me in November 1987, when I was diagnosed with a fibroadenoma in the left breast. The gynecologist had aspirated the fluid with a large needle, which was no picnic, but it filled up again. "Now I have no option but to remove the lump," Dr. Newhall said.

We were beginning a new school of ministry and I thought I just had to provide orientation for the new students. We set the surgery for a Friday, which would give me the weekend to recuperate. Everything went quite well and I was discharged the same day, only to suffer greatly at home during the night. But the Lord had done a miracle after the surgery. Why not before? Hadn't God's people been praying fervently for me to be healed supernaturally?

Doctor Newhall asked me to return daily for the nurse to treat the incision and apply fresh dressing. When I went on Wednesday, the nurse removed the drainage tube and applied the usual dressing. "We will be closed tomorrow for Thanksgiving," she said, "so I can't dress the incision. Don't remove any of the dressing, but take this gauze and pad the incision when it bleeds through," she said, handing me a sizeable amount of sterile gauze. I accepted the handful of gauze, but never needed to use it.

On Thanksgiving Day we attended a service at Christian Retreat. Evangelist Mike Shreve preached a powerful sermon and asked those with ringing in the ears to come forward for prayer. I came for prayer, but the constant ringing continued, and I was not aware that God had performed another miracle.

The next day when the nurse removed the gauze from the incision, it was as pure white as when she applied it two days earlier—not a drop of blood or a single stain. "I don't know if you believe in Divine healing, but I know the Lord stopped the bleeding," I said, remembering that the last thing I had seen was blood when the dressing was applied. "I know drainage does not stop suddenly, so the Lord must have done this," I said exuberantly. Neither the doctor nor the nurse seemed impressed, but at least I had given my witness.

Some fifteen years later, I mused on what the Lord had done and it increased my faith to believe that He is still God and would heal me, whatever the doctor's diagnosis. Doctor Branda jolted me back to reality with, "I have some bad news for you, Angie. There's a seven to ten millimeter region with ten or twelve irregular calcifications in the inner upper right breast. They are black and irregular, and that usually means they are malignant. I would be surprised if they are not malignant."

Doctor Branda, himself wheelchair bound, spoke with such empathy as he patted me on the knee. "Now, I'm not a surgeon, but here is what I think will happen. You will probably have a lumpectomy followed by radiation. It appears to be contained in a small area and not to have spread."

I'd been praying under my breath as the doctor spoke, but now he turned to me for a reaction. "The Lord will take care of me, and I will be fine," I replied.

Assuming I had not understood the profundity of his last statements, Dr. Branda began to repeat his earlier assertion that the calcifications were probably malignant and would have to be excised followed by radiation treatments. "There's a fifty-fifty chance of a malignancy, but as I said, I'd be surprised if they aren't malignant." Again he turned to me for a response and I sensed I had made him very uncomfortable.

"Doctor, you had bad news for me, but you have done your job well, and I thank you. I will be fine. God bless you," I said.

"I'll notify Dr. Trifoglio immediately, and you should see her as soon as possible so she can refer you to a surgeon," the sympathetic radiologist concluded.

Mentally reeling from this sudden heavy dump, I breezed out of the doctor's office. Pausing at the receptionist's desk, I said, "The doctor had bad news for me today, but he delivered it well. You all did your jobs well, and I thank you. God bless you." With that I was headed for my car, trying to process what I had just heard.

Since I was about a mile from our pastor's home, I called to ask if I might come over and talk with them. Praying all the way, I drove over and shared the news with his wife Helen. All I really wanted was someone to give me a reassuring hug and pray with me that everything would be all right. After she prayed for me, I headed home, determined not to call Rivers and deliver such news by telephone.

Once home, I didn't have to wait too long until my caring husband called and asked, "What did the doctor say about the test results?"

Still determined not to upset him, I replied, "Oh, they repeated the tests, and I'll tell you all about it when you get home." That was one of the most difficult moments of my day because the one I loved most was in the dark about my condition. When I needed his strong arms to hold and comfort me, I was trying to protect him instead.

I filled the afternoon with praying and carefully picking a list of persons who I believed would stand with me in faith. Knowing my sisters were Spirit-filled women who knew the power of God to heal, I was able to reach a couple of them who prayed with me by telephone. What a blessing to have family members who will agree in prayer with us when we hurt.

Scriptures offer so much comfort in the darkest hours. Speaking of the blessed state of the righteous, Psalm 112:7 (NKJV) says, "He will not be afraid of evil tidings; his heart is steadfast, trusting in the Lord."

Changed Priorities

Having had preliminary tests with a neurosurgeon, I was due to see a surgeon concerning the carpal tunnel syndrome, but that had to wait since the breast cancer diagnosis took priority. However, I decided to continue my normal activities that included teaching a candy-making workshop to children, and praying with the sick in the hospital. I would not sit at home and brood or fall into self-pity, but I would believe that God would take care of this one too.

Again I experienced the peace that passes understanding that the Apostle Paul speaks of in Philippians 4:6,7. I immersed myself in the Scriptures and meditated on them to renew my mind and increase my faith. Also, I called the Mike Murdock Evangelistic Association for prayer. Even though I had retired, I visited the FAA Christian Fellowship on the day I was to see the surgeon for the first time. The teacher, Pastor Lewis Anthony, anointed me with oil and prayed, specifically requesting that I not state the diagnosis because God knew the problem.

A precious sister, Bobbie Smith, who heads the group, was such a strong support. Knowing she had undergone breast cancer surgery a couple of years earlier, Bobbie would surely understand. She and I prayed by telephone and I asked God to surround me by saints who would walk with me in faith. Not having planned it in advance, I found myself asking God to keep anyone off our telephone and out of our home who would express negativism and lack of faith. The last thing I wanted was to have people rehearsing every tale of woe they knew about women who had experienced breast cancer, and especially those who had died from it. The Lord honored that request, as I would learn later.

I prepared an e-mail to some friends that said in part, "The Lord has given me such peace. If anyone had told me the doctor could say cancer to me and I take it so calmly, it would have been hard to believe. We don't get the grace until we need it."

Pastor Dave and Helen placed my name on their prayer list as did the Mount Olive Presbyterian Church, and we asked friends in different parts of the country to pray. The women from Windhaven Church and the pastor and others from New Beginnings Church diligently prayed and kept in touch. One encouraging e-mail message from Pastor Ed Heatwole and his wife Eileen said, "God is your strength and fortress, a very present help in trouble. To this I claim life, health and healing for you as you go for surgery tomorrow. May God put a song in your heart that will sustain you during the procedure."

Rivers and I felt so loved and blessed, and like Moses of old, God's people were holding up our arms and we were winning the battle. Several times during this period we discussed the sad plight of people who have no Christian friends when they face hard times.

Fine Needle Aspiration and Stereotactic Biopsy

Dr. Trifoglio recommended an excellent surgeon, and Rivers and I arrived in good spirits, fully expecting him to pronounce me healed. Doctor Duckett was patient, kind, and understanding, and I liked him immediately. He placed copies of the x-rays on the wall and pointed out the abnormalities. "There are fifteen to seventeen calcifications in the three o'clock position. Some of these appear to be malignant." But as he attempted to examine them in the breast, he could not locate them. "Lie down," he said, followed by "Now sit up." Back and forth he went, all the while trying to palpate the lump. With four magnifications on the x-rays before him, I felt sure a skilled surgeon such as Dr. Duckett could locate the tumor immediately.

Looking at Rivers who was grinning broadly by now, I interjected, "Is there a possibility that they aren't there any more?" I was full of faith because only a couple of hours before, I had been anointed with oil and prayed for. Determined to exercise my faith, I steadfastly refused to assume the tumor was malignant before tests proved it, and after having prayer I resisted the temptation of feeling to see if it was still there.

"Well, they're on the x-ray." He continued to probe, finally injecting the needle to aspirate the tumor. During those few humorous moments, I mentioned our faith in God and assured the doctor that Rivers and I knew God would heal me. "I know God does not cause cancer," the doctor had told us; "I pray when I'm in trouble!"

A few days later the results were in and the fine needle biopsy was negative. Praise the Lord, my healing was complete! Or was it?

The surgeon said he needed to do a stereotactic biopsy at the hospital to remove the calcifications. If they were not malignant that would be the end of it, but if they were, further surgery was indicated. I had only recently heard about the stereotactic biopsy as a strongly recommended procedure for removing calcifications, so I felt positive about having it. Only six hospitals in the metropolitan area were equipped to do the procedure, and we lived only a mile from one of them.

The outpatient surgery was scheduled for April 19, 2002. I was placed on a table face down, with an opening through which the doctor could operate. He was seated below, or as the nurse had described it—the way a mechanic repairs a car. Although local anesthesia was administered, I could feel each pinch, as Dr. Duckett snipped the tiny formations. I could also hear the sound of the vacuum as they were suctioned into the barrel of the giant-sized needle. Doctor Duckett completed the surgery by inserting a permanent clip to mark the site and taking x-rays to ensure he had removed all the calcifications.

Rivers and I were so happy the procedure was over. It had not been too invasive, required only a small incision, and would not require a lengthy recuperation period. This had been just a minor inconvenience. All we needed now was confirmation that the growths were benign.

As we awaited word on the test findings, I went about my normal activities. Since we were in the process of having our retirement home built some 150 miles away, we needed to visit occasionally. A few days later, a friend and I drove to Harrisonburg to choose cabinets, appliances, carpeting, vinyl flooring, and such. We were well on the way to having this home completed so Rivers and I could relocate to the peace and serenity of the Shenandoah Valley.

Diagnosis: Breast Cancer

Upon returning home on that life-changing evening of April 23, 2002, I listened to Dr. Duckett's message for me to call him. When we spoke he began, "I'm sorry, Angie, but the tumor is cancerous. But don't be scared."

"Oh, I'm not scared. It could be worse, Doctor," I answered. "Rivers and I have faith in God, and He will take care of me. I've been traveling and I'm tired. Rivers is at work until midnight, so I'm going to bed and go to sleep, and I don't plan to miss a meal."

"The cancer is not invasive at all—it's early stage. I'll remove the area only, approximately one inch. There is a ninety-nine percent chance of a cure," Dr. Duckett consoled.

Holding onto the telephone tightly, a lot was going

through my mind, not the least of which was thanksgiving to God. "Nothing can happen except what God allows, and Rivers and I will pray about this," I assured the doctor. Sensing he might think I was in denial rather than faith, I said for his benefit, "Doctor, I'm not in denial. I can even say the word cancer, but I know that God answers prayer."

"Your prayers are already working because you have such a positive attitude. You will be just fine. Now you know that God doesn't give people cancer," the doctor reiterated what he had said during my office visit. With that I thanked him and agreed to call and schedule the surgery.

Knowing that our son, Bert, was a pillar of strength even in the face of adversity, I asked him to come into our bedroom. As he sat on the bed, I told him what the doctor had said and asked him to pray. I was as concerned about Rivers as about my condition, so I prayed with Nehemiah, "O God, strengthen my hands." After recording my thoughts in a journal, I went to bed. The Lord was gracious and allowed His peace to pervade my spirit, and telling Rivers was not so difficult as I had imagined. He was loving, kind, and understanding as always and assured me that he would walk with me through whatever I had to endure.

When I saw the surgeon again he explained that the lump was about one inch in diameter and I would have a partial mastectomy or lumpectomy. Also I would have lymph node dissection for testing, and following surgery some thirty-five to thirty-seven radiation treatments. A mastectomy would be necessary only if tentacles were found, but it was not possible to determine whether the cancer was aggressive before surgery. He described each test I needed to undergo, and told me the surgery would take about one-and-a-quarter hours, and recovery one to three hours.

As Dr. Duckett talked about a date for surgery, I started to fudge a little, reminding him of speaking appointments and other commitments, but he would hear nothing of it.

Although it was not a matter of life or death, he made sure I understood that one does not leave malignant tumors intact very long.

Facing the inevitable, I determined to show the love of Jesus to anyone who crossed my path. If I needed to walk through and not around this mountain, I would talk about the Lord at every turn. The opportunity soon arrived as I went for various tests in preparation for the surgery.

My primary care physician, Dr. Trifoglio, a very concerned and caring woman, pulled up a chair close to me. Maybe it was coincidental, but I noticed a box of tissues close by, and I felt a slight choking sensation in my throat. She explained carefully what I could expect, assured me that she would be with me every step of the way, and asked if I had any questions.

When I started to respond with, "God will take care of me," I noticed her furrowed brow. Quickly attempting to put her at ease, I said, "Doctor, I'm a Christian and we will pray, but you can count on me to cooperate with you fully." Her face brightened up as she told me about those who speak of God's healing and refuse medical treatment until it's too late.

As Nurse Carey drew my blood that day, I talked with her about the upcoming surgery and how the Lord had given me peace. Being a bold Christian, she asked if she might pray with me, and I readily agreed.

While talking with Bobbie, the hospital nurse who conducts orientation for patients undergoing breast cancer surgery, she asked me to pray for another patient who was having a hard time with her diagnosis. The next day when I called, Bobbie said, "Your prayers have been answered because this woman's attitude has completely changed."

Meanwhile, I decided to look at the x-rays I had collected earlier for the surgeon's use. Much to my surprise, the tumor was in the shape of a heart—it looked exactly like a little black valentine. When I mentioned it to my surgeon he said tumors usually are jagged in shape and he had not seen a heart-shaped tumor before. From that time, I continued to show the x-rays to various people, and everyone said it was heart-shaped. I don't know the significance of this, but at least it has been a real conversation piece, and I've heard some very interesting theories.

Informing the Saints

Having told my pastor and his wife and a few select friends, I decided to inform the Board of Elders at our next meeting and then the congregation. The surgery was set for Monday, May 6, 2002. That Sunday I was scheduled to lead the main morning prayer. I asked Rivers to accompany me to the platform. He made a little impromptu speech and ended with words that really blessed my soul. "Of all the things that have happened to Angie, she always emerges with a smile on her face and a spring in her step."

I had earlier said to Rivers, "I won't let the devil get any mileage out of this one, so I will tell the congregation the same thing at the same time. Then no one will need to keep the phone hot asking if someone has heard that poor little Angie has cancer."

While this may sound a little extreme, if you have ever walked through any type of tragedy, you have likely been "comforted" by well-intentioned saints who had no idea what to say. Before I learned the tumor was malignant, a Christian friend had fired questions in rapid succession, "Do you have cancer? Are you all right? Is the breast still there?"

Determined not to allow any further misplaced sympathies, I had prayed, discussed it with my husband and pastor, and carefully planned what I would say to the saints. The whole speech was meant to bring glory to God, to comfort the saints, and to alleviate any fears about my well being.

With a smile on my face, I asked the congregation, "What is the worst diagnosis the doctor can give you?" I could hear several persons whisper cancer. I continued, "The doctor just gave me that diagnosis. I'm about to take a little missionary journey. Tomorrow by this time I will be in Doctors Community Hospital having surgery for breast cancer, and the Lord is already there. But don't feel sorry for me because I'm not sorry for myself." By now I could see a few red faces and hear a few sniffles. Some sat in what appeared to be stunned silence, completely in shock.

I relayed how God had allowed me to witness to medical personnel and quoted some comforting Scriptures. "The righteous cry, and the Lord heareth, and delivereth them out of all their troubles. Many are the afflictions of the righteous, but the Lord delivereth him out of them all" (Psalm 34:17, 19). "I waited patiently for the Lord; and He inclined unto me, and heard my cry" (Psalm 40:1).

It had been some two years since I had stood before the saints and requested prayer for my older sister who was dying of cancer. Because of this I told them I did not need to be reminded of the grim statistics on cancer. "Please don't come to me and say, 'poor little Angie has cancer.' Here is what I need from you—your prayers, your love, and your support."

I reminded them that, ironically, I was scheduled to lead our cell group in a study of the Book of Job that week, but I would have to practice it instead. There is no way to explain the perfect peace of God that pervaded my spirit as I spoke to the congregation. The pastor prayed for us, and I led the congregation in prayer, asking the Lord to heal those who were suffering and that the joy of the Lord be their strength. I sensed the love of God so strongly.

My Own Private Duty Nurse

One thing that had troubled me was the discovery that my insurance company decreed I could not remain in the hospital overnight. When the nurse informed me I responded, "I think it's cruel and inhumane to remove a malignant tumor from someone in the afternoon and send them home the same day. This is about money and not about my health!" Yes, I was an unhappy camper because I could not foresee how Rivers and Bert could care for me properly, especially the first night.

The Lord answered my need in a most remarkable way. My sister, Eunice Gilchrist, who was a nursing instructor for many years, had recently retired. She offered to come and take care of me. Eunice arrived the day prior to my surgery, and not only did she pray the prayer of faith with me, but she washed my feet and anointed them with oil. That saintly act of servanthood and love was such a blessing at a time of great trial.

Spring was in the air and the birds were singing on that Monday in May when I left our home for the one-mile drive to the hospital. We were all happy and optimistic as Rivers, Bert and Eunice accompanied me. Later my sister, Elsie Noel, Pastor Dave, Mom Brunk, Mary Minor, and Caleb Kaye also came. They lovingly stood by me as I went from one department to another for x-rays, sonogram, ultrasound, scans, and a very painful guided needle aspiration in nuclear medicine. Eunice held my hand and prayed me through that one, or I'm not sure how I would have made it.

As is often the case, it seemed the enemy of our souls was on hand in an unusual way. An anesthesiologist appeared in my room when it was time for my surgery. With medication in hand he began to query me. "You had a hysterectomy?"

"Yes," I replied.

"And last year you had your gall bladder removed?" the interrogation continued.

Bolting up in bed a little, "Who said I had my gall bladder removed?" I questioned.

"Says so right here on this paper," he replied, referring to some papers he had picked up from a desk in the room.

"Whose papers do you have?" I inquired.

"Aren't you Mrs. Wernick?" he asked as he drew closer, poised to give me an injection.

Now that did it! The doctor never asked my name, nor did he check my wristband. This was no orderly or nurses aide—he was a fully trained physician, an anesthesiologist who should have known better. My nursing instructor sister, being very keen on proper medical protocol, heard me raise my voice and began to listen up, hardly able to contain herself without intervening. We were happy when he left the room without giving me any medication and did not return.

Surgical Miracles

Looking at the wall clock I noticed it was exactly two-forty when I was being wheeled out of the surgical holding area into the operating room. When I awakened in the recovery room, I thought many hours had passed. Much to my surprise, I found that I was being discharged at six-ten, a mere three-and-one-half hours after I left the holding area!

Furthermore, we rejoiced that the doctor had not inserted the drainage tube with its unsightly bulb that the nurse had described to me earlier. She had given me a "Bulb Drain Record" to keep track of the output from the breast incision. "Wash hands, empty two to three times a day, record units, discard secretions, squeeze bulb, bring sheet to doctor's office." Thank God, the doctor had not found it necessary to insert that tube after all! Instead, he had applied an elastic bandage around my chest over the massive gauze.

Sister Eunice busied herself with my care and overall pampering, applying the ice packs and keeping me hydrated. When she removed my bandages on the third day, she noted that the bleeding was less than the size of a dime. Mind you, that was from a deep incision that was one-and-one-half inches across the breast, and another of one inch under the arm. We rejoiced at the Lord's care and how well I was getting along.

I had kept track of my progress with a few notes in my journal each day. The surgeon had prescribed Roxicet, "Take one tablet every four to six hours as needed for pain," the label read. He had advised the family to "set the alarm and give them to her around the clock." However, after the first night we stopped them because it was not necessary. By the second day my pain was minimal, and by day three, I had no pain except in my lower back from lying in bed.

When Eunice left, Brenda Wragg, a sister from our church, prepared freshly squeezed vegetable and fruit juices, laced with garlic, and others supplied meals. She saw to it that I lacked nothing, aided by my husband, our son, and several others from our church. I who enjoy giving so much, had to practice the grace of receiving. How humbling!

I was getting along so well that I called the doctor and asked if I could travel to Pennsylvania to attend a wedding on the fifth day after surgery. Months earlier the parents had engaged me to prepare a special surprise for the bride and groom. With the doctor's approval, we attended the wedding and I presented highlights from the couple's life in humorous poetic form at the reception. I had taken along our digital camera to get some really good shots, but after arriving I remembered the doctor had said I was not to raise my right arm. Into the trunk the camera went, lest I should be tempted. We traveled the ninety-five miles back home that evening. I was quite tired by then, but it did not seem to affect me adversely, so the next day we attended church.

Doctor Duckett was elated when he examined me a week following surgery. Gleefully he said, "Your case went perfectly from the beginning. Usually someone is having an off day, but everyone in the operating room was in sync during your surgery." He pronounced me "cured" and said there was no indication of the cancer having spread to the lymph nodes he had removed. "You have such a good spirit; your prayers have been answered."

I thanked him and added, "God was already in the operating room before you got there, Doctor." Although kind and very competent, Dr. Duckett's certainty about my needing some thirty-seven radiation treatments made me most uncomfortable. I was full of questions like, "If you got all the cancer and it had not spread into my lymph nodes, why so much radiation?" The doctor answered each question patiently and instructed me on how to regain strength in my right arm. On the eighth day I was to begin walk-the-fingers-up-the-wall and other exercises daily, as well as rolling my arm in circles to keep my shoulder from freezing. Having lifted some restrictions, I was now free to drive short distances.

The next day, I decided to see how high I could lift my right arm. I shot it straight up in the air over my head. "The doctor has to see this one to believe it," I said to myself. So I hopped into the car and drove the short distance to his office. "Tell the doctor I have something to show him," I said to the receptionist. When he came out, I threw both arms into the air and waved them around. He was completely surprised, so he gave me a great big bear hug.

I raced home to call a special friend and prayer partner, Malinda. Amazingly, as she rejoiced with me she said, "I had just prayed today that you would be able to raise your hands to praise the Lord!"

When I spoke with Eunice, she said she had prayed before my surgery that "the doctors would be confounded, astonished, and in awe and know what the Lord had done." Indeed, I had witnessed their surprise when I did not fall apart at the initial diagnosis of breast cancer, and how my expressions of faith in God's healing had amazed them. I also visited nurse Bobbie, to show her how I could lift my arms and talked to her about answered prayer.

During my next visit Dr. Trifoglio confirmed what I already knew—I was getting along quite well. "Your strong faith, positive attitude, and family support have made a lot of difference. You look great on the outside, but much healing is needed under the skin." She continued, "You might as well accept the fact that this surgery will cost you a year of your life." She followed up with warnings to take it easy, rest a lot, and not over exert myself with packing for the upcoming move. This would all pay off in the long run, she said. Doctor Trifoglio described the process for radiation treatments and instructed me on how to care for myself. "Now don't expect to do more than half of what you normally do. The radiation will make you very tired and you won't be able to do much." She wrote a referral for my first visit with a surgical oncologist.

Doctor Carolyn Hendricks was a warm, sympathetic and caring physician. As with the others, I mentioned the power of prayer and how God was seeing me through. She asked, "How did you discover the lump?"

I replied, "I thought I felt a lump a few months ago, but I put it off until it was time for my annual physical."

Much to my surprise, Dr. Hendricks said, "God works in mysterious ways. I don't know what you were feeling, but there is no way you were feeling that lump! But at least it got you to the doctor." She explained that because of the way it was situated, it would have been impossible for me to palpate it. "It was a low-grade tumor with a single area of micro-invasion, and your prognosis is excellent!"

The doctor wrote copious notes as she queried me about family members—parents, siblings, and close relatives who may have had cancer. I relayed a little to her about my sister, Bert, who was in the hospital for breast cancer surgery, and the Lord healed her before the operation began. She replied, "I'll put that one down as 'I don't know.'"

The doctor patiently explained some facts about breast

cancer and laid out my options, one of which was radiation. This was now the fourth physician to say I needed radiation, but because of the possibility of side effects, I was not yet content to accept this as a solution.

Pastor Ed Heatwole called from Harrisonburg to pray with me again by telephone, because the Lord had put me on his heart, and he had been obedient to call when I was facing a decision about radiation. God was showing His love and taking care of me in many ways. I again called several personal friends and relatives, along with the 700 Club and the Mike Murdock Evangelistic Association for prayer for wisdom regarding whether to receive the radiation. Christian friends had varying opinions, but ultimately I felt that Rivers and I must follow our collective hearts in making the decision.

When it seemed inevitable, I searched the telephone book and made no less than nine calls trying to reach the local radiation center for an appointment. Going in circles and completely exasperated by now, I gave up for the day, but still wanted a second opinion before subjecting myself to radiation.

Second Opinion

Suddenly I remembered an ad I had seen on television about Cancer Treatment Centers of America (CTCA). I called them immediately, and my heart leaped for joy as I spoke with a very friendly and caring oncology information specialist, Melissa Knox. In less than twenty-four hours I received a packet that contained all the information I needed to help us make a decision. It was complete with color photographs and brief biographies on the department heads. I knew instinctively that the Lord had allowed me to remember CTCA for a reason.

No waiting period to get an appointment; we'll purchase an airline ticket for you and your husband; we'll make reservations for your lodging; we'll pick you up at the airport; you may eat in our cafeteria free—on and on the amenities went. It seemed almost too good to be true, but Rivers and I both felt the Lord was in it.

Nine days later we flew to Chicago where a driver of a white limousine greeted us at the airport. From that moment, the royal treatment began. The place was unlike any medical facility I've seen and resembled an upscale hotel more than a hospital. Every physician and staff person seemed genuinely concerned about me. They were not treating cancer as much as they were treating me, and I felt safe and loved.

Monday, June 3, 2002 was a memorable day for me as I went from one department to another, following a typed itinerary Mary handed me. Dr. Mellijor, a surgical oncologist, examined me and explained the process. After I had seen all the specialists and my test results were in, they would get together for a consultation and decide what treatment option to recommend. I liked this multidisciplinary approach and felt they could give me the best that medical science had to offer.

Most of all, I sensed the Lord's presence—with all the medical procedures I've had, never before had the atmosphere been like CTCA. I was not a number, or a disease—I was a person! In the waiting room I closed my eyes and worshipped to the strains of "Be Exalted O God Above the Heavens," and "Surely the Presence of the Lord is in This Place" played over the sound system. Ruth LoCoco, a beautiful volunteer, offered the patients yogurt, crackers, juice, coffee, bottled water, and a listening ear.

From Monday to Wednesday I was tested—an electrocardiogram, an echocardiogram, x-rays, CT scans of abdomen, chest, brain, bone scan, total body scan—on and on. I had a consultation with a naturopathic physician, a nutritionist, and a psychoneuroimmunologist. Wow! Each person showed a genuine interest in me and allowed Rivers to sit in except when x-rays were taken.

I had never had an echocardiogram before and did not know what to expect. However, it turned out to be a joyful experience as Rivers and I talked about the Lord with John, a mature Christian who administered the test. Meanwhile, we watched my heart on the computer screen as John explained something about the valves and arteries.

Pastor Percy W. McCray, Co-Director of Pastoral Care, was a man full of the Holy Spirit and with a very engaging personality. We enjoyed talking and praying together, and I was impressed with their foresight in providing spiritual input for those patients desiring it.

At last it was time to see Dr. Mellijor for the final con-sultation to learn what they had found. The pathology slides had shown intraductal carcinoma with early invasion outside the duct; it was estrogen receptor negative. No chemotherapy was needed, but I should see a radiation oncologist to begin treatments when I returned home. I could return to the CTCA once a year for follow up if I wished. After the extensive testing, the best news of all was Dr. Mellijor's concluding statement, "There are no tumors anywhere in your body!"

Aboard American Airlines, flight 1524, some 33,000 feet above Ohio, the Lord reminded me of a Scripture. "For it was fitting for Him, for whom are all things and by whom are all things, in bringing many sons to glory, to make the captain of their salvation perfect through sufferings" (Hebrews 2:10, NKJV).

A Miracle In Motion

One morning while contemplating whether to get up or to turn over and continue resting, I felt the Lord was speak-ing to me, "You are a miracle in motion." Smiling broadly, I sprang up and wrote it in my journal. A few days later, I heard a television evangelist announce his sermon theme, that now familiar phrase, "a miracle in motion." Don't you just love it when the Lord confirms His word?

Radiation Galore

Doctor Larry Shombert, a radiation oncologist located about a mile from our home, became the principal in my next phase of treatment. He is the same physician I had tried to locate before I went to CTCA for the second opinion. Most likely I would have wondered the rest of my life how things may have turned out had I not had the second opinion by another set of professionals from different disciplines.

Having no previous experience with radiation, I thought I would breeze into the Greenbelt Radiation Oncology Center, get the treatment and head home. Instead, I spent about eight hours over a period of several days in preparation. Dr. Shombert explained that they would treat the whole breast as a preventive measure, and during the last week would concentrate on the area of the incision.

I was full of questions—in his professional opinion, what would happen if I did not take radiation? What if I did? What were the side effects? To be sure that I omitted nothing, I had made a list of questions to which I needed an answer. Doctor Shombert patiently listened to my questions and answered every one to my satisfaction, carefully explaining how to care for my skin during and after radiation. He assured me there would be no permanent damage to my normal cells, and that was comforting.

Now I was ready to begin the CT scans, simulations and planning sessions. When the head technician declared my plan complete, I was to begin radiation the next day. When I returned, the technician said the physicist had reviewed my plans and he says, "There's too much lung in it." So they had to re-work the plan.

While thinking that radiation would be administered to

the breast only, I was surprised to learn that more than half of my chest and my underarm would be involved. There were other surprises in store—use no deodorant or soap in the area, radiation every day, cease taking Vitamin E, keep the area dry, protect it from the sun, get regular blood draws from the left arm only, apply RadiacareGel three times a day, no heating pad to the area ever... No matter how inconvenient, I was determined to follow the plan and take care of myself. I wrote in my journal, "Radiation starts at 8:30," on June 24, 2002.

Meanwhile, God gave us a little reprieve. I rejoiced at His goodness in permitting Rivers and me to attend an "I Still Do" marriage conference in Washington with Carl and Judy Fredericks on the day of our and their thirty-ninth anniversary. That same week we enjoyed a wonderfully refreshing visit with our son Barth and his family from Idaho.

As I climbed onto the table for my first radiation treatment, I thought to myself, "This machine is so intimidating!" Like the proverbial itch where you can't scratch, being told to remain perfectly still only makes a person want to move. "Lord, please help me not to move," I prayed as I tried so hard not to hyperventilate.

Again the Holy Spirit brought a couple of Scriptures that had ministered in the past to my mind. During the successive thirty treatments, as I lay on the table, I quoted Scriptures that had built my faith in the past, "Don't worry about anything; instead, pray about everything; tell God your needs and don't forget to thank Him for His answers. If you do this you will experience God's peace, which is far more wonderful than the human mind can understand. His peace will keep your thoughts and your heart quiet and at rest as you trust in Christ Jesus" (Philippians 4:6,7, TLB). Then I would move to, "I can do all things through Christ, Who strengthens me" (Philippians 4:13, NKJV).

As in the past, the Lord gave me His perfect peace

throughout this daily routine, and this seemed to baffle the medical professionals. "You have such a positive attitude; you will heal very fast." While we know that attitude plays a powerful role in our well being, people who don't understand the power of God can easily attribute everything to a patient's attitude.

Radiation treatments bring a patient in contact with technicians and doctors five days a week, providing time to become acquainted more intimately than some other procedures allow. I talked with them about the Lord and prayed with one technician who was a Christian. Sometimes they brought compact discs of praise music for me to hear during my treatments. I made sure everyone knew I was praying for him or her, and often said, "God bless you."

"Perhaps my suffering will turn out to be a gift, and if I have to go through this, I will make the most of it," I had mused early on.

I reflected on how I had never felt more loved by medical professionals than when I had the cancer diagnosis and treatments. From patience in explaining what to expect to being sure I was handling the diagnosis well, the Lord placed many wonderful caretakers in my life who helped to make the episode a lot easier.

Rapid Recuperation

I knew my recuperation process was no less than a miracle, as throughout the entire ordeal of diagnosis, surgery and treatment, I had not become upset, nor had I questioned God in any way. It was only by His grace that I was able to remain hopeful and to witness to others about the power of God. Praise the Lord!

When people unintentionally spoke negatively about cancer, I tried to turn it into a discussion of what the Lord was doing for me. Since I never became ill at any time, it was hard for some people to accept the fact that I had a malignant tumor. I later realized that my expression of faith and confidence in God made some uncomfortable because they may have handled things differently after a cancer diagnosis.

When I realized that some friends had not shown up to visit, sent a card, or spoken with me about my situation, I felt a little hurt. Then I was reminded of a prayer I had prayed over the telephone with my friend, Bobbie Smith. "Lord, please keep off the telephone and out of our house, anyone who will speak negatively, anyone who will talk anything except faith." I realized that my prayers were answered. Be careful what you pray for—you just might get it!

Bidding the Congregation Farewell

We had been active members of Cottage City Mennonite Church, now Capital Christian Fellowship, for about fifteen years. During that time, we had developed some close friendships and had interacted with a lot of people. But now we knew the Lord was moving us on. Shortly after announcing the cancer diagnosis, we needed to tell our friends we would be moving soon, and it was a bittersweet time for us. While some friends cried, others offered encouraging words about entering this new phase in our lives.

I was to deliver the morning sermon on our last Sunday at church after singing a duet with Music Director Bobby Wragg, and then attend a luncheon in our honor. The August temperature had been in the high nineties that week, and this posed a potential problem for me. Since I was not allowed to wear deodorant, how could I remain fresh under those lights? Would the added stress of saying goodbye to our friends be too much?

The last time I had addressed the congregation was when I announced the upcoming surgery. Now I would tell them that, "Tomorrow I take my thirtieth and final radiation treatment!" I would also need to include a farewell message in my sermon to some very special people without breaking down and crying. Again, the Lord was faithful and it proved to be a day when He would change someone's life.

The topic was "Choose Life," and I spared nothing about what I felt was God's point of view on the sanctity of life. During the sermon I sensed a strong anointing of the Holy Spirit, and I would learn why later. The congregation seemed to follow me completely, and I was hearing some "amens" here and there. Then I noticed a young lady weeping, but I did not recognize her.

After church my friend, Ginny McGill, said, "Angie, today you saved someone's life."

Amused by her choice of words, I replied, "I can't save anyone's life, but the Lord can."

Ginny then brought a young lady to me who was her daughter's friend. Red-faced and still tearful, the woman explained that she had planned to commit suicide that week, but her friend had urged her instead to come and hear me speak. When I began to speak about choosing life, she felt I was speaking directly to her. But how could I know her problems, since we had never met? As I related my bout with cancer and God's abundant grace, she received strength to change her mind about taking her life because of her physical condition. If just one person would be drawn closer to Jesus, perhaps my suffering had been a gift after all. It had afforded yet another opportunity to practice Joy in Adversity!

Moving to Our Retirement Home

During radiation I was energetic, contrary to what the doctor had predicted. Although careful about my activities, I did not lie around and sleep a lot. I sorted, trashed, and packed our earthly treasures with a little help from a couple of friends.

Although Rivers and I were unable to visit the site of our new home often, we had several friends who lived next to it. Orval and Dorothy Shank and Dave and Joyce Eshleman watched over the project and reported to us regularly by telephone or e-mail. Randy Harman, our broker, touched my heart deeply when I called to explain why we could not visit for a while. "You take care of your health, and we will take care of the house." Associate Broker Sallye Trobaugh joined Randy in prayer for us. They tried to keep in touch and to help us overcome the many obstacles associated with home building.

On August 24, 2002, Rivers and I moved back to the Shenandoah Valley where we had lived from 1971 to 1985. We have many Christian friends in the area, and this was our reason for retiring in Harrisonburg. Joe and Betty Hottinger, who own a trucking business, drove a 45-foot rig to Maryland and moved us back. This one fits the category of more than we would ask or think!

We began a new chapter in our lives, and I resumed work on the book the Lord had impressed me to write several years ago.

Rivers offers comfort to Angie prior to her breast cancer surgery

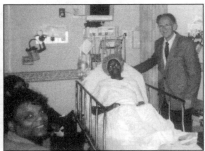

Mary Minor, Sister Eunice, and Pastor Dave wait with Angie prior to surgery

Application Questions:
Diagnosis: Breast Cancer!

Scriptures: Psalm 112:7, Psalm 34:17, 19, Psalm 40:1, Hebrews 2:10, Philippians 4:13.

1. What do you consider the most dreaded diagnosis you could face?
2. How would you change your priorities if you knew you had a life-threatening illness?
3. In light of your answer, what should you do differently now?
4. How would you inform others of a medical diagnosis that had the potential to upset them?
5. How have you experienced God's miraculous power in your life during times of crises?

Angie leaving hospital with sister Eunice 3 1/2 hours
after breast surgery began

Rivers and Angie attend church
six days after surgery

Angie wrapped like
a mummy for A
whole body bone
imaging at Cancer
Treatment Centers
of America

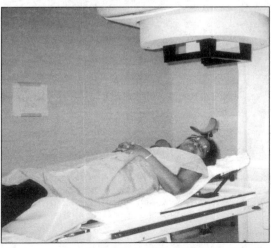

Angie preparing for the first of 30 radiation treatments

CHAPTER 12

FROM VICTIM TO VICTOR

How long it takes us to move from being a victim of our circumstances to having victory over them is largely dependent on us. If we have learned to trust God's wisdom when all is going well, why are we so prone to slip into unbelief when trouble comes? The faith that sustains us when the sun is shining should sustain us all the more when the clouds grow dark.

Knowing that no valley is so deep that God can't lift us out and no shadows so dark that His light cannot penetrate them can help us to move from victim to victor. Jesus prepared His disciples for the time when He would not walk with them as the Son of Man. Among the important things he said was, "These things I have spoken unto you, that in Me ye might have peace. In the world ye shall have tribulation: but be of good cheer; I have overcome the world" (John 16:33).

Upbringing Affects How We Cope

How we handle adversity is probably related to our upbringing. At least this is true in my case. Having grown up in a very strict Christian home, we were not allowed to question our parents. We had to obey without comment whether or not we agreed with or understood their reasoning. Our conduct had to be Christian because our parents took great pride in the Bass family name, and worked overtime to ensure we did not mar it. Unlike some young people today whose impetus to do almost anything is the knowledge that someone doesn't want it done, rebellion was not a part of our vocabulary. Respect was a very important component in our household, and all nine of us children most assuredly knew it.

It was not my privilege to shake my fist in my earthly father's face and ask him why he made a decision. I feared him too much for that, and I knew he did not tolerate insolence and back talk. My reverential fear of God has likewise taught me not to question Him. For me, "Why me?" is not the question. I don't have to know why I must walk through adversity; all I need to know is Who walks with me!

Trusting When You Don't Understand

During a period of great trial and suffering I came across this Scripture from Ecclesiastes 7:14, 15, "In the day of prosperity be joyful, but in the day of adversity consider: God also hath set the one over against the other, to the end that man should find nothing after him. All things have I seen in the days of my vanity; there is a just man that perisheth in his righteousness, and there is a wicked man that prolongeth his life in his wickedness."

I believe Solomon says there is a mixture of joy and sorrow in this world. As Solomon observed the apparent inequities the righteous endure, while the wicked seemingly flourished, he was left without definitive answers. When I realized the wisest man who ever lived had not figured out the whys of suffering, I decided to reserve my brainpower and not try. Sometimes God may reveal the reason, sometimes not. In either case, we must keep our eyes steadfastly fixed on Him in faith.

David, Solomon's father, wrote some very moving psalms that we find inspirational today; however, even a cursory glance at their context can be surprising. While hiding out in a cave in En Gedi and fearing for his life, he concentrated on God rather than on retaliation against King Saul. He penned the following words at a time when King Saul was unjustly pursuing him. In the midst of his distress we find him shouting praises to God and declaring his determination to remain faithful. "My heart is fixed, O God, my heart is fixed: I will sing and give praise...Be Thou exalted, O God, above the heavens: let Thy glory be above all the earth" (Psalm 57:7, 11).

One of the most beloved and familiar passages in the Bible, the Twenty-Third Psalm, gives us a view of David's ability to trust God in spite of adverse circumstances. As a sheep has no need for concern about where to eat or sleep because of the shepherd's steadfast love and sacrificial care, David also trusts God. He trusts God even in the valley of the shadow of death, which for us could be any particularly distressing episode we face.

In this psalm we read the phrase, "Yea, though I walk through the valley." I believe we do a disservice to new Christians when we don't prepare them to walk through the valleys in faith. We must teach them that valleys are inevitable, so they won't become discouraged and allow the devil to beat them up with unfounded doubts. As we recognize our own mortality and helplessness in the face of trials and hardships, we like David, can know that Jesus the Good Shepherd is with us when the valley is so dark we can't see our way out. Our Protector is guiding us through the most difficult and troubling situations to safety, and ultimately to our Heavenly home. "I will dwell in the house of the Lord forever" (Psalm 23:6b).

The Psalms of David also contain confessions, lamentations, and passages on suffering. In Psalm 25:16-18, in the midst of his sorrow, David pleads for God's mercy and forgiveness. "Turn Thee unto me, and have mercy upon me; for I am desolate and afflicted. The troubles of my heart are enlarged: O bring Thou me out of my distresses. Look upon mine affliction and pain; and forgive all my sins."

In the longest chapter of the Bible, Psalm 119, occupying

176 verses, David extols the blessings and benefits of following God's law. One of the benefits he lists in Verses 49,
50, and 52 is the comfort he received from God's Word.
"Remember the word to Your servant, upon which You have
caused me to hope. This is my comfort in my affliction, for
Your word has given me life...I remembered Your judgments
of old, O Lord, and have comforted myself" (NKJV).

Later in the same psalm, Verses 67, 71, and 75, David
credits his afflictions with helping him to remain resolute
in trusting God. "Before I was afflicted I went astray, but
now I keep Your word...It is good for me that I have been
afflicted, that I may learn Your statutes...I know, O Lord,
that Your judgments are right, and that in faithfulness You
have afflicted me" (NKJV).

I believe David struggled with the concept of his afflictions and suffering as a righteous man. However, as we read
through the Psalms, we see evidences of his steadfast faith
and undying love as he praises and exalts God in spite of the
circumstances. I have found no depictions of David as a victim because of the unjust treatment of his enemies.

No Guilt Trip Intended

When you read Scriptures about how Old Testament
saints responded to serious trials, you may be tempted to
feel inadequate. I'm not trying to place a guilt trip on anyone who may have succumbed to self-pity and depression,
but I do know that the same God Who sustained them has
the power to sustain us and deliver us from any trial.

Reading about some of the trying things Rivers and I
have faced and how we handled them, you may wonder if we
ever licked our wounds and felt sorry for ourselves. Looking
back on my life, I can honestly say that I learned very early
not to give in to the "poor old me's." In relating my response
to a cancer diagnosis, I'm not holding that out as a universal
response, but simply saying this is the way the Lord enabled

me to handle it and to avoid the pit of depression.

While I was unable to avoid having trials, I was certainly faced with a decision as to how I would deal with them. In adversity, the real me comes out. If you want to know what is in someone's heart, just turn up the heat a little. Like a tea bag in hot water, the hidden color begins to emerge. Let's consider some ways in which we deal with our wounds.

We can try to conceal them from others and pretend they don't exist by covering or patching them over with a positive confession. That's not dealing with the problem. If we conceal them, how can God heal them? One friend tried not to blow her nose so as not to admit she had a cold. If you insist you have no problem, how are the saints to join you in prayer? I believe there is a difference in making a bad confession and admitting to an existing problem. I encourage everyone to confess the Word of God and to believe Him for healing and anything we need. However, I see a distinction between, "Just as surely as I go outside in the winter I will get pneumonia" and "I've been diagnosed with pneumonia, but I am believing God for healing."

There are, however, people who constantly pick at their problems, rehearsing them to anyone who will listen. It's like removing the scab from a wound every time it almost heals, but continuously opening up old wounds won't aid in their healing.

As for me, over the years I became an expert at concealing my physical pain as I mastered the art of busying myself in serving others. While enduring pain that might cause some to double up in bed, I maintained the facade of well being behind a big smile as I went about business as usual. Only those close to me really knew my physical state. In fact, I thought I had earned undergraduate, graduate, and advanced degrees in the school of suffering patiently since I was able to hide it so well. BA – Being Afflicted; MA – Much Adversity; MS – Misery and Suffering; and PhD – Pain Hidden Deeply.

Pain is Universal!

During a time when I was stuck in bed for weeks that stretched into months, the Lord had taught me through my physical suffering that pain is pain, no matter what the source. That was a new revelation to me; however, I was now learning that pain is universal—it is no respecter of persons. Most of my suffering has been physical, but I can empathize with others who are enduring the myriad of hardships to which humans are heir. I learned to feel their pain and to believe God with them for healing.

Can't you usually tell when a person is teaching the Word of God and has not experienced what they are teaching? If they are speaking about healing and have suffered only minimally, it can be quite obvious. Sometimes they are unknowingly flippant and arrogant as they tell you how to do it—whatever it is. But when they have hurt, they can share how God has delivered them out of their pit of despair, thereby bringing encouragement to others.

Some years ago, God opened my eyes about spitting out spiritual platitudes without any "meat" that made them real to people. I felt very comfortable to stand up and tell others how to live, take the next plane out of town, and leave them in the dark about what I was going through. I believe I was coming across like a cocky kid who had her life presented on a gold platter. From my appearance no one could tell I had walked through any deep waters, much less any fire. How could people relate to a woman like that? What they did not know until the Lord convicted me about being more open, was that I lived with chronic physical pain.

I well remember the time when I was to be in Alberta, Canada to speak at a women's retreat. The whole trip had been fraught with one aggravation after another, barely arriving at the airport in time to catch the first flight because of a storm, running on the people mover to avoid missing a connecting flight, and the stabbing pains in my lower back.

Rivers had accompanied me and was spending the weekend with the husband of one of the women. I had never been in Alberta before, but the women were most hospitable and I felt as if I was among old friends. The Friday evening and Saturday sessions at Camrose College went fine, but during the night I became quite ill. While I had prescription medicines with me, I knew that I must take them with food. In a college dorm room, where would I find food at three o'clock in the morning? Not wishing to awaken anyone, I prayed, read my Bible and tried to sleep. When that did not bring relief, I got up and took a shower—that always helps! Not this time.

By morning I had a migraine headache, was nauseated, and feeling quite weak. Since my pride would not allow me to let the women know how sick I was, I sat very still during praise and worship. Every slight movement only caused the pulsating pain to increase.

The topic for the morning had to do with how not to faint when adversity comes into our lives, and I was expected to speak for an hour. Ironically, I felt as if I would faint physically when I rose to speak. How could I possibly ruin the service for a group of women who had paid a fee to attend a weekend spiritual retreat? The Lord would help me through this somehow. So I held on to the podium and delivered the message, with no one the wiser about my condition.

Not Appreciated?

I suspect every public speaker at some time can identify with thoughts of people not appreciating them. Leaders are expected to be infallible—they do the ministry, but need none; they do the listening and praying; they are judged by a higher standard. While I believe leaders should be held accountable for their lifestyle and actions, I think Christians must realize that leaders sometimes suffer severe attacks of the devil, and they need ministry also.

We had a lot of people praying for us as our family traveled by car from Virginia to California and Arizona where I led retreats. While the trip was bathed in prayer, I believe they forgot to cover the homecoming. After three weeks of an almost perfect trip and a happy family time, as soon as we arrived home I suffered a fall. After that, I began asking people to pray for the homecoming as well as for the ministry portion.

Then there were those times when I felt totally unappreciated and taken for granted. I had left my family at home and traveled to the Midwest for a retreat. When I arrived I was bone weary but knew the Lord had called me to be there. The assumption seemed to be that if I had traveled that far to minister, surely I needed nothing. One lady further insulted me with, "As much as that ticket cost, we will get all the mileage out of you we can." It is difficult to stay in the Spirit in the presence of such insensitivity.

Once when I attended a retreat led by Pastor Christine Dunk, she came into the audience and prayed with me. Without asking where I hurt, Christine said, "You are like a desert flower—unrecognized and unappreciated. God is going to bless your socks off; just walk through the doors He opens for you."

Why Me, Lord?

When things are going well, why don't we ask, "Why me, Lord?" We just assume that, as His children, we are entitled to a life of happiness and ease—a life full of blessings. Why don't we feel sorry for ourselves, or at least guilty, when we have everything we need? Did you ever hear anyone complain about that? Probably not.

Conversely, why have we not learned that because we live in a fallen world, we are subject to the same trials and tribulations as others? Why are we so surprised when they come? The Holy Spirit resides in us, and He gives us coping mechanisms unbelievers don't have. But if God never allowed us to suffer, how could we minister to the hurting, the downtrodden, or the outcast?

The Holy Spirit is described as a Comforter in John 14, and 16. The Apostle Paul suffered piteously, as recorded in II Corinthians 4:7-11, and 11:23-27. Reading about his persecution, distresses, beatings, imprisonment, shipwrecks, stoning, hunger, thirst, and various perils, makes me ashamed to complain. At no time do we read that Paul succumbed to the victim mentality. Instead, he counted it a joy and privilege to suffer for the sake of the Gospel of Jesus Christ. In his second epistle to the Corinthians, Paul mentions comfort in the first chapter no less than seven times in three verses. Do you detect any depression, self-pity, or 'why me' questions? Paul keeps his eyes fixed on Jesus; he remembers his Damascus Road experience and his apostolic calling, and the Holy Spirit propels him on.

We groan, "But, Lord, I want the comfort, encouragement and consolation, but I could do without the sufferings." I believe they come as a package deal—God gives us His gift of comfort in order that we might comfort others in their times of trouble. How do we become comforters? It's by having walked through tribulation or distress, and having learned from God's comfort how to encourage and comfort others. A comforter who has never experienced any adverse circumstances is an inept one.

When God allows you or me to suffer, we need not consider ourselves victims of circumstances. Did not Jesus suffer to "bring many sons into glory?" No one of us has been called upon to suffer the atrocities that the sinless Son of God suffered because of our sin. The writer of Hebrews says that Jesus learned obedience through His sufferings. But He endured the cross because of His love for us, knowing that victory awaited Him—returning to God the Father and sitting down on His right side.

Perhaps you are not walking through any trials right now, or have never had any serious problems, but keep living. Sooner or later, something comes our way that we cannot ignore—we have to deal with it. We may not understand why God has allowed this awful thing to happen to us or to our loved one. But it is very important to walk in obedience and trust His discretion, even in the darkest times when we can't make sense out of the situation.

"But, Lord, You promised," I can almost hear someone saying. Like a nagging child speaking to Mother, we sometimes wonder why God is taking so long to answer our prayers. Did Mother ever reply, "Yes, I'll give it to you when the time comes, but not yet?" I believe our all-knowing Heavenly Father sometimes says the same thing to us, "Just wait for My timing; trust My love and wisdom."

Maybe you're saying, "Lord, I've had it!" You feel like Moses, that God has you waiting on the back forty. Or perhaps you can identify with Elijah, sitting under his juniper tree lamenting and complaining to God when Jezebel was after his neck. Discouraged and ready to die, he thought he was the only one left who was faithful to God. Or maybe you're in Jonah's shoes—the worm has just come out and destroyed your shade tree, and you're sitting unprotected from the sun, about to perish. Then there is Zaccheus, sitting up a tree waiting to see Jesus pass by. Are you like the woman with the issue of blood—if only you could reach Jesus, but pressing through the crowd, or through your problem, seems impossible?

You may be hurting desperately, and don't even know what's wrong. You can't even articulate it to anyone. I have had physical pain so intense that I could not describe it, but your pain may be emotional. You may feel no one understands and no one has walked through such an experience. When the devil can convince you that your problem is unique—no one has ever had it before, and maybe even God can't or won't fix it, then depression will dog your heels.

God loves you with an everlasting love, and Jesus can identify with your pain. Whether under a tree, up a tree, out on a limb, or no tree at all, God is right there ready to minister to you. He wants to give you strength as you walk through your fiery furnace, or through your deep waters, and He will deliver you just in time. As the Gospel song suggests, we must, "hold on to God's unchanging hand."

Do you want to move from victim to victor? The choice is yours. An old song says: "On Jordan's stormy banks I stand, and cast a wishful eye, to Canaan's fair and happy land, where my possessions lie." Maybe your Jordan is overflowing its banks, or the waters are frighteningly turbulent. You may be like the Israelites, standing on the banks of the Jordan River waiting for it to part? "Step in," God says. "As soon as the soles of your feet touch the waters, I will part them."

Faith steps in without seeing the waters parted first. Even if your Jordan looks foreboding or unnecessarily deep, launch out; stretch out on Jesus. Get your feet wet. God won't let you drown. If you are ready to make the transition from victim to victor, you will need to take a step of faith.

Between the time when I had breast surgery and when I began radiation treatments, I wrote this in my journal. "Do you have a joy-despite-adversity faith—a faith that only grows stronger when the heat is turned up a few degrees, when the water overflows, or when you feel as if you're in the lions' den? That's the kind of faith that can impact others and encourage them to dare to believe God in times of testing, knowing He will deliver them as He has delivered you."

Coping Mechanisms Jesus Gives

Since we are all different, we must find what works best to bring us out of the victim mentality. Bill Gaither suggests in a song, "Just throw back your head and sing." It is hard to listen to praise songs or to sing them and stay depressed.

When we assume a posture of worship and take the time to be still and allow God to be God, the whole atmosphere changes. The problem may not have vanished, but our attitude changes when we turn it over to Him and rest in His promises. Praise songs are wonderful, but many of the old hymns are profound.

In How Firm a Foundation, the writer assures us that God's Word is a firm foundation on which we can stand. It continues with God's promise to strengthen and hold us up. In the context of Joy in Adversity, the following lines express it so well.

> *"When thro' the deep waters I call thee to go,*
> *The rivers of sorrow shall not overflow;*
> *For I will be with thee thy trials to bless,*
> *And sanctify to thee thy deepest distress."*

> *"When thro' fiery trials thy pathway shall lie,*
> *My grace, all sufficient, shall be thy supply;*
> *The flames shall not hurt thee, I only design*
> *Thy dross to consume, and thy gold to refine."*

(From "Life Songs, Number Two," Mennonite Publishing House, Scottdale, Pennsylvania, 1938.)

Jesus and the disciples sang a hymn as they left the Passover meal and headed for the Mount of Olives for that agonizing night in prayer to God before the crucifixion. Paul learned early in his ministry to be joyful in times of persecution. Therefore, he could write with authority while in a Philippian prison, "Rejoice in the Lord always. Again I will say, rejoice!" (Philippians 4:4, NKJV). Paul found his sufficiency, not in the expectation of being released from prison, but in the strength of Christ. His body was imprisoned, but his spirit was free; he was content even though he was facing execution, knowing he could do all things through Christ.

In the midst of our most trying times, we are to rejoice. Our joy is not dependent on outward circumstances, but is based on a faith firmly rooted in God's providence. Can we not rejoice while in the trial, knowing that God will use it to develop character in us?

During my career, I have had many colleagues who were not Christians, but some of my strongest witness was an outgrowth of the tough things I faced. Often someone would ask questions that opened the door to tell him or her that Rivers and I were praying about a situation and believing God. It also opened the door for people to come to me for prayer when they were confronted with illness, a loved one's death, or some other matter over which they had no control. Our attitude in times of adversity can be a powerful testimony to those who don't know Jesus as Savior and Lord.

Solomon knew the value of coping skills as he affirms in Proverbs 18:14 (NKJV), "The spirit of a man will sustain him, but who can bear a broken spirit?" Our bodies may respond to medicine, but not the spirit. Medical personnel have told me repeatedly that I would get well quickly because of my positive attitude. Some have not learned how to delineate between a positive mental state and faith in God.

Stuff Happens

Things still happen that disturb my peace from time to time. When walking through a particularly frustrating or trying experience, sometimes I suggested to Rivers, "Let's go somewhere and laugh." Our friends, Bob and Twila Charles, from Pennsylvania were prime candidates for this assignment. Thoroughly Christian, very hospitable, and extremely funny would describe them. A weekend at their home is totally refreshing and exhilarating.

Most of the problems I have related were physical in nature, but for those who have healthy bodies, let me relate a story about a recent practical aggravation with which we dealt.

Rivers and I were celebrating our thirty-eighth anniversary and had invited my former pastor, Nelson Burkholder and his wife Dorothy to accompany us on a trip out of town. Reservations awaited our arrival, and all was well, until the day before we were scheduled to leave when I noticed some dampness in a storage closet. The plumber found that our polybutylene pipes had sprung a leak. We were faced with several options—stay home, go away and hope it was a slow leak, or postpone our trip and have it repaired.

We chose to have all the pipes replaced with copper ones, not knowing what an expensive and trying ordeal this could entail. It was the worst mess we had ever encountered, but two months and many thousands of dollars later we had the house back in order.

I'm sure you have your own stories about similar occurrences; however, we all have choices in the way we respond. While Rivers and I were not at all happy about ruptured pipes at such an inopportune time, we were so grateful that we were not away when it occurred. Again, we discussed how it would have been much worse had all our furniture been soaked and needed replacement. Also, while the drywall was being repaired, I had some quality time witnessing to the contractor's wife and helping with her newborn.

My best ministry to others has come out of painful experiences through which the Lord taught me important lessons. I decided a long time ago that God does not allow me to teach beyond where I have lived. When we share the Word of God through the lens of through-the-fire experiences, it has a ring of authenticity. The trying of our faith produces patience and dependence on God.

You may feel as if your life is spinning out of control like a merry go round and you cannot get off. God is with us even when we ride the roller coaster of life with its many ups and downs. The climb uphill may be strenuous, and we coast on the downward ride sometimes too fast, but we must hold on in prayer until the ride stops. By faith, we can outlast our bumpy rides.

We are not to be caught by surprise when trials come, because as we read the Bible, we learn that our faith is tried and we prove our faithfulness by walking through trials successfully. Don't you just love the word through? That's my favorite part of a trial—knowing this too shall pass.

Dorothy and Nelson Burkholder with their "adopted girls" Eunice and Angie at their home 5 weeks after Angie's TMJ surgery

Even though the valley may be dark, it won't last forever, and I shall walk through triumphantly and emerge unscathed. By His help and grace we can move on to victory every time. So when you fall into life's temptations, as the Apostle James says, "Count it all joy!"

His Hand My Stay

When pain and suffering come our way,
It's sent to make us strong.
But we still beg and groan and sigh,
"Lord, don't let it last too long!"
I just can't stand discomfort;
And pain is not my lot.
When tribulation comes my way,
I just feel so distraught!
But I will lean on Jesus;
I know He'll lead the way.
For when with faltering steps I tread,
His hand will be my stay.

February 2003

Application Questions:
From Victim to Victor

Scriptures: Ecclesiastes 7:14, 15, Psalm 23, 25:16-18, Psalm 119: 49, 50, 67, 71, 75, II Corinthians 4:7-11, 11:23-27, Philippians 4:4, Proverbs 18:14.

1. How does your upbringing affect the way you cope with adversity?
2. In what ways have you learned to trust God when you did not understand what was happening, or the end was not in sight?
3. Discuss the universality of pain and how this affects your thinking.
4. Discuss why you do/do not consider it sinful to ask God why.
5. What coping mechanisms has God taught you for dealing with trials?

Dad and Mom,
Bruzer and Caressa Bass,
with grandchildren La June
and Barth two months
before Dad's sudden death

Older sister Cress a few
months before her death

CHAPTER 13

ADVERSITY, NO STRANGER TO ME

Looking back on my life, I realize that obstacles and hurdles were always there for me to overcome. While I enjoyed a normal, happy childhood for the most part, there were also instances of pain and suffering. My humble beginnings include birth into a Christian home as sixth daughter and seventh child. At a mere three-pound birth weight, keeping me alive was problematic in the years prior to the technology we now enjoy in neonatal units of America's hospitals. Over the years my mother enjoyed relating the story of my birth to me, and I was fascinated to hear it. She suffered a fall in the seventh month of her pregnancy, and I seemed to stop growing after that. Other complications set in, but the family lacked funds for regular obstetrical care. Besides, most women at that time did not undergo the many tests and have the prenatal care of today's mothers, and often sent for the doctor after their labor began.

I was born at home, and that is where I stayed, but I wonder how my parents managed to keep me warm through the winter months in a house with no central heating system. Lacking a modern bassinette, my mother improvised a way to protect my fragile body by carrying me around on a pillow. My oldest sister Cress, then twelve years old, cared for me a lot also. This memory was still so vivid to her that when she was hospitalized in the final stages of cancer, she fondly recounted the story again to her children and me. She must have told a lot of her friends about it because at her funeral I was approached with, "Are you the one she used to carry around on a pillow?"

At work when we were asked to write something about ourselves that others did not know, I didn't have to think very long. I wrote the following riddle for the guess-who exercise at the employee training session.

Who Am I?
I was born at home and weighed three pounds.
My parents used a pillow to carry me around.
Such a modest beginning, you would never guess,
Since my body weight is now equal to the rest.

Childhood Trials
As far back as I can remember I was smaller than most girls my age, and as a young child this bothered me a lot. When I entered public school I was shy because I somehow equated size with importance. My best friend, Virginia Alston, was a little shorter than me, and I would cry when she did not come to school. To make matters worse, my second grade teacher, thinking she was doing me a favor advanced me to third grade after a few weeks of school. The size gap not only widened, but now I was younger than the others. I felt defenseless when someone teased and taunted me, and nicknamed me "Virgin Mary" in high school.

At home I was used to having older siblings who parented me along with Mom and Dad. I also remember when my grandmother lived with us, and I was clearly her pet. She unapologetically favored me and affectionately called me "sweet pea." Our upbringing was very strict, and little foolishness was tolerated in our home; however, we learned to match wits and to mouth off at one another. I learned to make vituperative comments that could cut a person in shreds verbally. So when I was really backed into a corner, I could be counted on to mutter some wisecrack remark.

Having a competitive spirit and being no match for my

peers physically, I became fiercely competitive academically. I figured if I could not beat anyone physically, I could exercise brainpower over him or her by staying at the top of my class. I would sit in the front of the classroom, earn good grades, and win all the spelling bees. My teachers considered me a model student, and this made me feel important. I felt like a runt because whenever sides were chosen for some physical activity, I was never among the first, but when it came to academics, everyone wanted me on their team.

Living in the south, I learned "my place" early, as we were forced to attend segregated schools and to live as second-class citizens. As we walked some three miles to school on winter mornings, buses carrying Caucasian children passed by, and they would yell racial insults out the window.

My Dad worked so hard to earn a living for his family, but as a child I watched my parents and older siblings endure numerous inequities. We learned to work hard and to be high achievers despite the obstacles placed in our path. When I was quite young I determined to make positive contributions, and no one would make me bitter; their unfair treatment would only make me better. I would excel at any cost! I believe this is when my perfectionist traits began.

My Dad was a "Bible thumper" if ever I knew one, and he had organized Righteous Grove Baptist Sunday School, the first in our community. However, it was in Saint John Baptist Church that I responded to an altar call to accept Christ and be baptized at nine years old.

My parents loved the Lord and were a Godly influence in the lives of their children. Some of my best memories of my Dad are watching him sitting at the dining room table early in the morning reading the Bible and humming his favorite hymn, "In the Garden," under his breath. I used to say my Dad would "talk to a sign post about the Lord if it would listen." He became a licensed minister in the Methodist church when he was middle-aged, and he seemed to enjoy nothing more than preaching. I always felt a certain sadness that our sons never knew him because he died when Barth was only a few months old.

A Tribute to My Dad
"Pretty is as pretty does," my wise Dad liked to say.
He drilled that truth into my mind and taught me to obey.
All that the Lord commanded, he did with all his might.
And walking in true holiness was noble, good, and right.
He told us children how that God supplied our every need.
And to be happy throughout life, God's Word we all must heed.
He read his Bible faithfully, yes, in the early morn.
He'd talk to others about the Lord—on his sleeve his faith was worn.

February 2003

Introduction to the Mennonites

When I was fifteen years old, I visited a Mennonite church for the first time, and this would change the course of my life. While I had been brought up in a Christian home, Sunday morning church services were as segregated as the public schools. It never made sense to me that people claimed to worship the same God but could not do so in an integrated setting.

Pastor Nelson Burkholder and his wife Dorothy were the most loving people I had ever met. They taught the Scriptures diligently, and treated everyone with dignity and respect in an integrated church. This was unheard of in Newport News, Virginia, in the mid-fifties as far as I knew. Before the Supreme Court decision to integrate the public schools, they risked a lot to begin a church in our neighborhood. I never knew until recently when I edited a book for Pastor Burkholder that their lives were threatened and they suffered a lot of abuse in order to follow the call of God.

While our family continued to attend the Baptist

church, my Dad allowed my sister Eunice and me to join the Calvary Mennonite Church. We learned so much from the Scriptures in our teen years and enjoyed the constant loving support that church members offered. Eunice and I were both deeply involved in the life of the church and were growing spiritually. However, as is sometimes the case, the devil was lurking around seeking someone to devour, and young Christians can be a mighty tempting target for him. My faith would be tested in ways I never thought possible, and I was about to learn a powerful lesson about strife and falsehood in the church.

Falsely Accused of Promiscuousness

Pastor Burkholder was a man of impeccable integrity, always on guard against actions that might give the appearance of evil, and taught us to do the same. While he was kind and loving, his Christian convictions dictated that when he shook the hand of a lady or girl at church, it was always at arm's length. As a teenager, I well remember his teachings on purity and the importance of a strong testimony for the Lord. He was the last person I would have suspected of impropriety.

Sometimes I thought it almost extreme, but he never brought girls to church in his car if his wife was not present. We were taught not to indulge in mixed swimming events because of the attire involved and to dress modestly at all times. While "Brother Burkholder," as he was affectionately called, teased us verbally in the presence of his wife, he never touched us. He was absolutely above board in every respect. Careful not to offend, he was the kind of pastor we all admired and respected—well most of us.

People were coming to know the Lord, and members were being added to the church. During that time some Mennonites conducted services in the prisons, and several men accepted Christ through this ministry. One such person is a man I will refer to as John, who became a member of our congregation.

While John loved the Lord, he seemed to have a controlling spirit, an intense desire to take things over. Although John was not very capable, Pastor Burkholder tried to accommodate his desire to preach and to serve in other capacities. For John, it was all or nothing, so he cooked up a scheme designed to "defrock" the pastor and destroy one of the young women. I always wondered why I was chosen for this "honor." It was so diabolical that I felt it was birthed in the pit of hell.

John accused the pastor and me of having an affair. You must know that a Mennonite pastor found guilty of any type of immorality or impropriety would have lost his license and suffered other serious consequences, so this was no light matter. John recruited a younger brother in the church to follow me around and report back to him. Since I drove my car mostly to work and church, there wasn't much to report, so the details were fabricated.

When John brought the accusation and refused to recant his lie, the Bishop called a meeting with the congregation. The pastor and I would be examined based on the "evidence" which was nonexistent. However, without their knowledge, prior to the meeting I was asked to submit to a physical examination by a local gynecologist to certify my virginity. How utterly humiliating!

With much embarrassment, I explained to the physician why I needed the check-up. I asked him if I could type the letter so his secretary would not see it. Doctor Gregory P. Carter kindly consented, writing the information out and signing his name on letterhead paper so I could type above it. The letter actually included measurements of my private parts and a certification that it was not possible that I had indulged in sexual intercourse with anyone.

Thankfully, this letter was not to be shown to the

congregation, but was a trump card of sorts in case John persisted with his lie. The kind Bishop and all the members knew this allegation bore no resemblance to truth, but this was a process they felt they must go through.

To add to the problem, you must place this accusation in its context. This was southeastern Virginia in the turbulent early sixties when marches and sit-ins were staged to integrate public places. Our church had been integrated for several years, and we had proven that all people could worship God and that eleven o'clock on Sunday morning need not be the most segregated time of the week. We also had meals together and spent time in one another's homes. But some people were still suspicious and would freely say that any Caucasian man who established a church in a segregated neighborhood was there for only two reasons—money and women. Pastor Burkholder served without salary, building homes to earn a living, and his commitment to the Lord was unquestionable. Such a story was completely without merit, but it still had the potential for volatility.

Since the perpetrator and his assistant refused to admit to their lies during the meeting, the Bishop told the group about the contents of the doctor's letter in general terms. This not only cleared my name where the pastor was concerned, but it laid to rest any possibility that I was promiscuous with anyone.

As in all types of adversity, even this one had a redeeming factor if one is open to searching for it. Dorothy, the pastor's wife said, "If they had to do it, I'm sure glad they chose a virtuous girl to accuse."

It was so hard to return to church knowing that lies, once spread, can never be brought under control completely. However, God gave me the grace to continue, and the loving support of the other members never wavered. When John's plan to take over the church failed, he left in anger. Pastor Burkholder continued in the pastorate for many more fruitful years of winning souls for Jesus.

Although I lacked the spiritual maturity to understand how powerfully the enemy of our souls could motivate a professing Christian to do such a thing, I was learning more about adversity and how the adversary uses it to discourage us. But surely there must be a blessing in this somewhere, for Jesus said, "Blessed are ye when men shall revile you, and persecute you, and shall say all manner of evil against you falsely, for My sake" (Matthew 5:11).

Discrimination at the Pinnacle of Power

Two months after Rivers and I were married in June 1963, he and thousands of others were laid off from the Newport News Shipbuilding and Dry Dock Company. This was a trying time for us newlyweds, but we pulled up stakes and moved to Washington. Rivers eventually landed a job with the Federal Bureau of Investigation, and since I was tenured with the government at Fort Monroe, Virginia, I transferred to the Pentagon.

My competitive spirit and perfectionism served me well as a government secretary stenographer because accuracy was of paramount importance. Sometimes I was called upon to take notes at military briefings of two hours duration. Often I had no idea what they were talking about, but it was my duty to record it accurately and type briefs without error, not on computer, but on an electric IBM typewriter in multiple copies. Much of my output had to be letter-perfect without the benefit of even one erasure.

I was known as an excellent stenographer by the military brass, and was showered by comments like, "You're the best secretary I've ever had in my military career." Yet, I began to notice that when promotions and awards were given, I got only verbal affirmations. Since I had been taught not to talk back to authority, I took it meekly and just worked harder, sometimes skipping lunch and bathroom breaks. When my reputation as a stenographer got around, I was asked by other officers to work on holidays and Saturdays for them.

After completing a particularly difficult task that included hand-drawn graphs and charts, a high-ranking officer said to me, "I don't know anyone who could have done that in two days!" In the office of a Brigadier General, I was assigned the most difficult work with such encouragement as, "Well, I wanted it done right, so I gave it to you." By now it was too late to correct the misconception that "Angie will do it gladly, and in half the time."

Accusing someone of racial discrimination was something I never liked to do, so I looked for other reasons for unfair treatment. Many days I went home and cried to Rivers about the way I was treated. I worked with two Caucasian women who were two grades my senior and less qualified. The general would comment to me secretly that I was the best, but he never used his mighty pen to back it up. To make it worse, I was required to type letters of commendation and awards for the other women, while I received a six-line evaluation with no monetary award.

I would apply for other positions and notice the surprise on the faces of the interviewers when they saw I was a person of color. Sometimes it unnerved them so much they bungled the interview, and one blurted out, "How do you get along with white people?"

When I went for an interview only two doors away from my office, the lieutenant colonel said, "I have a list of thirty best-qualified persons. In order to weed them out, I'm going across the hall and dictate a memo to you by telephone." He bolted out the door and began what was a clear violation of accepted practice. The personnel office had already certified me as a very qualified stenographer, and telephone dictation was not appropriate.

Having been turned down for many promotions for no acceptable reason, I asked God to help me do my best. My tendency toward excellence rose up and I said to myself, "I'll show him how good I am. I'm the most qualified person on the list." This time it worked because I did so well on the illegal test that I got the job.

Later when a friend learned of my promotion she exclaimed, "You are so lucky." Little did people understand the stress and inequities I had endured to land this promotion. Every time someone discriminated against me or made racial slurs because they forgot I was around, I just worked harder and prayed more. I would not allow anger to consume me despite the actions of another.

In utter disgust and tears, but determined not to become bitter, I said to Rivers, "One of these days someone will recognize me for my work rather than for the color of my skin." Little did I know it would take several years to find a supervisor who would treat me fairly. During my first two years in the Pentagon, I worked a lot of overtime, and eventually became exhausted and ill. After I fainted and exhibited some symptoms of a heart attack, my physician sent me to one of Washington's top cardiologists who treated me, but I never learned for sure what occurred.

During the Vietnam War the pressures only escalated and I became quite concerned about some of the material I was forced to type, as some of the responses to soldiers in the field were less than honest. As a Top Secret Control Officer I had to affix my signature on forms and take responsibility for a lot of classified military documents. Security procedures were so stringent that sometimes at home I would ask myself if I had followed them correctly, as I did not wish to be cited for security violations.

Then one day I fell in line at the snack bar next to Paul Peachy, a fellow member of Hyattsville Mennonite Church. He had been demonstrating with the Friends who had attempted to circle the Pentagon in some type of protest against the war. "What are you doing here?" I asked. He rephrased the question and asked what I was doing there. "I work here," I replied. That set me to thinking why members of the same church were on opposite sides of the issue—why one was on the inside working and one saw fit to demonstrate outside.

No matter how hard I worked it was never enough, and I came to resent the constant string of verbal compliments without monetary backing. When I felt I could handle the pressures no longer, I began to pray for deliverance. I knew that if I found another job, I would never look back in regret. So I prayed, "Lord, if You deliver me from the Pentagon, I will never ask You that again." In near desperation, I took a downgrade in another government agency to escape the pressures of the Pentagon in 1966. God does all things well. On September 11, 2001, I rejoiced that I had left the Pentagon many years earlier. The two offices where I had worked were directly in the path of the jumbo jet that slammed into the heliport area just outside my window.

When I left the Pentagon I went to work at the Armed Forces Institute of Pathology, Medical Museum. It was a joy to work in the fascinating field of forensic pathology, and the doctors for whom I worked were kind and accommodating. However, the museum was relocated, and since I did not wish to go along, I went next door to the Smithsonian Institution.

Mr. Durant was Director of Astronautics at the National Air and Space Museum, and I became his secretary stenographer. He had the reputation of being a difficult man to work for, and this presented a challenge to me. When someone from the personnel office confided to me, "You will just hate him," I responded, "No, I will just love him." I knew that with prayer and hard work we would get along if he gave me half a chance.

Behind that gruff exterior was a brilliant man who excelled in his work. He said to me one day, "You are the first person I've ever had that I could trust." With such encouragement, I did everything to make him shine in the eyes of others. When he traveled abroad, I made sure he had everything he needed and that the office ran smoothly in his absence.

Mr. Durant respected me completely, and he recognized me for my accomplishments. He was responsible for space artifacts in the museum, and through him I met such renowned persons as Norman Rockwell, Bob McCall, Werner von Braun, Mrs. Robert (Esther) Goddard, and Astronaut Michael Collins, commander of Apollo 11 space-craft. He later entrusted me with Astronaut Collins' space suit that Rivers and I transported to Lake Placid for exhibit at a Lapidary and Mineralogical Sciences Convention.

His complete trust in me was demonstrated when I applied for a promotion in a high-level office. The inter-viewer called me and said, "Your boss really loves you. He said you are excellent in every way, 'but you will get her over my dead body!'" Could it be that someone would finally recognize me for my abilities?

The Lord had finally answered my prayer and given me a supervisor that others disliked, but who only wanted a trust-worthy employee. He liked to say to me, "No one in Washington will take you from me." To ensure that I remained with him, he treated me quite well and rewarded me monetarily. When we moved away he insisted on writing a letter of reference in which he praised me highly and said, "She is completely devoted to the fine tenets of her faith." What a surprise from a man who was not a Christian.

Discrimination in Real Estate

All that overtime in the Pentagon paid off because Rivers and I began to save money for a down payment on a home. We tried to live frugally while we watched our passbook sav-ings grow. During our second year of marriage we began to look for a home in the Maryland suburbs. Armed with the conviction that neighborhood is everything, we naively began to call in response to newspaper ads. By telephone, I could extract promises of good deals on attractive properties, and this worked fine as long as we did not show up.

One realtor was so excited. "Mrs. Williams, the owner is desperate to sell, and I can get this house for you even cheaper. Just meet me at my office at six o'clock and I'll take you out to see it," he gushed. Overjoyed, Rivers and I drove to his office. As we waited upstairs we could hear him talking to someone downstairs about this nice young couple he planned to show the house.

Rounding the stairs and seeing us the realtor asked, "What do you want?"

Rivers replied, "We are Rivers and Angie Williams, and we're here to see a house."

Without missing a beat, he replied, "Can't show it to you."

We thanked him and turned to leave, whereupon he followed us outside. He shook Rivers' hand with both hands and started to relegate us to properties in a not-too-desirable neighborhood. "We have what you are looking for over in the XYZ area," he suggested.

We declined his offers, thanked him, and left in disgust as I muttered to Rivers, "He couldn't sell me the White House now."

One weekend we were baby sitting with Mom and Dad Brunk's five children. We noticed signs for open house at a new housing development not far from their home. Excitedly, we entered the office and eagerly awaited some type of greeting. We milled around with the children for a while and no one greeted us or offered to help. This seemed strange, but giving them the benefit of a doubt, we decided that in the busy Sunday afternoon traffic they had inadvertently overlooked us.

We returned on Monday when no one else was there. Smiling broadly, we entered the office only to be ignored again. This time, we had decided in advance to stay around and see what they would do. We sensed that our presence made the young man very uncomfortable, so when he could ignore us no longer he asked what we wanted. He responded to our questions about the property in short staccato sentences while he shined his shoes, barely looking at us. He did, however, give us a key and allow us to walk through a model home on our own. Clearly, we were not welcome in Kettering! They obviously attempted to discriminate against someone who decided to fight back, as a lawsuit later forced them to integrate the development.

During the mid-sixties, discrimination in housing in the Washington metropolitan area was quite common, but we were determined to live in the best neighborhood we could afford. We learned of instances where realtors would jack up the price of a home when they showed it to people of color. So when we sensed unfair treatment, we asked friends to look at the same property to see whether a realtor would quote them the price they had quoted to us.

Being slapped in the face and our dream for a home nearly squashed this way was difficult for us newlyweds, but the I'll-show-you attitude reared its head. I said, "We pay taxes just like everyone else, and we won't be told where we can live." But whom would I call, and where would I find help when faced with this giant monster of housing discrimination?

I began by calling the White House and stating our concern about finding suitable housing. As is often true with government agencies, I was passed from one agency to another. Completely undeterred, I placed some twenty calls until I ended up with the Greenbelt Citizens for Fair Housing who were anxious to help. A few months later, Rivers and I were the first to integrate what was known as "old Greenbelt."

We lived peacefully in Greenbelt for several years; however, it was uncomfortable to be patronized, which we considered another form of prejudice. From calling the hospital when our son was born to inquire about his color to expecting me to know every person of color they had ever met, some well-intentioned neighbors tried to adjust to our presence. When I took the baby out for a walk, I'd be approached with, "Oh, you're Mrs. Williams. Your husband works for the FBI..." Appearing to know all about me, sometimes they did not give me their name unless I asked.

We were invited to a reception where we were introduced to city officials—the mayor, city manager, chief of police. While they were all kind, we knew other neighbors did not enjoy such celebrity, and surely this had something to do with our skin color. When there was a city meeting of some sort, several people would call to see if we planned to attend, some offering to give us a ride. I joked to a neighbor one day, "They don't care whether you come, but they do want to make sure we are there."

When I decided to return to work, I placed an ad in the Greenbelt paper for a baby sitter. A mother of young children responded immediately, and I took Barth and visited her at home. She appeared cordial and accepting; however, by the time I arrived home a few minutes later she called to say a relative was terminally ill, and a few other things I found hard to believe. My righteous (I hope) indignation was stirred because I felt she had assumed I was Caucasian based on where I lived.

One amusing thing that happened several times was people's surprise when I answered the doorbell. By this time, we had relocated to a much nicer home in Greenbelt in Boxwood Country Estates. The subdivision included a few persons of color, both Americans and internationals. My youthfulness and skin color took a lot of people by surprise, and I was greeted more than once with, "I'd like to speak to the lady of the house." Despite any unpleasant experiences, living in Greenbelt was a wonderful phase in our lives, and we cultivated some lasting friendships.

When we left Greenbelt, we did not want race to be a deterrent to selling our home. After realizing people could be

swayed by skin tone, we felt justified in removing family photographs from the walls and shelves before someone came to
view our home. It seemed to work well, so we repeated it
when we moved from a home in the deeper south where we
had "provided the only integration" for the neighborhood.

Other Minor Annoyances

Our good friends, Aaron and Sally Schlossenberg, lived
about fifty miles around the Washington Beltway from our
home, so we spent weekends with one another. One weekend we went out to play tennis on a court owned by the
cooperative where our friends lived. As soon as we returned
to their home, someone telephoned and asked, "Who were
those colored children at the tennis court?"

Aaron replied, "Those were no colored children; they are
our friends," whereupon he hung up the telephone.

* * *

In the early seventies I operated the Student
Employment Office at EMC. This necessitated making a lot of telephone contacts with excellent results
for the students. However, I noticed that some people made racist remarks to me. I jokingly relayed
some of this to President Augsburger who asked,
"How can you laugh about that?"

I replied, "The joke is on the person on the other
end of the line, but there will be some red faces if
they ever see me in person." In order to help the students, I avoided personal contact with local busi-
nessmen even when they suggested meeting me.
One day when a student was injured on the job I
knew my anonymity had come to an end as I heard a
familiar voice ask the secretary if he could see me.
Reluctantly, I appeared smiling and invited him into
the faculty lounge for coffee, pretending not to
notice his shocked look.

Later Paul told me he went back to his office and said to his secretary, "You have been talking with Angie Williams for a long time. Tell me, what do you think she looks like?"

The secretary described a rotund middle-aged Mennonite lady wearing a plain dress and having her hair up in a little bun in the back. "You could not be more wrong," he replied. "Would you believe Angie Williams is young, attractive, (pause) and black?"

Some Christians Discriminate

In 1971, when Rivers and I moved to Harrisonburg, Virginia, we would again be the first to integrate a neighborhood. We learned after purchasing a home that a covenant existed that excluded "Negroes and chicken coops" in Park View. Our neighbors, almost exclusively Mennonites, treated us with respect; however, several persons asked some pretty inappropriate questions at times that exposed their stereotypical thinking.

We were asked to present something on race relations for the Virginia Mennonite Conference. Uncomfortable with such a topic, Rivers and I had a hard time finding a venue. We decided to use inappropriate remarks made to us, but turn them around and ask them to an ethnic Mennonite. My friend Shirley Yoder agreed to assist. After explaining that these were not fabricated, but were remarks made to us, I began to fire questions at Shirley. As fast as she could answer, I asked another, and then walked away without telling her my name or any information about myself. The audience got the message quickly because it seemed inappropriate for me to ask Shirley such ridiculous questions. My admonition to them was, "Before you make a remark to someone of another race, think whether it would be appropriate for them to say the same thing to you. If not, then don't say it."

* * *

One day the office staff at the college surprised me with a lovely birthday cake. We were having a wonderful time until a faculty member came in and sat next to me. Peering into my eyes she said, "You people look so young. How do we tell your age?" She obviously thought I should be flattered by her "compliment."

I replied, "By the wrinkles in the face just like everyone else!"

* * *

One Sunday I was near the door at New Covenant Fellowship where I served on the Board of Elders. I greeted a visiting couple and extended my hand. They refused to shake my hand and walked past me. My friend, Janet Hostetler, was standing nearby, so she introduced herself and ushered them back over to me. "This is Angie Williams," Janet said.

The visiting lady had not recognized my face, but the name she knew. "Oh! Angie Williams!" she exclaimed, as she began to praise me for my work as an officer with the denominational women's group. I was, of course, left wondering why my position had suddenly earned me the right to be respected.

* * *

Often people representing the church asked me to accept various positions until I became overburdened with responsibilities. An "important man" called me from another state requesting that I join a group representing a cross section of the Mennonite Church. He tried to impress upon me what an honor this was and what a fine contribution I could make. When I still refused, he asked a colleague to approach me about it. In his over zealousness to twist my arm he crossed the line when he said, "We need a woman on the group and a minority, and you can meet both requirements."

* * *

I was asked, "What do you prefer to be called, colored, Negro, black or African-American. Smiling broadly, I replied, "Try Angie!"

* * *

An author was commissioned to interview me and write my biography for a church publication. This man knew me, and there should have been no doubt about the close-knit family life we enjoyed. However, when he visited our home with camera and pen in hand, he wanted to exclude Rivers from the photographs. When he wanted to picture me reading to the boys and playing games with them without Rivers, I protested, "That's not the way it is! We play games together as a family." I felt he had assumed our family was matriarchal and that Rivers did not relate closely to the boys, and it was difficult to disassociate himself from that stereotype. What resulted was a fairly accurate portrayal of our family that included a lot about Rivers in the article, so I could live with this compromise.

* * *

Some years later, Rivers and I sat at the front of our congregation in Maryland listening to a visiting speaker. The young woman represented a local Crisis Pregnancy Center that our congregation supported annually. As she spoke of the problems of illegitimacy, I felt she overstepped her bounds by this statement. "This is a part of the black culture."

We continued to smile, but inside I was unhappy at such a comprehensive statement that did not represent my family's moral values at all. During the discussion period, I reminded the lady that whatever "black culture" meant, this behavior was never a part of my upbringing. I said, "This has nothing to do with color of the skin; it's a matter of sin."

Completely unapologetic, the lady reinforced her stereotype, "I've studied sociology, and I know what I'm talking about."

Knowing the grim statistics, I replied, "I've been a part of the race for over forty years, and my six sisters and I were never immoral. There are also a lot of others like us."

Helping the Cause of Integration

Although Rivers and I were reared in a segregated environment, we both determined early not to allow the misconduct of others to embitter us. We have our own way of contributing to integration and equal treatment of all people. While some chose to participate in sit-ins and marches, we chose to cultivate relationships that we believe in the long run build bridges among different ethnic groups. God has called us to be peacemakers and ministers of reconciliation, and this has taken the form of developing deep lasting friendships with a diverse group of persons. A cursory glance at our guest book reveals a wide range of guests from many ethnic backgrounds who we have hosted for meals and overnight lodging.

We agree with Dr. Martin Luther King in that we do not judge people "on the color of their skin, but on the content of their character." I was quoted in a magazine article as having said, "To love Jesus is to love people." Consequently, our two sons learned at an early age how to relate to persons from different countries, some of whom have lived in our home. This has been a very enriching experience since God has given us the gift of hospitality and service to others. How do we know whether we have "entertained angels unawares," as the Scripture says?

Rivers and I made many friends through traveling to my speaking appointments, often staying in homes, and our sons experienced a lot of diversity that way also. We taught them to appreciate and accept people without judging based on ethnicity.

Affirmative Action, Not So Affirming

I do not doubt that some persons have benefited from affirmative action; however, I believe it has worked to my disadvantage both in the workplace and in the church. The very premise around which it was conceived can be a source of reverse discrimination. Why should I expect to be accorded some particular advantage because of the atrocities heaped upon my ancestors? All I ever asked for was half a chance to prove my abilities.

As I was bemoaning the subject and discussing it with my friend, Barbara Brown, I said. "Suppose I ask you to race with me around the FAA building? Since it is a square block, I will expect you to allow me to run a full block before you start. Did I not, by such a request, admit that I think you are a better runner than I? Or why would I expect to start ahead of you?"

That is how I view affirmative action—offering an unfair advantage to someone in a vain attempt to placate their supposed need for it. If a Caucasian friend assumes he or she needs to give me a head start, I would think they viewed me as inferior—someone who could not compete equally with them. Why would I desire to be thought of as inferior? When we request special programs, have we not admitted our inferiority by claiming to be different and in need of more help than our Caucasian counterparts?

Once when I was asked to write a magazine article on race relations, I steadfastly declined. The editor called and urged me to write because, "you have influence in the church." I finally agreed on the condition that I be allowed to write an objective opinion piece. It has been some twenty years since I wrote that piece, but I believe it still holds true. "You cannot compensate for the inequities of the past by overcompensation in the present!" I stated. No amount of unfair advantage can erase the horrible history of slavery and segregation in this country; however, constant reminders can only embitter descendants of slaves if we allow it.

When affirmative action arrived on the scene, I felt it was never meant for those of us who could compete with the masses, and I never accrued a single benefit from it to my knowledge. Instead, employers made it pretty clear to me that I was capable of competing with anyone, and therefore, not eligible for any special programs. Sometimes I felt it a distinct disadvantage to be considered capable because some of my colleagues seemed to view me as a threat.

I noticed how they sometimes opened opportunities for minorities who were not ready for the challenge. In those instances, the person performed miserably, which led me to believe they only reinforced already imbedded stereotypes. This in itself, I view as a type of discrimination. It is not only unfair to every Caucasian colleague who was more qualified, but it is also unfair to every person of color who could have performed admirably if given the same opportunity. I concluded that since I was not considered anyone's "project," I was passed over frequently for positions for which I was qualified. When I queried a human resources specialist, she said, "You are over-qualified for these positions; they are designed for someone who needs on-the-job training." This is why I see affirmative action as not so affirming for those of us who can compete with the majority.

It is no secret that there are many types of discrimination, and some of them do not pertain to skin color. Sometimes I believe people are too quick to think race upon the slightest mistreatment. I've decided that the devil is color blind, and he sends his imps to harass Christians for other reasons as well. When we become too touchy about race, we can attribute it to situations where it does not belong and it can hinder building sound relationships.

The trials I endured in the Pentagon were not the first I had faced in the workplace, nor were they the last. The most serious one occurred just a few years ago after I returned to Washington to work at the Federal Aviation Administration.

Most of my supervisors and colleagues respected me highly and complimented me generously. One manager referred to me as a "consummate professional." Another manager who treated me disrespectfully, nonetheless wrote, "Angie has the exceptional ability to conceptualize and formulate creative campaigns from the mere germination of a thought or idea. She has done an exemplary job in developing and organizing large pieces of data and presenting them in a clear, succinct fashion...Her oral presentations and written word are above reproach...She is truly an asset to any organization she is affiliated with, and would be a serious loss to ours." They wrote such glowing appraisals; however, it took me some time to realize that some of the compliments were designed to make me work even harder to reflect favorably on my supervisor. It was no secret that with a little appreciation I would produce even more.

In less than three years after I arrived at the FAA, a top executive hired me. I was fiercely loyal, and was known to say, "As long as I work for you, you'll be taken care of better than any other executive in this building." Risking my own health, I lived up to that commitment, working long hours and many weekends. When I realized that some of my less-qualified colleagues were promoted equal to me and then past me, I started to wonder why.

Meanwhile, this high-level executive wrote glowing performance appraisals for me, "She is a rare gem and a model for the agency." Every outgoing document had to pass my scrutiny even though the writer was generally paid at a much higher level. "You are the best writer we have," my brilliant supervisor had told me repeatedly. A model for a big federal agency, best writer in an organization of about one hundred people? But what was it getting for me?

For several years this worked fine until one day I exclaimed to my friend Malinda, "I'm tired of being patted on the head. My hair is wearing thin from all the rubbing on the head, but that doesn't buy my groceries." Malinda Battle was a special buddy I had known for many years, and she was a dependable Christian friend and confidant. We spent much time discussing my job situation, and I tried hard not to believe my supervisor, a man of color, would dare discriminate.

At last I transferred to another office in the same organization. I applied for several positions and was certified by the personnel office as best qualified. My supervisor, a Caucasian female, adamantly refused to promote me from the certificate. After holding it for several months she marked it that I was "best qualified" but added a stipulation that personnel not give me the customary raise. When the personnel folks told her this was illegal, she persisted and cancelled the certificate to avoid promoting me.

Now I knew exactly what some staff meant when they said, "No good deed will go unpunished." Indeed, I felt I was being punished for being a good employee. My personnel advisors suggested I lodge a formal complaint, but I refused to accuse my supervisor of racial prejudice. Instead, I felt it was age discrimination since she often affirmed me verbally in the presence of my colleagues. To make matters worse, she assigned me to do the work of others who were two grades my senior. I am not sure why, but it took over two years and an administrative law judge to get the two-grade promotion I had already earned. By that time, it had worn on me emotionally and physically. Ironically, the notice to appear before an administrative judge to testify came the same week when I was scheduled to conduct a women's retreat in Indiana on "Joy in Adversity."

When my supervisor was confronted concerning my allegations, she affirmed me as an excellent employee, but her excuse for not promoting me was that I lacked appropriate technical skills for the higher position. Having done my research carefully, I knew the regulations clearly stated that technical skills were not a requirement for that series. The experts in our personnel office had scrutinized my records and certified me qualified already, so she could not establish a solid basis for her decision.

Eventually, I applied for a position in another organization and was accepted. Much to my surprise, the executive argued to keep me while steadfastly insisting that I lacked technical skills. When the director of the hiring organization pressed for my transfer and they could hold me no longer legally, they struck an agreement requiring me to work for them several hours a week to complete a project. Being less than perfect, I complained to a friend, "I wasn't good enough to promote, but they don't want to give me up."

God's Word Gives Strength

Filing an equal employment opportunity complaint required more negative energy than I had anticipated, and took its toll on my health. How do you face a belligerent supervisor every day when they know you have lodged an official complaint? As always, I turned to the Word of God for promises to which I could cling.

I often read Psalms about how David cried out to God when he was being treated unfairly. By the inspiration of the Holy Spirit, he recorded words that strengthened me and encouraged me to trust in God and not to retaliate against those who hurt me or told untruths to get their way. Psalm 37:1, 7 says, "Fret not thyself because of evildoers, neither be thou envious against the workers of iniquity...Rest in the Lord, and wait patiently for Him: fret not thyself because of him who prospereth in his way, because of the man who bringeth wicked devices to pass."

Many times I was tempted to give up my quest for the promotion I had earned, but the following verses gave me hope. "I have seen the wicked in great power, and spreading himself like a green bay tree. Yet he passed away, and, lo, he was not: yea, I sought him, but he could not be found" (Verses 35, 36).

One day when I was reading the Psalms, I came across a verse that made me laugh at a time when it appeared that the ungodly had the advantage over me. I had decided that the system was designed to wear a person out, make them sick, or discourage them into silence. On the very day when I was scheduled to appear at the Equal Employment Opportunity Commission, I marked this verse in my Bible. "...But the mouth of them that speak lies shall be stopped" (Psalm 63:11b).

I had asked my praying buddy Malinda to accompany me, and her role was to sit in the room and pray silently. During the conference I heard lies put forward that I was able to refute, and the judge was clearly convinced that I had been discriminated against. After over two years of procrastination, while they admitted no wrong, they had to promote me.

I do not pretend that my attitude was always holy during this stressful time when I also battled some physical problems. Even though I had prayed early in the process that God would help me to love my enemies, at times this was very difficult. When I lost my focus, the Holy Spirit often brought Psalm 73 to my mind. It seems the writer became envious as he observed the prosperity of the wicked. They appeared not to have any problems in life or in death. He thought his righteousness was in vain until he "went into the sanctuary of God," and regained his perspective. I noticed that when I got my eyes off the Lord and concentrated too much on the inequities I faced, they seemed to loom even bigger. Like the Psalmist, I wanted to see God in the dry and thirsty places as I experienced Him in the sanctuary (Psalm 63:1,2).

Discrimination Against Christians

Working for the federal government has many advantages, and I thank God for the privilege. I did learn, however, that virtually all minority groups except Christians have protective rights. Surely it was all right for me to have my ears polluted by persons using God's name in vain and sprinkling their speech with expletives all day. But what if I had pulled the Bible from my cabinet and started quoting Scripture or saying "Hallelujah" and "Praise the Lord" every time another Christian came to my office? I knew this would not be tolerated, and I figured that conversely, I should not have to put up with someone's ungodly speech.

After hearing all I thought I could take of two colleagues' foul-mouthed language, I devised a plan. I would go to them individually and kindly remind them that their conversation was "not fit for holy ears." This I did, and both took it graciously, although it was so engrained that they sometimes fell back into the practice. However, most of my colleagues would not swear in my presence.

On one occasion I attended a staff retreat where we were asked to participate in a get acquainted astrological exercise. Praying under my breath, I glanced around the room at the other Spirit-filled Christians, expecting that some of them would object. I was disappointed to see that everyone chose to participate except me. This was a team building retreat, and I knew I was in jeopardy of being accused of not being a team player. However, there are times when we must stand on our convictions even if we must do so alone, and this was one of those times.

Most people in the workplace respected me highly and I was able to pray with a lot of employees, especially when they had problems. There are a lot of strong Christians working at the FAA, and I believe this makes it one of the best government agencies.

When I return to visit I am greeted warmly by the guards, hugged, and referred to as a spiritual mother. I can still talk about the Lord to them, and they accept it graciously. I was so blessed when a former colleague confided, "You are the best Christian I know."

Application Questions:
Adversity, No Stranger To Me

Scriptures: Matthew 5:11, Psalm 37:1, 7, 35, 36, Psalm 63:1,2, Psalm 73.

1. Have you ever been discriminated against because of ethnic background, age, weight, socioeconomic status, etc.? Discuss ways of coping with such inequities.

2. In what ways might you be guilty of discriminating as a Christian?

3. Why do you think Christians in the workplace are the unprotected minority?

4. How have you relied on God's strength to overcome the trials you have faced?

5. Have you ever felt that the wicked are somehow advantaged and exempt from suffering? If so, discuss how Psalm 73 can return you to proper perspective.

CHAPTER 14

PERSEVERANCE, ENDURING UNDER PRESSURE

Two years ago when I was asked to return as guest lecturer for a class at Evangel Theological Seminary, after a good laugh, I began to pray about what I would teach. It became clear that I should deal with the subject of "Joy in Adversity." Now, you need to know that I never attended seminary, but have lectured at seminaries a few times over the years. Each time it humbles me that God should open such a challenging door, and knowing my inadequacy only causes me to depend on Him more.

"Perseverance is the ability to endure under pressure," I announced to the class of attentive seminarians. Occasionally during the next three hours, I would elicit their input by repeating, "Perseverance is..." and wait for these present and future ministers' response. While I knew the seminary held what I considered a balanced position on accepting God's miracle-working power for today, I was unsure how the students felt about my spending a whole class period talking about how to deal with adversity.

I had spent many hours preparing my notes and an outline and other handouts for the students. Since I knew the class was made up of pastors, persons aspiring to be pastors, and other Christian workers, I felt they could benefit from a teaching on adversity. Having persevered through so many trials, I felt what I had to share was legitimate.

Once in the classroom, I found myself wondering how many of these pastors-to-be had been taught that to accept Jesus was to escape a life of trials, temptations, and adversity.

How would they deal with situations when the church prayed for a family and the child died, or when someone lost their job because they stood up for righteousness? How would they explain to a new Christian that God does not always answer our prayers quickly or in the way we pray them?

Knowing this teaching would not bring a lot of "hallelujahs" or cartwheels in the aisles, I had approached the subject reluctantly. Throughout the next three hours, I continued to emphasize, "We are what we are in adversity!" and, "Perseverance is the ability to endure under pressure." During the lecture I related instances of how God helped me to withstand pressure without falling apart. The students really seemed to resonate with what I was teaching, and at the end gave me a standing ovation and much verbal affirmation.

Lord, I Want It Now!

"Call upon Me and I will answer thee," says the Lord in Jeremiah 33:3. But, when, Lord? The problem is that we want answers right now. Perseverance in prayer is too hard. We don't want to wait on the Lord or anyone else—it's not a part of our lifestyle.

By all means, we should pray the Word of God, but what do I do if the problem keeps hanging around? Sometimes we have no option but to wait, but we can determine how we behave while we wait. Growing up in Christ requires learning how to wait patiently on the Lord.

The Psalmist put it well as he spoke of how to persevere in faith during a trial. "I waited patiently for the Lord; and He inclined unto me, and heard my cry" (Psalm 40:1). After he had waited, we don't know how long, he continues in Verses 2, 3, "He brought me up also out of an horrible pit, out of the miry clay, and set my feet upon a rock, and established my goings." This is the part I really like because the Lord gave me this promise concerning my jaw joint dysfunction some years ago. "And He hath put a new song in my mouth, even praise unto our God: many shall see it, and fear, and shall trust in the Lord."

Trust in God results from learning to wait upon Him in prayer. When we reflect on how He has answered prayer in the past, it emboldens us to hang on in faith. We can learn from Psalm 55:17, "Evening, and morning, and at noon, will I pray, and cry aloud: and He shall hear my voice." Our heart may cry out, "O Lord, how long?" As long as it takes is how long we persevere in prayer.

Hope and Patience in Suffering

When we are hurting deeply it is blessed to know that God loves us too much to leave us helpless or hopeless. He offers us the tools to have hope and patience in suffering. The Apostle Paul suggests that suffering in this world will bring later glory. "...If indeed we suffer with Him, that we may also be glorified together. For I consider that the sufferings of this present time are not worthy to be compared with the glory which shall be revealed in us" (Romans 8:17b, 18, NKJV). Paul also says that we are saved by hope. "But if we hope for what we do not see, we eagerly wait for it with perseverance" (Romans 8:25, NKVJ).

Further, Paul poses two questions so profound they virtually answer themselves. "Who shall separate us from the love of Christ? Shall tribulation, or distress, or persecution, or famine, or nakedness, or peril, or sword?" (Romans 8:35, NKJV). The answer screams back to us, "Unequivocally, no!" Through the remainder of the chapter, Paul affirms that absolutely nothing in Heaven or hell can separate us from God's love through Christ Jesus.

If you want to know what is in someone's heart, just watch what they say during turbulent times, when adversity rocks their faith boat. We are what we are in adversity!

Before retirement I worked at the FAA whose mandate,

simply put, is the safety of the flying public. They assure you a safe flight, but don't guarantee a turbulent-free ride. The ride can be bumpy at times, but the captain announces any predictable turbulence beforehand. He also ensures the passengers' safety by requesting that everyone fasten his seat belt. The pilot doesn't say, "At 35,000 feet over Ohio, I'm planning to bail out and you can land this aircraft yourself."

Likewise, God does not promise a smooth flight through life, but He does promise His presence during the bumpy times and a safe landing when life's flight is over. Sometimes when adversity comes, you may feel as if you are headed for a crash landing. But fasten your spiritual seat belt and hold on. You are in safe hands because God is still piloting your aircraft.

The Apostle Peter said that perilous times would come, and I believe they are already here. Those who will survive are the ones who have learned to endure under pressure, because endurance produces hope. Endurance enables us to hold on when things look hopeless.

I believe God allows suffering in our lives for a purpose that may not be immediately apparent. We must all walk through suffering of some sort, but suffering has a purpose—the power to produce perseverance, character and hope. If only we can learn to endure under pressure, God can produce the character of Christ in us. If we go through adversity, we can grow through adversity, and I believe that is always God's ultimate purpose in allowing it. To a women's group I said, "I don't know any saint who has not walked through some deep waters."

"Sometimes it takes a painful experience to make us change our ways," says the writer of the Proverbs. What is there about having a life free of significant trials that seems to lead to complacency? We can easily take God's blessings for granted because prosperity often breeds ingratitude. Sometimes what we label as "faith" is already fact. I don't have to believe for a paycheck if I have worked all week; I just assume it's on the way.

In The Furnace, But Not Feeling The Heat

When faced with trials, we typically try to figure things out and come up with a plan. It's a different matter altogether to profess faith in God's power when a situation looks so dark and hopeless that you can't even formulate a solution in your mind. Let's consider the three Hebrew young men who faced a fiery furnace in Babylon for refusing to bow down and worship the king's idol.

When the furnace heat is turned up seven times, how do you respond? Are you tempted to denounce the true God and bow down and worship Nebuchadnezzar's golden image, or whatever it might take to relieve the pressure you feel?

Shadrach, Meshach, and Abednego were well trained in the laws of God, and though they were in a foreign land, when faced with this awful circumstance, their faith was unwavering. They declared, "If it be so, our God Whom we serve is able to deliver us from the burning fiery furnace, and He will deliver us out of thine hand, O king. But if not, be it known unto thee, O king, that we will not serve thy gods, nor worship the golden image which thou hast set up" (Daniel 3:17, 18). What do you mean, "if not?" Were they making a negative confession, uncertain of whether God would deliver them?

At these words the king became very angry and his countenance changed against these men he had formerly respected and promoted to high positions. To make sure the fire would devour them, he had the heat turned up so high that those who threw the men in were killed. We speak figuratively about being in the furnace and not feeling the heat, but these young men were literally in the furnace, fully clothed and bound. There was no physical means of escape.

But God, the Omnipotent One, the One Who keeps His covenant, knew their hearts.

The king was very miserable as he agonized about his inability to retract his decree about throwing anyone into the furnace who did not worship his idol. He hardly thought some of his choice Hebrew subjects would fall heir to this awful fate. Anxious to know their outcome, and I believe exercising a sort of faith, he rose early and rushed to the furnace. He was not prepared for what he saw when he looked in. He knew they had cast three men in, but he confessed, "Lo, I see four men loose, walking in the midst of the fire, and they have no hurt; and the form of the fourth is like the Son of God" (Daniel 4:25).

These men could have reasoned that they could bow down and pretend to worship, but their commitment to God was so strong that being burned to death was a better option than worshiping an idol. First they affirmed God's ability to deliver them; then they affirmed His willingness to do so. God delivered them from the fiery furnace; He did not prevent their going into it. What a miracle God performed in protecting them in the furnace, and bringing them out without the smell of smoke on their garments. They were in the furnace but not feeling the heat. God can, God will, and God did!

I suspect Shadrach, Meshach, and Abednego were tempted to doubt God. But God brought them from prisoners in a furnace to promotion in the province. God can change the heart of a king, and He did, according to Daniel 3:30-4:3.

Jesus was with the men in the furnace; He was the fourth man in the fire. How about you and me? When we are in the heat of the furnace or the thick of the battle, do we remember to move beyond seeking the purpose of the trial to standing on the promises and seeking God's presence? When you emerge from your fiery trial, what is your condition? Are you charred and scarred beyond recognition? Are you burned and bitter, or has the furnace made you better? Has the experience purified and perfected you, or has it just petrified and provoked you to the point of self-pity?

Rejoice In Tribulation?

The Apostle Paul seems to indicate in Romans 5:3,4 that we are to rejoice during trials and tribulation because we know they build strength of character. But you say, "I don't want to experience any pain!" Neither do I. But how do you know that your faith will stand the test if it has never been tested? Sometimes those who belittle others and accuse them of having no faith behave worst of all when faced with unexpected tribulation. They may have become spiritual brats who have no place in their theology for anything but a life of ease and answered prayer.

The phrase, "tribulation produces perseverance" is a puzzling one. Tribulation means suffering and distress, and may include physical challenges. But who wants to "tribulate?" If we will wait in faith upon the Lord, exercising patience during the hard times, the result will be the ability to endure. We will learn to trust God in ways we never thought possible, and this develops Christian character. We can endure the present trial because we see our future potential in Christ.

But we live in an instant throwaway society. Waiting is not applauded—it's just not natural. We confess what we think we need and expect God to make good on it. We observe someone else's problems and give them frivolous solutions like, "If you just had enough faith." "That would never happen to me." "I'm a King's Kid." Just keep living—sooner or later you will face something you can't confess away. What will you do when God allows you to wait? Will you have persevering faith?

We all know the pat clichés—"name it and claim it,"

"blab it and grab it," "say it and see it," "speak it and seek it." We're like a bunch of spiritual babies, whining to the Lord and telling Him what we want. When you get what you want, will you want what you get? God forbid that some of us even demand of God how it must be, when we should instead throw ourselves on His mercy.

While positive confessions may sound nice in theory because it makes the Christian feel in control, in the vernacular of the streets, "it ain't necessarily so." It takes a lot more than my screaming, "It's mine!" What about God's sovereign will for me that I don't always see? Have you ever thanked God that He did not say yes to some really far out prayer you prayed? Weren't you glad that the Omniscient God knew that what you wanted was not His best for you?

God Pacifies Babies

Did you ever notice that when you were first born-again, it seemed as if God answered your prayers more quickly? In a spiritual sense, He diapered you, stuffed a pacifier into your mouth, and rocked you to sleep. Why is He allowing you to wait for answers to prayer now?

Our son, Barth, weighed only five-and-one-half pounds at birth. His sucking ability was not fully developed, so feeding was difficult, and he lost weight. For several weeks I had to feed him small amounts every half-hour around the clock. Although Barth was a newborn, he knew exactly how to keep his parents on the run twenty-four hours a day, caring for his every need. All he had to do was to cry, and no matter what time the clock indicated, I sprang into action. I did it gladly because he was a helpless newborn baby. But now Barth is thirty-four years old, and we expect him to act like an adult. He has a full set of teeth, and he can grind a steak.

Does God expect us to grow up spiritually? I suspect He does, for He will not allow us to remain babies forever. The writer of the Hebrews illustrates this beautifully in chapter five, stating those who have reached "full age" can ingest solid meat.

Do babies grow up overnight? Of course not, and neither do spiritual babies. It takes the sincere milk of the Word and the Holy Spirit to feed and guide them into all truth. Instant sainthood? Perish the notion! It takes a lot of walking through and persevering under pressure to become a mature Christian, and I have discovered no way to short-circuit the process.

Instant Answered Prayer

Sometimes when we hear about a miracle we mistakenly fail to realize this person may have been waiting on the Lord for a while. If it's an instant healing or a financial miracle that God bestows on someone we don't know, we can even become jealous. Why did God answer their prayer and I'm still waiting for my miracle?

Do you ever feel like asking, "Lord, just what are You waiting for?" When I was speaking on prayer, I asked the audience an innocent-sounding question. "How many of you are waiting right now for the Lord to answer a particular prayer?" Surprisingly, some folks did not raise their hands.

I continued in this vein. "I have experienced God's miracle-working power in my life, so I am not trying to talk you out of praying for miracles, but how many always get instant answers to prayer? Have you prayed for something you did not receive immediately? You have been on your face before the Lord pleading for a long time. It seems as if your prayers are caught somewhere in the ceiling, and that the heavens are brass as far as your getting a prayer through."

Recognizing that some folks still did not raise their hands to indicate they were waiting on the Lord, this was my opportunity to exclaim, "There are only two categories of

Christians—those who are waiting for God to answer their prayers, and those who are not praying. There isn't anything in between." Their giggles indicated that some were feeling as if I had tricked them.

While I firmly believe in instant miracles, through studying God's Word and observing the experiences of many other Christians, I've been led to believe that God does not jump at our every demand. Some people treat God as if He were a celestial errand boy. "Give me this, bring me that." Some even pray and ask God to "go into the jails," or to "go into the hospitals" and do this or that. I think I understand what they mean, but did Jesus not commission us to go into the world and preach the gospel? How then can we turn it around and assign our duties to our Heavenly Father? How presumptuous!

By their confession the super-spiritual crowd would have you believe they always get instant answers to prayer. They claim it in the Name of Jesus and it has to manifest itself. I don't fall into the category of the super-spiritual because the Lord allows me to wait for answers to prayer.

Sometimes when God gives us a specific promise, He may allow us to wait for a long time to see it fulfilled. As I've studied the Word, I have become increasingly aware that most of God's promises have no timetable attached. God gives a vision, and we get all excited. But God may be saying, "Wait! Wait for My timing. Wait until I work out some other situations that have a bearing on the answer to your prayer. You don't know all that I know; you don't see all that I see."

Sometimes it seems that God is taking too long, so I take matters into my own hands. Don't you? Waiting is painful, and we don't like to wait. We have no option but to wait, but we can decide how we wait. Having done all to stand, we stand firmly. God comforts us in our afflictions, but He allows us to wait—to walk through adversity and not around it.

A popular speaker and friend of mine told about her son, a Bible College student, who had been given some type of hallucinogenic drug in a soft drink. Although he became schizophrenic, the Scripture he had memorized when he was very young began to come out. He could not speak an intelligent sentence, but to the dismay of his psychiatrists, quoted Scripture in response to whatever they asked him. He really drove them mad! His healing was gradual and took seven years, but his mother never gave up.

While she told the story at a women's meeting, I noticed that the moderator began to squirm. She later reprimanded the speaker for telling the group it took seven years for her son's healing. It appeared the moderator wanted her to tell the miracle, but to imply that it occurred instantaneously. That is dishonest! And it may even discourage other Christians who are not experiencing instant answers to prayer. What I saw in her story was hope and perseverance through adversity and not a lack of faith in God's miracle-working power.

Adhering to God's Timetable

A motto taped to my office filing cabinet reads, "Wait on the Lord; be of good courage, and He shall strengthen thine heart: wait, I say, on the Lord" (Psalm 27:14).

If you are believing God for your miracle and waiting for its manifestation, be encouraged. I can hold out hope to you that God has heard your prayer, He has the answer on the way, but it will come in His own time, which may not be in sync with yours. When God allows us to wait He is teaching us patience so the devil can't sabotage our destiny through our lack of perseverance.

God may be testing me to strengthen my faith, because we cannot reach our destination in Christ without adequate preparation. When we want to accomplish great exploits for

Jesus, we sometimes have to undergo a pruning process, an elimination and concentration exercise from which we emerge more mature. When God prunes out everything that is a deterrent to our spiritual growth, we are then ready for Him to take us to higher heights and deeper depths.

Two years ago when I arranged for early retirement, I knew that God had put it in my heart to write a book to encourage others as they walk through life's many adversities. Since God had confirmed His Word to me through several believers, I expected that everything should go off without a hitch, but this has not been the case.

Having worn those cumbersome braces faithfully for almost two years, I realized that I still suffered repeated radiating pain in my arms and wrists, and the braces had not helped. My condition had worsened, and when I had barely begun my manuscript, I realized the keyboard was not my friend. After a few minutes of typing, I would experience excruciating pain in my wrists and arms. Also extending my arms to drive the car aggravated my wrists and brought pain.

But Lord, how can I get this book on paper if I cannot type? I need strength in my wrists to pound a computer keyboard. And isn't that part of the reason I was so sure that You were leading me to retire? Furthermore, this condition has resulted from repetitive work on computers in a federal government office, and since I'm no longer there, how can I get them to take responsibility for it? I was full of questions, but I knew I had to persevere through this also.

I would be dishonest if I did not admit that I felt a tinge of discouragement, but then the Lord opened my eyes. "Lord, I must be in Your waiting room again," I surmised. "My timing is now, but I must of necessity, wait for Yours." So I went back to a tried and tested Scripture verse and started to sing. "They that wait upon the Lord shall renew their strength...." I have no choice but to wait; however, I can choose how I wait. Will I rest in the Lord, or will I wrestle and complain before Him? This one had the potential of being a real challenge, but my God will get the glory out of it yet, and He will heal me completely in His time, I mused.

Still sometimes I vacillated back and forth, "Is this the Lord's timing or the devil's attempt to discourage and hinder me?" Considering the message of this book an urgent and much-needed one, I wanted to get it out post haste. Furthermore, I had registered for a top-notch Christian Writers Conference, a benefit of which was a coupon that entitled me to a consultation with a seasoned editor or agent. I viewed this as an opportunity to have my manuscript critiqued by a professional. Had I chosen to meditate on my inability to work on the manuscript and my other physical limitations, depression would have been my constant companion.

I reflected on previous conversations with several unbelievers who had asked me what I intended to do after retirement. I had mentioned my plan to write a book on how to have Joy in Adversity. Now as they asked me about my progress on the book, I knew that my attitude and demeanor about the carpal tunnel syndrome and tendonitis would make a great testimony on how to endure hardship. Holding up one wrist in a brace, I'd exclaim, "I guess I have to practice being joyful in adversity a little longer before the Lord allows me to complete the book." Sometimes we have to negotiate our way around detours when we set out to do God's work. Like the Apostle Paul, I felt as if the Lord had given me a task and Satan had hindered me.

Waiting In Scripture

There are many examples in Scripture of God's faithful servants being put into a holding pattern and allowed to wait for His perfect timing. Did not Abraham, a friend of God, wait patiently for many years before he finally held the son God had promised him?

According to Hebrews 6:13-15, through faith and
patience, Abraham inherited the promises, but what of you
and me? "For you have need of endurance, so that after you
have done the will of God, you may receive the promise"
(Hebrews 10:36, NKJV). This verse is in the context of faithfulness in times of suffering and tribulation. You may ask,
"But, Lord, how long after I have done Your will can I expect
to see Your promise fulfilled?" My Bible prescribes no
timetable, and that is what I believe true faith is all about—
we wait in hope for what we cannot see.

Joseph, whom God had shown through a dream that he
would become a powerful ruler some day, had to wait some
seventeen years. Meanwhile, his dream had turned into a
nightmare when he was tossed into the pit by his brothers
and then sold into slavery in Egypt. Psalm 105 recounts
Israel's history and encapsulates it in poetic form in the context of God's faithfulness. Joseph's brothers thought they
were selling him and disposing of a dreamer, but God was
sending him and supplying a deliverer! The word of the
Lord tried Joseph, and he remained faithful. What of his
dream? What of God's promise? When Joseph was thrown
into prison unjustly, "The Lord was with him; and whatever
he did, the Lord made it prosper" (Genesis 39:23, NKJV).

The prophet Daniel, who was beloved of God and used
mightily in His kingdom, knew a lot about waiting on the
Lord. In one instance when Daniel prayed, the Lord dis-
patched the answer but it took twenty-one days to get
through. Why? The Prince of Persia, or the devil interfered
and waged battle in an attempt to thwart God's plan. What
if Daniel had given up on God because he didn't want to
wait any longer?

Even Jesus waited for the Father's perfect timing. How
often we read the phrase in the Gospels, "His hour was not
yet come." Jesus steadfastly refused to do anything apart
from God's foreordained plan.

Chastisement, God's Correcting Tool

Chasten and chastise are words not in common usage today; however, they are used in some versions of Scripture to describe the way God administers discipline to His children. Some years ago, I became convinced that one function of the Holy Spirit is that of Divine Disciplinarian (John 16:8). While there are a number of Scriptures that bear this out, I believe the most extensive text is Hebrews 12. After chapter eleven praises a number of Old Testament heroes of the faith for their ability to persevere and overcome, chapter twelve begins by referring to them as a "cloud of witnesses."

If you have read their stories, you know about some of the severe trials they endured while waiting for God's deliverance. Their examples encourage us to strip off anything that hinders our ability to "run with endurance the race that is set before us." Though the race of faith is sometimes quite difficult, we win when we keep our eyes fixed on Jesus, Who is our supreme example and model of endurance. Through His death, resurrection, and ascension to Heaven, Jesus made it possible for us to persevere and to win our race through this world.

When we compare our sufferings to the extreme torture that the sinless Son of God endured for our sins, these earthly trials seem pretty trivial. We need not become discouraged and faint in our minds, or give up without a fight. This is spiritual warfare, and the enemy of our souls wants us to lose our focus and succumb to defeat. The writer of Hebrews encourages us, like Jesus, to look beyond the immediate suffering or persecution to the joys of Heaven that will be ours.

Earthly fathers discipline their children in order to train them. Why does God discipline us? I believe we can glean at least three reasons from Hebrews 12. First, the Lord disciplines us because He loves us (Verse 6). Second, He disciplines because we are His true sons and daughters with an inheritance in Him, and not illegitimate children (Verses 7, 8). Third, He disciplines us because He wants us to partake of His holiness. The reward of discipline is that when we are trained by it we profit by producing the fruit of peace and righteousness that pleases God.

"You should know in your heart that as a man chastens his son, so the Lord your God chastens you. Therefore you shall keep the commandments of the Lord your God, to walk in His ways and to fear Him" (Deuteronomy 8:5, 6, NKJV).

"My Son, do not despise the chastening of the Lord, nor detest His correction; for whom the Lord loves He corrects, just as a father the son in whom he delights" (Proverbs 3:11, 12, NKJV).

When God disciplines us, by whatever means, He always does it for our good. I once heard someone say in reference to God's correction that we should be immediately responsive and pleasantly obliging. Just as we would not leave a two-year-old without correction, God does not leave us to our own devices. His Word is the standard for life, and when we disobey it, there are consequences. "Harsh discipline is for him who forsakes the way, and he who hates correction will die" (Proverbs 15:10, NKJV).

The Psalmist says he was chastened upon his bed with sickness, and that before he was afflicted, he went astray. While I don't view every illness as God's way to discipline the one who is suffering, I believe that sickness comes from sin in the world because of Adam's fall. It is comforting to know that no matter why we are hurting God says, "I will never leave thee, nor forsake thee" (Hebrews 13:5b). No matter how strong the chastening, how hot the furnace, or how deep the water, God is with us by the Holy Spirit.

The Lord, My Fortress in Adversity

It was almost midnight on Memorial Day, and in defiance of the doctor's orders not to type, I was "stealing" a few moments to make some notes for this book. Rivers had just questioned what I was doing, and I assured him I would not work very long. But I was on a roll, and all writers know that you had best capture the words when the inspiration is flowing. Shortly after the clock struck twelve, I reluctantly turned off the computer and started to open my Bible for guidance. It seemed the Lord was saying, "Read Psalm 31." I have read that psalm many times, but its content did not immediately register. So I said out loud, "Lord, I don't have the foggiest what that is about."

When I opened my Nelson Study Bible, I was surprised to see the psalm was titled, "The Lord a Fortress in Adversity." It begins, "In You, O Lord, I put my trust; let me never be ashamed; deliver me in Your righteousness. Bow down Your ear to me, deliver me speedily; be my rock of refuge, a fortress of defense to save me. For You are my rock and my fortress; therefore, for Your name's sake, lead me and guide me" (Psalm 31:1-3, NKJV). I also read, "My times are in Your hand," and "Be of good courage, and He shall strengthen your heart, all you who hope in the Lord" (Verses 15a, 24).

When I read Verse 7b, "You have known my soul in adversities," my immediate response was, "Thank you, Father, I will persevere."

"But, Lord, how long must I wait?" That question has many answers, but they may all be summed up by saying, "Father knows best." He does not delight in depriving us of good things—rather He withholds them until He knows the time is perfect. Be encouraged in His love as He cultivates patience in you. Adversity breeds character while uninterrupted success breeds pride. Those who have not experienced the trials of this life have difficulty relating to those who are currently walking through them. The most unempathetic Christians I know are those who spout faith-filled words that have never been tested in their own lives.

Whether you are a pastor, a layperson, or are involved in

some other facet of ministry, you will need the gift of encouragement. When others become frustrated and impatient while waiting for the Lord to answer their prayers, you can apply a little spiritual salve to their pain. Your ability to minister effectively will largely depend on your ability to deal with people's hurts, their mixed-up lives and propensity toward falling into sin. You will face situations you never thought possible and deal with persons who fall into the same sin repeatedly; some of them may be pastors. Don't be shocked; be ready!

We need to teach people how to avoid discouragement that the devil can use to breed defeat. David, after observing the pride of the wicked, describes them this way, "He hath said in his heart, I shall not be moved: for I shall never be in adversity" (Psalm 10:6).

We are what we are in adversity! The world and the church will quickly see what we are when we are called upon to persevere, to endure under pressure.

Chapter 14: Perseverance, Enduring Under Pressure

Scriptures: Psalm 40:1, 2, 3, Romans 5:3,4; 8:17b, 18, 25, 35, Hebrews 6:13-15; 10:36, Deuteronomy 8:5, 6, Proverbs 3:11, 12; 15:10, Psalm 10:6.

1. What does it mean to have hope and patience in suffering while waiting on the Lord in prayer?
2. How is it possible to be in the furnace without feeling the heat?
3. What does the Scripture teach about the ability to rejoice during times of tribulation?
4. What is the difference in how God deals with new Christians and mature Christians in answering their prayers?
5. How has God used correction in your life?

CHAPTER 15

PRACTICAL RESPONSES TO ADVERSITY

A few years ago when the subject of adversity loomed heavily on my mind, I began to think of what advantages it might offer. Since we Christians must walk through adversity, surely we could glean some good from it. If God could use it in my life to help me grow up spiritually, then it was actually my friend. I began to pen these words that burned in my heart.

Adversity Can Be Your Friend

Adversity can be your friend,
If on the Lord your soul depends.
When around you the battle is raging wild,
Just remember you are His beloved child.

Turn to Jesus, for in Him is perfect peace.
You'll soon experience a sweet release.
As in your heart He says, "Peace be still,"
And you calmly submit to His sovereign will.

Yes, fear not, fret not, faint not, my friend.
On the strength of God's Word you can surely depend.
The battle is not yours, for He's on your side,
If in His loving arms you will safely abide.

You'll be sheltered during storms, hurt and strife,
When you let the God of all comfort rule your life.

"Stand still and see My salvation," Father says to thee.
"The Lord will fight for you, and you shall hold your peace."

So fear not, fret not, faint not, my friend.
On the strength of God's Word you can surely depend.

July 1987

When Formulas Seem To Fail

We've looked at Biblical examples of perseverance in adversity, but how about us? Have you tried everything you know and your mountain seems to get even higher? Has your faith been tried, stretched, tested, and re-tested? Will your faith stay firm in the furnace or in the deep waters? Would you buckle under persecution? Do your prayers seem to fall to the floor like lead balloons? Do you heap condemnation on others when they don't get the victory over a habit or addiction you may have struggled with for a long time?

Rather than searching the Scriptures for yourself, do you run from one person to another seeking a word of knowledge? We all need the body of Christ, as Moses needed Aaron and Hur to hold up his arms during a fierce battle. However, for a Christian this should not be a substitute for spending time with the Lord in Scripture reading and prayer. Waiting on the Lord is sometimes neglected because we want to rush into His presence out of breath and get a quick blessing.

When I was an instructor at a school of ministry, it was not uncommon for a student to come for prayer or counseling. One day a student asked me, "Do you have a word from the Lord for me?" She anxiously searched my face for some profound spiritual utterance.

Not wanting to appear unspiritual, I could have done

what I had suspected some others were guilty of—tell the person what you know they want to hear. Instead, I was painfully and shockingly honest when I laughed and said, "No, I don't have a word from the Lord for you, but I can make something up if you like."

After teaching seven hours on "Renewing the Mind Through Meditating on Scripture," I dedicated the eighth hour in the school of ministry to "Testing the Prophetic Word." Some people look outside the written Word of God for some favorable word that agrees with what they want to do. While I know that God still speaks to and through His people, we know that every "word from the Lord" does not emanate from the Throne Room. If it doesn't agree with the written Word of God, beware because false prophets proliferate this land!

There are a lot of spoiled Christians in our churches who expect to receive good from God's hand, but won't accept whatever discipline He metes out. Because we have led people to believe that nothing adverse can happen to Christians, it is easy to imagine ourselves sailing through life on a bed of roses. Psalm 50:16-17 (TLB) says: "But God says to evil men, 'Recite My laws no longer, and stop claiming My promises. For you have refused My discipline, disregarding My laws.'" What we mistake as an attack of the enemy may sometimes be the correcting hand of the Lord.

Like spiritual brats, some of us are shouting, "I'm standing on the Word, and God has to..." When our one-two-three formulas fail, we realize we don't have God figured out, and sometimes we won't understand His ways.

Real faith demands that we trust God even when we don't comprehend what He is doing or why we are in a holding pattern. When we have confessed every Scripture we can find on the subject, have prayed and had others pray, have cast our care on the Lord, and the problem is not resolved, we may be in God's waiting room. We have no option but to be there, but we can choose not to struggle or strain, but to rest in the knowledge that God has a purpose, a plan, and a process that we must go through. Mature faith rests on God's promise to deliver us by His methods and in His time.

We don't enjoy walking through trials and tough times, and it is difficult to wait upon the Lord. While we must be instant in prayer, the answers belong to God. Waiting involves a sacrifice to the flesh, and we cannot reduce God to a formula!

Don't Be Offended By Trials

When one trial after another comes into your life, it is easy to succumb to Satan's temptation to lose hope. Sometimes your trials may seem to get progressively worse, and when you pray you see no improvement in your condition. Hold on! Your faith is being tested, and you must not despair. Do not be offended because you don't understand why God is allowing these trials.

Our own personal walk through adversity has been a lengthy one. Every time we thought nothing more could possibly happen, it seems as if some new thing reared its head. However, we learned to dig around in the trial and look for the blessing. When things were at their worst, we absolutely knew that we were blessed in our mourning because Jesus said so. We might as well accept the fact that as long as we live in a fallen world, we will be tempted, tried, tested and proven. We cannot avoid having trials, but by His help and grace, we can respond to them in faith and reliance on the power of Jesus to bring us through.

Jesus told a parable in Matthew 13:1-23 about a farmer who sowed seeds into various types of soil. While he used the same seeds, the outcome was different because of the soil into which it fell. The seed in the good soil produced fruit in abundance while that on the stony ground produced immediate fruit that did not last. Jesus explained the parable's meaning as it concerns the Word of God. The stony ground represents those who receive the Gospel joyfully but have no root, and where there is no root there can be no fruit. So they continue in the faith until tribulation or persecution comes. The seeds that fell among thorns represent those who allow worldly cares and the deceitfulness of riches to choke the Word out of their hearts. Weak or carnal Christians are not prepared to withstand severe trials, and are tempted to turn back to the old life of sin.

Fear Not! Fret Not! Faint Not!

Some years ago when we were walking through some very deep waters, I thought I was really praying, when God spoke to my heart, "What are you doing?"

Very pleased with myself, I responded, "Lord, I'm praying."

The answer came thundering back to me, "No, you are not praying; you are complaining!" Ouch! Right between the eyes.

The Psalmist said, "I complained and my spirit was overwhelmed" (Psalm 77:3). This is precisely what happens when we whine to God about every slight inconvenience and fail to thank Him for His many blessings. Our problems begin to overwhelm us, desperation sets in, and we live on the verge of despair and defeat. Thinking life has dealt us an unfair hand, we become chronic complainers and grumblers. We become bitter and ungrateful, but we are warned in Scripture not to allow bitterness to take root, and we are not to become jealous of those who seem to have an easy life. We moan, "Life simply is not fair!" But Jesus never said it would be.

When Jesus told the disciples that He was facing the cross, Peter began to say this would not happen to Him. If Peter, who walked with Jesus for three years could miss Him, is it not possible for us to do the same? Peter's rebuke to

Jesus concerning the cross was likely well intentioned although misguided. He was speaking out of the flesh, so his attempt to protect Jesus from the cross was, in essence, an attempt to thwart God's plan. Like us, Peter, had no idea what he was talking about!

Are you spitting out great spiritual platitudes, giving pat answers or preaching at people who are walking through adversity? It's a lot easier to condemn than to walk through a trial with someone. I believe God is well pleased when we drop the rapid-fire answers, and place our arms around a brother or sister and stand with them during difficult times.

After the Apostle Paul discusses some of the unspeakable persecution he suffered, he encourages young Timothy to stand firmly for the faith. While still instructing Timothy, Paul names some of his detractors and says that at first, "no man stood with me, but all men forsook me...the Lord stood with me, and strengthened me." Paul remains focused on what God has called him to do and ends the book by affirming his faith that, "The Lord shall deliver me from every evil work, and will preserve me unto His heavenly kingdom" (II Timothy 4:17, 18). I pray that our faith will be steadfast despite how our friends respond to our trials.

The Lord placed three phrases on my heart, and I began to meditate on them as our family walked through difficult times—fear not, fret not, faint not. When we are faced with adversity, we are tempted to do all three. If we allow fear to consume us, we will be tempted to fret and complain or to faint and give up, which can render us ineffective in ministry.

While some fear is healthy, other types can fill us with inertia and virtually cripple us as Christians. If we fear failure or what others might think, we may be unwilling to pay the price of success. When faced with such fear we become our own worst enemy, but we can pray, "Lord set me free from myself, for I am the only one who can bind me."

When we fear the opinions of others, we can quote Hebrews 13:6b, "The Lord is my Helper, and I will not fear what man shall do unto me." Another Scripture I have found helpful is II Timothy 1:7, "But God hath not given us a spirit of fear, but of power, of love, and of a sound mind."

Then there is the tendency to fret when faced with suffering or trials. The Scripture tells us not to fret. In the Amplified Bible, Philippians 4:6-7 says, "Do not fret or have any anxiety about anything, but in every circumstance and in everything by prayer and petition (definite requests) with thanksgiving continue to make your wants known to God." Here's the good part, Verse 7. "And God's peace (be yours, that tranquil state of a soul assured of its salvation through Christ, and so fearing nothing from God and content with its earthly lot of whatever sort that is, that peace) which transcends all understanding, shall garrison and mount guard over your hearts and minds in Christ Jesus." The essence of this Scripture is, don't worry or fret; but pray, give thanks, and walk in peace.

According to Isaiah 26:30, the Lord will keep us in perfect peace when our minds are fixed on Him. This leaves us with an option if we wish to experience His perfect peace— we must look to Him, no matter what the circumstances.

Jesus commanded—not suggested—in Matthew 6:25-34, that we not worry about our life. Since He cares for the birds of the air and the lilies of the field, we know that He cares even more for us because we are made in His image; we were created for His pleasure. We are to seek His kingdom first and trust Him to supply our physical needs. While He knows what we need before we ask Him, we are still commanded to ask, seek and knock in prayer.

Another human tendency when facing difficult circumstances is to faint, but the Lord reminded me of the many times when I had fainted physically and lost consciousness.

My eyes rolled back, and I lost all awareness of what was happening around me. As far as I was concerned I had totally lost control. What happens if we lose control? We fall—hard! When I fell someone had to take charge and pick me up, and I sometimes ended up with a lump on my forehead. Isn't this true of the Christian life? When we lose our focus or take our eyes off Jesus, we lose control and faint spiritually. But we don't have to faint!

The writer of Hebrews says, faint not! "For consider Him [Jesus] that endured such contradiction of sinners against Himself, lest ye be wearied and faint in your minds. Ye have not yet resisted unto blood, striving against sin. And ye have forgotten the exhortation which speaketh unto you as unto children, My son, despise not thou the chastening of the Lord, nor faint when thou are rebuked of Him" (Hebrews 12:3-5).

When facing a trial, all we want is out, and now! I found it hard to empathize with a friend who was red-faced and crying because her baby had a cold, since my husband was hospitalized and quite ill at the time. She had never had any serious health problems, so the child's cold was a big deal. If we haven't learned to trust God in small matters, when serious adversity comes, we buckle and fold up.

Sometimes when the Lord is dealing with us, we mistake it for the devil's interference. Therefore, I believe our first response to adversity should be prayer—seeking the Lord to determine whether our Father wants to teach us something. God graciously demonstrates His love, confirms He is our Father, and produces righteousness in us. When we understand it to be the Lord's rebuke or His correction, we can quit our whining and thank Him that He loves us enough to correct us.

Was I ever tempted by the big three—fearing, fretting, or fainting? You bet! When horrific adversities came into our lives, I found the grace to endure joyfully by reading and meditating on Scriptures. When Rivers and I were both suffering from a long-term physical problem—the second time in less than ten years—I drew great strength from recalling how God had healed us and supplied every need in the past. We had become accustomed to waiting on one another, but what do you do if you are both ill? We felt we had again tasted old age while we were still young.

Since I know that within my own strength I would fear, fret and faint, I find great comfort also in Isaiah 40:28-31. "Hast thou not known? Hast thou not heard, that the everlasting God, the Lord, the Creator of the ends of the earth, fainteth not, neither is weary? There is no searching His understanding. He giveth power to the faint; and to them that have no might He increaseth strength. Even the youths shall faint and be weary, and the young men shall utterly fall: But they that wait upon the Lord shall renew their strength; they shall mount up with wings as eagles; they shall run, and not be weary; and they shall walk and not faint."

At the First Sign of Adversity

"When we face adversity, how shall we behave?" I asked a class of future ministers several times. Soon they were with me, and in unison, they shouted: Fear not! Fret not! Faint not! What can I do when the furnace starts heating up or the waters are about to flow over me? Several practical responses that have helped me are: sing, pray and look to Jesus, hold fast in faith, and meditate on Scriptures. Jesus should be our first resort, not our last resort!

I pray alone, but it helps to pray with Rivers or a friend. When I am not constant in prayer, I buckle in despair. When I hold fast to God's remedies in His Word, I am reminded that suffering brings perseverance, and perseverance brings hope. I can even count it all joy when I remember that patience results from having my faith tried.

Not Wrestling, But Resting

Sometimes it is amazing what praising can do. When I sing songs of praise to my wonderful Lord, I stop wrestling with my problems and begin resting on His promises. I cast my care on Him, and when I'm tempted to take it back, I remind myself that God is carrying it now.

Our tendency is to dwell on our problems, to elicit pity from our friends, and sometimes to enjoy the attention it gets us. Have you ever ministered to anyone who did not want the Lord to deliver them from their situation because it got them so much attention? It is a sacrifice to the flesh to give up control of our problems and to offer praise to God.

We must never allow the devil to intimidate us by his lies. We want to escape our pain so much that we sometimes take God's promises and try to fit them into our own carefully crafted plans. When we run ahead of God, little wonder we don't see God's promises fulfilled in our lives. God does not engage in politics, and we cannot make bargains with Him in order to get what we want. We must throw ourselves on His mercy. It's not, "Lord, give me what I deserve." If He did, we could not stand it.

I believe Romans 12:1,2 provides a five-step response to adversity when it says we are to present ourselves to God as living sacrifices and not be sucked into the world's customs.

- Throw yourself on God's mercy.
- Present your body sacrificially to Him.
- Renew your mind and let the Word transform it.
- Avoid conformance with the world.
- Prove God's will for your life.

Firmly Rooted Faith

When our faith is firmly planted in the finished works of Jesus Christ, we can pray and believe God in every situation. Real faith faces the adversity head on without becoming discouraged. One day when I was reflecting on how to have tenacious faith, the Lord gave me an acrostic about the meaning of faith.

F – Finding
A – Answers
I – In
T – The
H – Heavenlies

Are you finding answers in the heavenlies, or do you choose to respond to adversity by blaming God or some person? I believe God honors the faith of those who look for His hand in every situation. The psalmist said, "Unless thy law had been my delight, I should then have perished in mine affliction" (Psalm 119:92). We must be steadfast in our faith and hope in Jesus when we see no way to overcome the trial. "And let us not be weary in well doing, for in due season, we shall reap if we faint not" (Galatians 6:9). Don't grow weary or get tired of living a Godly life, even when it appears that unrighteous people around you are more prosperous and healthy. Hold on, knowing that help is on the way because God has promised that He will neither leave us nor forsake us. Don't lose heart; don't lose faith; don't give up. Overcome adversity or be overcome by adversity!

The battle is the Lord's, no matter what you may be facing. While this does not excuse us from taking responsibility for doing what we can to alleviate a problem, ultimately we must be firmly established in our faith. As God said to the Israelites, "The Lord shall fight for you, and ye shall hold your peace." Do you and I have the faith to believe that? We may need to check our faith level. When all the veneer is stripped off and all the facade is peeled back, the real person comes through. What the world sees in our times of adversity is what we really are, and with the proper response we can teach others.

I have a friend who prayed for her husband over twenty years before he saw the light and allowed God to change his life. She remained steadfast and continued to pray and rejoice in the Lord, and it was well worth the effort.

Let's not become a softie—always expecting God to keep trials, persecution or affliction out of our lives. Someone has aptly said we need to seek God's face more than seeking God's hand. What if your husband remains unfaithful, your children continue to rebel, or your physical body is not healed yet, even though you are praying fervently? Will you be able to rejoice in tribulation, knowing it produces patience?

I Will Rejoice!

When Paul and Silas preached at Philippi, a slave girl with a spirit of divination followed them around saying, "These men are the servants of the Most High God, who proclaim to us the way of salvation" (Acts 16:17). What she said was true, but she was motivated by an evil spirit, so Paul rebuked the devil and cast him out. Angry because their hope for further profit had vanished, her owners started a riot. Paul and Silas were severely beaten and imprisoned without legal consideration under Roman law.

Some of us may have been tempted to ask God whether we had really heard Him correctly when we went to Philippi, especially since these trumped-up charges had resulted in such unspeakable cruelty. My first inclination would probably have been to beg God to get me out of that prison—fast. Instead of falling into self-pity, at midnight they gave a Gospel concert to all the prisoners. Surely the chains must have been bruising their ankles. These men were following God's leading and look where it took them. If ever anyone had a reason to complain, they did. But what did they do?

They rejoiced and sang praises to God because they considered it an honor to be persecuted for righteousness sake.

While the prisoners listened to their wounded cellmates, the Lord sent an earthquake to shake the foundations of the prison, to loose their chains, and to swing the prison door open. What the devil meant for evil, God turned around for good, as this whole episode resulted in souls being saved. What adversaries could withstand the power of God when He chose to move on behalf of Paul and Silas?

When Peter was imprisoned for preaching the Gospel, the church had a prayer meeting. Was Peter complaining and groaning about his predicament? The Bible says he slept—in fact, the angel had to awaken him to escort him out of the jail supernaturally.

Paul, Silas, Peter, John and others were living out the words of Jesus in Matthew 5:10-12 (NKJV): "Blessed are those who are persecuted for righteousness' sake, for theirs is the kingdom of Heaven. Blessed are you when they revile and persecute you, and say all kinds of evil against you falsely for My sake. Rejoice and be exceedingly glad, for great is your reward in Heaven, for so they persecuted the prophets who were before you." When they obeyed God, they incurred the wrath of man.

Paul would later write in Romans 12:12 that we are to be "joyful in hope, patient in tribulation, continuing steadfastly in prayer." He closes out the chapter by an exhortation to leave vengeance to God and to overcome evil with good.

How do you and I know when we respond to adversity in faith whose life may be enriched and encouraged, or whose soul will be saved? If you have been in the thick of adversity, are you to assume you have somehow missed God? Are you outside of His will and that's why you're suffering? Sometimes yes, sometimes no. When we don't see evidence of answered prayer, will we still believe God? We can't always control what touches our lives, but we can control our response.

In the Prophet Habakkuk's day the wicked Chaldeans were exploiting and plundering the Israelites. How could God possibly allow this? After he poured out his complaint, he prayed and affirmed his faith in God's sovereignty. "Although the fig tree shall not blossom, neither shall fruit be in the vines; the labour of the olive shall fail, and the fields shall yield no meat; the flock shall be cut off from the fold, and there shall be no herd in the stalls; Yet will I rejoice in the Lord, I will joy in the God of my salvation. The Lord God is my strength, and He will make my feet like hinds' feet, and He will make me to walk upon mine high places" (Habakkuk 3:17-19a). During a period when Rivers and I were both ill, I wrote in my Bible next to this Scripture, "Trust God, no matter what comes!"

Lord, You expect me to rejoice when my friends are irritating me, my children are acting up, the grocery money is low and my energy level is even lower, when there's no money in the bank, my husband is on the verge of losing his job, and my in-laws have become outlaws? Real prayer is waiting on God when in the natural we see nothing happening. It's trusting His discretion, His sovereignty, and His all-knowing love.

Jeremiah was dismayed as he watched Judah's captivity because of disobedience and Jerusalem's fall to its enemies. After pouring out his complaints, he is still able to affirm God's goodness and the hope we have in Him. "This I recall to my mind, therefore have I hope. It is of the Lord's mercies that we are not consumed, because His compassions fail not. They are new every morning; great is Thy faithfulness. The Lord is my portion, saith my soul; therefore will I hope in Him. The Lord is good unto them that wait for Him, to the soul that seeketh Him. It is good that a man should both hope and quietly wait for the salvation of the Lord" (Lamentations 3:21-26).

After King David's clandestine affair with Bathsheba, God sent Prophet Nathan with a message that exposed his sin. While God spared David's life, he made it clear that the child born of the illicit union would die. Heartbroken, David fasted and prayed, begging God for mercy; however, when the child died David responded in a most unusual way—he rose up and worshiped God. We too can worship God when we don't understand His decisions—let's stop trying to get our way and start dying to God's will.

David put it well in Psalm 50:15. "And call upon Me in the day of trouble; I will deliver thee, and thou shalt glorify Me." We can glorify the Lord while still in the furnace, or while we are yet walking through the deep waters. Sometimes God has to allow us to be in the furnace, to walk through the rivers or to be in some type of adversity in order to rid us of our independence and teach us to trust Him. Have you walked through the valley of the shadow of death? You are His beloved child, and He has walked through it with you.

Singer Andre Crouch, sings that trials are sent to make us strong; if we never had a problem we would never know that God could solve them. As we persevere through a trial we learn patience, which is courageous gallantry in the face of hardship. When you overcome one trial you become stronger for a more difficult one. If you will rehearse God's power to deliver you from past adversities, you will find your faith growing to trust God in the current situation.

Jesus told a story about two men who built houses—one built on a rock and the other on the sand. When the storms came the one built on sand was swept away while the house on the rock stood firmly. While both men faced storms and severe winds, only one was able to remain standing because of the solid foundation on which he built. That foundation is Jesus Christ, and a life built on anyone else will not withstand the adversities to which we are heir.

When the disciples were caught in a severe storm in a boat out on the lake and their lives were in jeopardy, they cried out for Jesus to save them. Although they could not see Jesus, He was there all the time. Will you believe that Jesus is with you in the storms of life even when it feels as if your boat is about to capsize?

When you are suffering affliction, being persecuted, or have been attacked by the enemy of your soul, acknowledge your position in Christ, appropriate God's promises in the Word, and accept God's provisions for your deliverance. But remember, when the most severe adversity threatens to destroy your life, fear not, fret not, faint not, because we are what we are in adversity!

Fear does not emanate from God; fretting represents inability to wait on God; and fainting is total loss of control.

First impressions may be fallacious.
Even disappointments can be used by God.
Adversity can turn out for my good.
Resist temptation in the name of Jesus.

Follow the leading of the Holy Spirit.
Rely on the promises of the Word.
Every adversity is an opportunity to trust God.
Take time to pray and wait on the Lord.

Fears are often unfounded.
Adversity can be a powerful teacher.
In everything give thanks.
Never allow adversity to cripple you.
Turn to the Word of God for instructions.

Application Questions:
Practical Responses to Adversity

Scriptures: Matthew 13:1-23, Hebrews 13:6b, II Timothy 1:7, Isaiah 26:30, Proverbs 24:10, Isaiah 40:28-31, Romans 12:1,2,12, Habakuk 3:17-19a, Lamentations 3:21-26.

1. In what ways can adversity turn out to be a friend?
2. Why do some people become offended by life's trials?
3. What should I do at the first sign of adversity?
4. How can I avoid, fearing, fretting, and fainting, but rest in the Lord when everything seems to be falling apart?
5. How is it possible to rejoice during trials when I don't feel like it?

MINISTRY IN FLORIDA

Angie teaching in Tabernacle at
Christian Retreat

Kingdom Living Institute - Gospel Crusade President and Founder,
Dr. Gerald Derstine and his wife Beulah, in center,
teaching staff (seated) with students

CHAPTER 16

WHEN YOU WALK THROUGH VICTORIOUSLY

It's when you walk through, not if you walk through because we cannot always get around a situation, but must walk through it. However, we can find great comfort in the words of the prophet Isaiah. "But now thus saith the Lord that created thee, O Jacob, and He that formed thee, O Israel, fear not: For I have redeemed thee, I have called thee by thy name; thou art Mine. When thou passest through the waters, I will be with thee; and through the rivers, they shall not overflow thee: when thou walkest through the fire, thou shalt not be burned; neither shall the flame kindle upon thee. For I am the Lord thy God, the Holy One of Israel, thy Saviour" (Isaiah 43:1-3a).

God said to His chosen people, when you walk through the waters or the fire, not if you walk through. If they had to walk through, why do we think we will walk around? Why do we assume we won't have to deal with any difficulties while we are still in the world?

Remembering Small Miracles

While it may sound negative to suggest that people prepare for trials, we Christians have them just like our unbelieving neighbors. However, the way we deal with persecution, suffering, affliction, adversities, and trials is entirely different. One thing that has helped me immensely is remembering how God has worked miracles in our lives before.

When Barth was in junior high, during a practice session a student accidentally poked him in the eye with a music stand. Patrick Bopp, his teacher at Trinity Christian School, held a prayer meeting with the students for Barth's healing.

When Dr. McDonald put the yellow drops into Barth's eye, I could see the crescent-shaped indentation the music stand had left. I could also see the concern on the doctor's face as he completed his treatment and applied a patch. We left with a prescription for some drops and an appointment to return. However, the Lord healed Barth's eye, and we returned to testify to the doctor about what the Lord had done. As a reminder, I kept the unfilled prescription for many years.

Barth with eye patch before God healed him

On another occasion, Barth's usual asthma flare-up was in full force. I called my friend, Sue Miller, to come and pray with me. While Barth rested on the sofa, Sue and I sat by the fireplace and prayed and quoted the Word. After a couple of hours, Barth began to feel better, the vomiting and coughing stopped, and he could breathe well. Unlike all those trips to the emergency room when they administered two injections and waited for them to work, this time Barth had no residual cough and he returned to school the next day.

Metro Miracles

Whenever I shared "Metro Miracles" in our congregation I received positive feedback. For several years when I worked in Washington, I boarded the Metro rail in Maryland and rode into town. If you have never boarded a packed subway train in a big city during rush hours, you probably cannot fathom what it is like. When people are going to or from work they are often in a hurry and sometimes impatient and rude. This never seems more evident than when they wait along the tracks for the train. Most people forge ahead with little consideration others, and that is why I call a simple act of kindness like giving me a seat a miracle.

Having left home around six-thirty in the morning, only the Lord knew how I felt by five o'clock in the afternoon following a stressful day at work. My back and legs hurt so much that sitting was difficult, and standing while holding my belongings was out of the question. To make matters worse, the train moves very fast, sometimes jerks, and stops suddenly. However, often there were not enough seats to accommodate the masses. I would stand by the track and pray for a seat when I saw the train approaching, knowing full well that unless God intervened I would have to stand. The Lord answered my prayers so many times, and I record-ed some twenty incidences in my journal.

You need to know that I did not look sick or crippled, and nothing from my physical appearance suggested that I needed a seat more than anyone else. This is how I know for sure that God was working, because I watched men of all ages sit while women stood. I watched young people occu-py seats reserved for senior citizens while allowing older people to stand. Rarely did I see anyone get up and offer a seat to someone; however, people of all ages, male and female, and different races yielded their seats to me. When they did I would thank them for their kindness and end with "God bless you." Then I would spend time praying silently for them. There is no logical explanation except that God gave me favor.

There were also instances when people were packed in the train so tightly that they were actually pressed together body to body. One vacant seat remained, and people would stand around it, but no one would sit on it. Assuming God had reserved that seat for me, I would excuse myself and press my way through the crowd to reach the seat. Knowing that God cares about the little things, I would thank Him profusely for my Metro miracle each time.

One particularly interesting incident included a middle-aged man who gave me his seat. Six trains had gone past toward Virginia, but the train to Maryland was late and hundreds of people were complaining while they waited impatiently. I was praying, but in my head I was thinking, "No way!" Several persons pushed their way in and I barely made it through the door. Immediately, a man leaped from his seat on the front row and asked if I wanted to sit. I thanked him and sat. The lady on the seat beside me was laughing so hard, and although I did not know her, I finally asked, "What is so funny?"

She replied, "You wouldn't believe how that man pushed everyone out of the way to get that seat. As soon as you came in, he jumped up and gave it to you."

I was not surprised, so I said, "I was praying for a seat. The Lord knows that I would never push anyone out of the way, so He sent 'Pushy Sam' ahead to do it for me." After we both enjoyed a good laugh and I told her about my physical condition, I added, "He probably doesn't know the Lord told him to get up and give me that seat."

On another occasion when someone rose very quickly so I could have a seat, a lady asked, "Why did they give you a seat? I have been riding this train for six years, and no one ever gives me a seat. Even when I was on crutches I sometimes had to stand."

Value of Adversity

When we come out on the other side of the trial we can see the value of adversity, which is difficult to do while enduring a trial. However, even while you're in the midst of the storm you can experience:

1. The presence of Jesus.
2. The peace of Jesus.
3. The protection of Jesus.
4. The promises of Jesus.
5. The provisions of Jesus.
6. The potential for spiritual growth.
7. The power to face the next trial victoriously.

When we have experienced Jesus' presence, peace and protection while walking through some type of adversity, we are then able to minister to other hurting individuals. In addition, when we have appropriated His promises, received His provisions, and recognized the potential for growth, we have the power to face the next trial with complete assurance of victory. We can trust God's integrity!

"For His anger is but for a moment, His favor is for life; weeping may endure for the night, but joy cometh in the morning" (Psalm 30:5). We endure the pain in order to reap the gain. Jesus endured the cross because beyond it He could see the crown. He suffered patiently and He did not become weary and give up when He faced the most heinous death known to man, crucifixion on a Roman cross.

Trials by their very nature contain some intrinsic value. A trial is useful in proving the worth of something. In the case of an individual, we prove our strength as we walk through joyfully. When Jesus restores us to wholeness, we can emerge unscathed knowing the pain and tribulation have worked for our gain. What do you see beyond your painful trial? Do you view your trial as a means of gaining wisdom, knowing that strength is increased through struggle? An old Chinese proverb says, "The gem cannot be polished without friction, nor man perfected without trials."

Recently I attended a Women's Aglow meeting and listened to a man of God speak. After the service we spoke briefly. He pulled a "gold nugget" out of his pocket and placed it in my hand. "When you are tried, you shall come forth as gold," Bill Yount said. This was such a confirmation to me, as I was at that very moment battling some physical maladies.

Pure gold melts at 1063 degrees Celsius, and boils at 2966 degrees. Gold has to be processed to separate the impurities before it is of any value, because gold is worthless before it is refined. Gold must withstand intense heat to bring out its value, and this means a great deal of discomfort to us when we are left in the refining fire for a while.

God's prophet Isaiah said to the Israelites: "Behold, I have refined thee, but not with (for) silver; I have chosen thee in the furnace of affliction" (Isaiah 48:10-11). Where, Lord? In the furnace of affliction? Yes, it is in the furnace where impurities are separated from valuable substances. The writer of the Proverbs said: "Take away the dross from the silver, and there shall come forth a vessel for the finer" (25:4).

When we have walked through our trial victoriously, spiritual growth is evident. Why has God allowed us to be there? Remember that Daniel was brought up out of the lions' den; God did not spare him from going there. Shadrach, Meshach, and Abednego were not spared the fiery furnace, but God delivered them out of the fiery furnace. Paul was pruned through his trials, and his imprisonment proved to be of great value in that he wrote some powerful epistles while there. Through suffering unjustly Paul proved his ability to imitate Christ, so he could say, "Follow me as I follow Christ." Peter and John were delivered out of jail by an angel, but God did not prevent their going to jail. Guess what? God will allow you and me to suffer too, and we may not understand why, but if we wait on Him we will see the value added to our lives.

What I have shared in this book is only the tip of the iceberg, and it would take volumes to describe all the instances of adversity we have walked through. I don't have to know why—I just need to know Who walks with me.

Don't Lose Focus

To walk through victoriously, we must keep our eyes on Jesus, the author and finisher of our faith. How did Jesus respond to the devil's temptations in the wilderness? He responded with, "It is written! It is written! It is written!" When we find Scriptures that relate to our particular problem, our faith grows. Reading what the Word says about perseverance in suffering helps us to be steadfast in faith while waiting for our miracle. It helps us to focus not on the problem, but on God's ability to meet the need. The enemy of our souls wants to wear us out so we become so fatigued and exhausted that we give up on God.

Although I had read about Jesus' temptation in the wilderness many times, a spiritual principle dawned upon me as new revelation came. After great spiritual exaltation comes temptation and testing. The devil tempted Jesus following great honor and blessing bestowed by God. I have seen this in our family, and I believe that when God has used us in some way, we need to be aware that the enemy may show up quickly with a temptation.

When we have been successful in resisting the devil's attempts to cause us to give up, to faint, or to become frustrated, we are well on the way to victory. He tempts us to focus on what we have lost rather than on what we still have. Since Jesus said the devil is a liar and the father of lies, why would we listen to a pathological liar? Be wise—keep your eyes on the prize—Jesus Christ.

Meditate on the Word

Allow the Word to bathe your spirit and renew your mind. When I face serious problems, tribulation, adversity, I go to the Word and camp out. I find out what the Word says about the situation, and this builds my faith.

Meditating on the Scriptures has been the single source of the most spiritual growth for me.

Recently I led a retreat on renewing our minds. When we fast words and observe a period of corporate silence, God speaks some pretty spectacular things. At one such retreat in a remote location in Illinois, the Lord healed a lady of serious eye problems that the doctor said would blind her. While in the stillness with the Lord, He showed her how bitter she had become against her mother-in-law. When she purposed in her heart to forgive, the Lord healed her eyes and she had the victory.

In Wooster, Ohio, God healed a young man who attended a seminar I led on "Renewing the Mind By Meditating on Scripture." He had been in a state of deep depression and hopelessness, and was ready to commit suicide because his many doctors were unable to help him. I cannot take one iota of credit—the victory came to the young man because God saw fit to heal him as he listened to the Word. His time had come, and God delivered him without anyone laying hands on him. This is yet another example of what can happen when we look to Jesus in faith.

A lot of people have affirmed me in the gift God has given me to teach the Word. However, we must realize that every gift has a negative side, and the enemy will tempt us to indulge in the negative side of the gift. If we don't keep our minds renewed with the Word, our blessing can be our bane.

One day when I was bemoaning the unfairness of the way I was being treated at work, I began to play a tape over and over in my mind. Setting this man straight was long overdue I mused. As I stood at the copy machine rehearsing my speech mentally, the Lord brought this Scripture to mind. "Let no corrupt communication proceed out of your mouth, but that which is good to the use of edifying, that it may minister grace unto the hearers" (Ephesians 4:29). All I could do was to repent even though I had not uttered the words in my heart. Things had not changed outwardly for me, but the Lord had changed my heart, and I had victory over temptation.

Sometimes when I really hurt, I lose perspective. Like the psalmist, when I see how the wicked prosper, if I don't "go into the sanctuary" and see the wicked from God's perspective, I can lose it. He realized that although God is gracious and long-suffering, the wicked would not go unpunished. The Psalms came to my aid many times when I worked in the stress-laden nation's Capital, with all of its opportunities and inequities.

Hold Fast

Most of us experience times when we feel our good works are in vain. We have striven to obey God, yet everything still seems to blow up in our faces. Victory over one trial only seems to give way to another more difficult one, but be encouraged that God has seen your faithfulness. The writer of Hebrews reminds us that God is not unrighteous to forget our work and labor of love we have done in His name. While we may not see an immediate reward for righteousness, it comes in God's time and the victory is just around the corner. When you weep through the night, expect God's joy in the morning.

Our faith is really tested when we cling to God's promises, when we hold fast in the face of adversity. God always makes good on His Word, even though His timing is not necessarily synonymous with ours. The writer of Hebrews exhorts us to draw near and to hold fast, not losing confidence after we have done the will of God. "Lord, how long must I hold on in faith?" you may ask. As long as it takes, we continue in prayer and trust God's character because He is faithful. We acquiesce to His will even when we can't predict the outcome. When we are ill, we accept the answer God brings, whether by an instant miracle or by medical intervention.

Paul tells us to, "Be joyful in hope, patient in affliction, faithful in prayer" (Romans 12:12, NIV). The chapter begins with total commitment to God as our spiritual act of worship. To remain faithful, I have to remain in His Word and to delight myself in obeying His laws. God told Joshua to keep His laws on his lips, to meditate on them day and night, and to obey them. To walk through victoriously I have to meditate on the Word of God and not be consumed by whatever I'm going through. To meditate is to allow someone or something to dominate our thinking, and when I allow a problem to dominate my thinking, I lose the victory every time.

Because of all that my family and I have endured, I am able to empathize with others who hurt. God has enabled me to minister comfort to them in their affliction.

If we desire to do great exploits for Jesus, we must be willing to pay a price; be willing to accept inconvenience sometimes; be willing to suffer if it comes to that. How can we minister to hurting people effectively if all we ever had is the proverbial hangnail or a stubbed toe? Our ministry may lack depth, empathy, and authenticity. If you want to get results in ministry, you must be able to bear up under adversity. If called upon to suffer, learn to do so joyfully. God said to Paul, "My grace is sufficient"—whatever the disputed thorn in the flesh represented, it was not beyond God's abilities. **Joy in Adversity** means:

1. Joyously suffering calamity, affliction and adversity.
2. In the furnace but not feeling the heat.
3. In the fire without being burned.
4. In the storm, but not being struck by lightning.
5. In the river without drowning.
6. Walking through the Red Sea on dry ground.
7. Crossing the Jordan River when its banks are over flowing.

8. In the pit, but destined for the palace.
9. On the cross, awaiting the resurrection! Glory to God!

Unfortunately, some want to get to the palace without going through the pit; they try to reach the Promised Land without trusting God through the Red Sea or the sandy desert. We want to receive the blessing without first enduring whatever waiting period God imposes. The Apostle Paul said if we suffer with Him, we shall also reign with Him. We want to reign, but we don't want to suffer. We want the victory, but we don't want to walk through anything.

Jamie Buckingham said, "Because I can see the potential, I can tolerate the apparent." By faith I can see and smell the sweet victory that God will bring through this trying situation. Some trials are so severe that it is hard to imagine any good coming from them, yet I know it's there.

The Last Why Answered

Jesus never promised Christians a life of ease and freedom from trials. In fact, when He instructed His disciples on many things right before His crucifixion, He warned them that they would suffer tribulation while in the world. Jesus left to return to Heaven, a place of perfection, but we must first learn how to live victoriously in a world of sin and suffering.

How can you and I have victory over adversity? It helps to know that trials are a part of the human experience. They come to test our testimony and reveal what is in our hearts. Trials come to humble us, to increase our endurance, and to bring us to maturity in Christ.

Annie Johnson Flint expressed it well in a song, "He Giveth More Grace," based on James 4:6b, "God resists the proud, but gives grace to the humble" (NKJV). She says that when the burden grows greater, when the labors increase, or when the trials are multiplied, He gives strength, mercy and peace. It is not possible to exhaust God's grace and mercy no matter how often we come before His throne with our petitions. The victory is always found in Christ Jesus.

In John's vision of things to come as recorded in the Book of Revelation, the white-robed multitude of people from every nation who will stand before the throne and the Lamb of God are said to have come out of great tribulation. We may be encouraged that no matter what we have to endure in this world, the joys of Heaven await us. When it seems that our adversity is interminable, we might need to remember that this life is short when compared to eternity with Jesus!

If you still wonder why God has allowed suffering, affliction, tribulation, adversity, trials, or any other discomfort in your life, this scripture, I believe offers comfort to the fifth power. "Blessed be God, even the Father of our Lord Jesus Christ, the Father of mercies, and the God of all comfort; Who comforteth us in all our tribulation, that we may be able to comfort them which are in any trouble, by the comfort wherewith we ourselves are comforted of God" (II Corinthians 1:3,4). God gives us the gift of comfort in order that we might become comforters able to speak encouragement and hope to others.

The Bottom Line For Me

Every time I thought no further adversity could come our way, I was in for a rude awakening. We have had an extended walk through adversity that has taken us through the fire and the deep waters, and I have related only a portion of it in this book. But we can say without equivocation that Jesus has been with us every step of the way. As long as we are in this world, we can expect trials to come, but we can decide how we deal with them. We sometimes enjoy complaining so much that we call a friend to agree with us and join us in a pity party. The more we complain, the worse the problem seems to become. God judged and punished the Israelites for their murmuring and complaining when the going was tough.

The writer of the Proverbs says the spirit of a man will sustain him in bodily pain. The Apostle Paul says that our inner man is strengthened day by day even though our bodies are perishing. Trials bring out patience, steadfastness and endurance, according to James. When we endure, we can outlast the devil until the trial is over. Paul also said we should rejoice in the Lord always, and then he repeats it, "Rejoice!" Remember that he was writing this from a prison cell where the peace of Jesus was his constant companion.

When I stand before the Lord, I want to be able to declare with Paul, "I have fought the good fight, I have finished the race, I have kept the faith" (II Timothy 4:7, NKJV). I long to hear Jesus say, "Well done, good and faithful servant, enter into the joys of the Lord."

Like the Apostle Paul, Rivers and I choose to focus on what we still have, not what we have lost, although I don't claim that is easy. As of this writing, less than a year after surgery for a malignant breast tumor, I continue to deal with many other physical problems. After three bilateral surgeries, although I have achieved a degree of improvement, the TMJ problem still exists, while Rivers' health remains an ever-present concern. However, by God's grace, none of life's tragedies have overtaken us, and we are still walking through our trials victoriously.

He Gives His Peace

God never promised you, my friend,
That skies would always be blue.
But Jesus uttered in the Word,
"My peace I leave with you."

"Not as the world gives you its peace,
Would My peace vainly flee.

But in and throughout all your trials,
My peace will govern thee.

So when the sky seems dark and gray,
And you nearly stumble and fall,
Look up to Jesus and speak His name,
He'll hear you when you call.

He'll soothe your hurt and ease your pain,
He'll say you'll be all right.
He'll whisper peace to your troubled heart,
Even on the darkest night.

March 2003

Jesus can...

"Come unto me, all ye that labour and are heavy laden, and I will give you rest" (Matthew 11:28).

"These things I have spoken unto you, that in me ye might have peace. In the world ye shall have tribulation: but be of good cheer; I have overcome the world" (John 16:33).

The Apostle Paul affirms in Romans 8:28, not that all things are good, but that in all things God is able to work for our good when we are in Christ Jesus. Be encouraged that no matter what the problem or how difficult the trial, Jesus can turn it around; therefore, we can have Joy in Adversity!

Application Questions:
When You Walk Through Victoriously

Scriptures: Isaiah 43:1-3a, Psalm 30:5, Isaiah 48:10, Romans 12:12, II Corinthians 1:3,4, II Timothy 4:7, Romans 8:28.

1. Discuss some of the past miracles God has performed in your life and how this has encouraged you.
2. What value do you discern in the adversity you are facing or have faced in the past?
3. How can meditating on Scripture help you to keep the proper focus and find the good in each trial?
4. Can you answer why adversity comes into the lives of Christians?
5. How has this study helped you to be victorious in spite of what trials you have to endure?

Angie delivers sermon at Gospel Hill
Mennonite Church

Angie with Music Director Bobby
Wragg sings prior to her sermon at
Capital Christian Fellowship while
still taking radiation treatments

Angie delivers sermon at
Mt. Olive Presbyterian Church

APPENDIX A

Scriptures for Weary, Worn-Out Saints

"I have told you these things so that in Me you may have peace. In this world you will have trouble. But take heart! I have overcome the world" (John 16:33).

"Praise be to the God and Father of our Lord Jesus Christ, the Father of compassion and the God of all comfort, Who comforts us in all our troubles, so that we can comfort those in any trouble with the comfort we ourselves have received from God. For just as the sufferings of Christ flow over into our lives, so also through Christ our comfort overflows" (II Corinthians 1:3-5).

"Dear friends, do not be surprised at the painful trial you are suffering, as though something strange were happening to you. But rejoice that you participate in the sufferings of Christ, so that you may be overjoyed when His glory is revealed" (I Peter 4:12, 13).

"Therefore, among God's churches we boast about your perseverance and faith in all the persecutions and trials you are enduring...But the Lord is faithful, and He will strengthen and protect you from the evil one" (II Thessalonians 1:4, 3:3).

"Not only so, but we also rejoice in our sufferings, because we know that suffering produces perseverance; perseverance, character; and character, hope...Be joyful in hope, patient in affliction, faithful in prayer...For everything that was written in the past was written to teach us, so that through endurance and the encouragement of the Scriptures we might have hope..." (Romans 5:4, 12:12, 15:4).

"Consider it pure joy, my brothers, whenever you face trials of many kinds, because you know that the testing of your faith develops perseverance. Perseverance must finish its work so that you may be mature and complete, not lacking anything...Blessed is the man who perseveres under trial, because when he has stood the test he will receive the crown of life that God has promised to those who love Him" (James 1:1-4, 12).

"We are hard pressed on every side, but not crushed; perplexed, but not in despair; persecuted, but not abandoned; struck down, but not destroyed. We always carry around in our body the death of Jesus, so that the life of Jesus may also be revealed in our body. Therefore we do not lose heart. Though outwardly we are wasting away, yet inwardly we are being renewed day by day. For our light and momentary troubles (afflictions) are achieving for us an eternal glory that far outweighs them all" (II Corinthians 4:8-10; 16,17).

"When you pass through the waters, I will be with you; and when you pass through the rivers, they will not sweep over you. When you walk through the fire, you will not be burned; the flames will not set you ablaze" (Isaiah 43:2).

"For unto you it is given in the behalf of Christ, not only to believe on Him, but also to suffer for His sake...I know what it is to be in need, and I know what it is to have plenty. I have learned the secret of being content in any and every situation, whether well fed or hungry, whether living in plenty or in want. I can do everything through Him who gives me strength" (Philippians 1:29, 4:12,13).

"The Lord knows how to rescue godly men from trials and to hold the unrighteous for the day of judgment" (II Peter 2:9).

"That you may walk worthy of the Lord, fully pleasing Him, being fruitful in every good work and increasing in the knowledge of God; strengthened with all might, according to His glorious power, for all patience and long-suffering with joy" (Colossians 1:10,11, NKJV).

"For the eyes of the Lord are over the righteous, and His ears are open unto their prayers: but the face of the Lord is against them that do evil" (I Peter 3:12).

"I will say of the Lord, 'He is my refuge and my fortress, my God, in whom I trust. . . ' If you make the Most High your dwelling—even the Lord, Who is my Refuge—then no harm will befall you, no disaster will come near your tent. For He will command His angels concerning you to guard you in all your ways" (Psalm 91:2, 9-11).

"In my anguish I cried to the Lord, and He answered by setting me free" (Psalm 118:5).

"Cast your cares on the Lord and He will sustain you; He will never let the righteous fall" (Psalm 55:22).

"O Lord, be gracious to us; we long for you. Be our strength every morning, our salvation in time of distress" (Isaiah 33:2).

"I will lie down and sleep in peace, for You alone, O Lord, make me dwell in safety" (Psalm 4:8).

"Weeping may endure for a night, but joy comes in the morning" (Psalm 30:5b, NKJV).

"A righteous man may have many troubles, but the Lord delivers him from them all" (Psalm 34:19).

"In the day of my trouble I will call upon thee: for thou wilt answer me" (Psalm 86:7).

"Praise be to the Lord, to God our Savior, who daily bears our burdens" (Psalm 68:19).

"God is our refuge and strength, an ever-present help in trouble. Therefore we will not fear, though the earth give way and the mountains fall into the heart of the sea...Be still and know that I am God" (Psalm 46:2, 3, 10a).

"Those who trust in the Lord are like Mount Zion, which cannot be shaken but endures forever" (Psalm 125:1).

"No temptation has seized you except what is common to man. And God is faithful; He will not let you be tempted beyond what you can bear. But when you are tempted, He will also provide a way out so that you can stand up under it" (I Corinthians 10:13).

APPENDIX B

Tips for Assisting Those Who Hurt

Someone has said that people don't care how much you know, but they want to know how much you care. Do you want to develop a servant's heart toward others? Do you ever desire to help others when they fall upon desperate times but don't know how—what to do or say? Perhaps, you are the one in need and have not yet learned how to receive answers for your prayers that God sends through His people. If you are in either category, you may find the following tips useful, or at least enough to provoke you to think of ways to minister to others or accept ministry from them.

The grace of giving

1. Pray first so that your attitude is appropriate for the occasion.
2. Avoid saying, "If you need anything, please call." Very few people will call you and ask a favor. Instead, suggest something specific like, "I'd like to bring your lunch, what day would suit;" or "I'd like to baby sit so you can do some errands, what time is best for you?"
3. Don't use a visit to a sick person as an occasion to get your own needs met.
4. Resist the temptation to try to solve all their problems, i.e., making flippant suggestions that insult their intelligence. (Often they have already tried what you suggest, or have heard it from many others.)
5. Avoid tiring hospitalized patients by overly long visits.
6. Test the waters for conversation, i.e., does the patient

want to talk about his/her condition, or does it upset them?

7. Never rehearse episodes of tragic illnesses to a patient, especially when their disease is life threatening and you know others who have died from it.

8. For post-operative patients, don't try to "keep them in stitches" because their actual stitches can be very painful and laughing only exaggerates the pain.

9. Always keep in mind what is good for the patient and not what you prefer to do.

10. When someone is very ill, don't depress him/her with all manner of bad news.

11. Don't speak negatively in the room of an unconscious patient.

12. Be sure the gift or act of love fits the occasion and the person—not everyone has the same needs even in similar situations.

13. Pray for and take care of the caretaker; they may hurt more than the ill person.

14. Never talk down to a person who is physically ill or going through a serious problem.

15. Don't discuss the patient within earshot as if they can't hear or understand what is being said.

16. Refrain from being a know-it-all by answering questions the patient isn't asking.

17. Never make remarks that assume sin is the cause of a person's illness, thereby producing guilt.

18. Be sensitive by not making people feel ingratiated to you because of a gift.

19. When possible, give monetary gifts anonymously to protect the dignity of the recipient.

20. Pray about and look for the needs of others you can meet that are not at first obvious.

21. Volunteer to serve as liaison between the persons in need and those who wish to assist so kind deeds may be of optimum benefit.

22. Check with the caretaker on special dietary restrictions of the patient before preparing and delivering meals.

23. Organize givers in order to maintain a proper flow of intake so that five meals don't arrive on one day and none the next.

24. Watch for signs of fatigue, restlessness, and disinterest as an indication that it's time for your visit with a sick person to end, or ask them discreetly.

25. Remember: Looks can be deceiving—people may have nice clothes, car, home, but no cold cash for everyday necessities.

26. Remember: Whatever you have—good health, ample finances, a loving marriage—are gifts from God and are temporary.

27. Learn to minister to people across social stratas—well-educated, high-income people have needs just as those on the lower rung of the socioeconomic ladder.

28. Remain positive and encouraging in the presence of a hurting person, even if they are prone to negativity.

29. Pain is pain, and it happens to the best of us!

The grace of receiving

1. Learn to accept God's answers to prayer sent through His children.

2. Don't make excuses nor try to cover up needs because of pride.

3. Never allow self-pity to overtake you.

4. Assign someone as a liaison to coordinate meals and other needs in order to keep the flow of assistance at the

right pace.

5. Look for God's hand in every circumstance, no matter how painful.

6. Recognize that anyone can have a need, and there is no reason for shame.

7. View every gift as from God, and be thankful, but never feel ingratiated to the giver.

8.   Don't express displeasure at the quality of a love gift, even if it does not quite meet your expectations.

9. By God's help and grace, move quickly from victim to victor.

10. Never take the kind deeds of others for granted, but accept them graciously.

11. Allow friends to use some creativity in assisting you; i.e., never express ingratitude by criticizing how they assist you with tasks.

12. Remember God's marvelous acts in the past to build faith for your current situation.

13 Share your victories with others in order to build their faith.

14. Keep your eyes on Jesus, knowing that He will see you through this adversity.

15. Remember: People don't owe you anything, so every kind deed is a special gift.